Start Your Own

VENDING BUSINESS

Additional titles in *Entrepreneur's* Startup Series

Start Your Own

Entrepreneur
MAGAZINE'S

start up

3RD EDITION

Start Your Own

VENDING BUSINESS

Your Step-by-Step Guide to Success

Entrepreneur Press and Ciree Linsenman

EP
Entrepreneur®
Press

Entrepreneur Press, Publisher
Cover Design: Beth Hansen-Winter
Production and Composition: Eliot House Productions

This publication is designed to provide accurate and authoritative information in regard
to the subject matter covered. It is sold with the understanding that the publisher is not
engaged in rendering legal, accounting or other professional services. If legal advice or
other expert assistance is required, the services of a competent professional person should
be sought.

Library of Congress Cataloging-in-Publication Data
Linsenman, Ciree.
    Start your own vending business/by Entrepreneur Press and Ciree Linsenman.—
3rd ed.
        p.   cm.
    Rev. ed. of: Start your own vending business : your step-by-step guide to success
/Entrepreneur Press and Rich Mintzer. 2nd ed.
    Includes index.
    ISBN-13: 978-1-59918-436-4 (alk. paper)
    ISBN-10: 1-59918-436-2 (alk. paper)
    1. Vending machines. 2. New business enterprises—Management. 3. Entrepre-
neurship. I. Mintzer, Richard. Start your own vending business II. Entrepreneur
Press. III. Title.
HF5483.G33 2012
658.8'7—dc23   2011051346

Printed in the United States of America

16 15 14 13 12   10 9 8 7 6 5 4 3 2 1

Contents

Chapter 3

Buy a Business or Start from Scratch 31

Chapter 4

Finding Your Niche 43

Chapter 5

Structural Strategies 61

▲

Chapter 12

Chapter 13

Chapter 14

Chapter 15

Always Treat 'Em Right 241

Chapter 16

Monitoring Progress. 255

Chapter 17

Words of Wisdom 265

▲

Preface

If you're reading this, you're most likely interested in starting a vending business or at least finding out more about what owning one would be like. Either way, we know from experience just what you need.

You need information, but not written in a manner that causes you to nod off. You need facts, the ones that'll get you up and running. You need advice, but only the best and most relevant. And you need reassurance that the leap you're about to take is more than just one of faith.

So let's start with that last bit first. Indeed, you're repeatedly going to hear how much work owning a business is and how difficult it is to be successful. However, this country was founded on the principle of controlling one's own destiny and being one's own boss. While some folks focus on the negative, we'd like to stress the positive: Owning a business is a tradition in this country, and you can be proud to be a part of it.

As for the rest of what you need, we've sifted through literally piles of information and spent hours talking to successful entrepreneurs and industry experts. Many of the messages we heard were repeated over and over by people who don't even know each other. We've taken all that data and distilled it into a solid source of information for you.

In addition, you'll find in the Glossary all the lingo you'll need to speak like a pro as well as contact information in the Appendix for everyone we spoke to. If there's one common theme we heard again and again, it's to call on those with experience—they'll be happy to help answer your questions and give you additional advice.

One problem with this book is that it suffers the limitation of any two-dimensional resource. The written word requires taking a very nonlinear world and putting it into a linear format. While we've put lots of thought into organizing the flow of topics in a logical fashion, reading each page in sequence may not work for you.

Instead, we encourage you to jump around as much as you like, seeking out related information when you're ready to learn it. We'd even encourage you to flip first to Chapter 17 for some of the most valuable advice you'll find between these covers.

After you're finished with the last chapter, consider skipping next to Chapter 2, where you'll learn whether vending is the glamorous affair you've always imagined or perhaps not quite for you. Then, if you're still with us, start in again from the beginning and work your way through.

No matter how you use this book—whether you read it cover to cover or simply refer to it as questions arise—we know it'll serve you well as you embark on what's sure to be one of the most exhilarating experiences of your life: being your own boss.

Finally, we'd like to tell you upfront that the business owners and experts we interviewed gave most generously of time, energy, and resources. They also provided this book's sample forms, documents, worksheets, etc., which you're sure to find invaluable for adapting to your own business needs. It's to them that we owe our most sincere gratitude for making this guide possible.

So sit back, get comfortable, and let your journey begin.

1

Introduction to Vending

Before investing time, energy, money, and, most important, yourself in any business, it's just plain good sense to know something about what you're getting into. History, current issues, and future trends all impact the steps you take toward becoming a successful entrepreneur.

In the case of this book, it's also important to know who's giving you the advice. How and why did they or did they not succeed in certain areas of the vending industry? Does the geographic area where they live demand the same products as yours? How do their businesses compare to the one you're planning to start?

The more you know, the more likely you are to prosper. So without further ado, let's answer the questions we've already asked as well as a few more.

What Are We Talking About?

If you visit your dictionary (we used *American Heritage*), you'll likely discover the definition of "vending machine" is "A coin-operated machine that dispenses merchandise." Of course, if you've purchased food, beverages, or sundries from a vending machine lately, you know that paper money and even plastic are used for purchases.

Perhaps a more thorough description of vending is the one suggested by the National Automatic Merchandising Association (NAMA) in its booklet *Vending 101: The business of buying, placing on location, filling with product, removing cash, and maintaining vending equipment.*

Just like boiling down the theory of gravity to "What goes up must come down," the day-to-day realities of a successful

Berdoll Pecan Candy and Gift Company Pie and Candy Vendor

Health Is On Our Minds

The International Food Information Council Foundation 2010 "Food and Health Survey" uncovers some hints about the U.S. population's food choice motivators. For those of you vending edible products, consider these facts when deciding what products will appeal to your audience.

What kind of eaters are we this year?

○ 70 percent of Americans say they are concerned about their weight status.

○ 77 percent are trying to lose or maintain their weight.

○ To lose weight, 69 percent are changing the amount of food they eat, 63 percent are changing the types of foods they eat, and 60 percent are engaging in physical activity.

○ Weight loss is the biggest motivator for 65 percent of Americans improving the healthfulness of their diet.

○ 72 percent of those Americans embracing dietary recommendations are trying to consume more fiber and 73 percent want to eat more whole grains.

What are the biggest influences on our purchasing decisions?

○ 86 percent of Americans say taste.

○ 73 percent say price.

○ 58 percent say healthfulness.

○ 55 percent say convenience.

If you are able to carry products that satisfy a lot of these preferences, chances are you'll be received well by 77 percent of the population.

vending operation are also a bit more complicated. But NAMA's definition is an excellent place to start.

Where It All Began

According to *A Concise History of Vending*, written by respected professor, prolific author, and NAMA president emeritus G. Richard Schreiber, the earliest known vending machine was an Egyptian liquid-distribution device dating from 215 B.C. Not surprisingly, the device dispensed holy water at places of worship when a coin was deposited.

In the United States, it is generally accepted that vending began in 1888, when the Adams Gum company introduced its penny machines. From this humble beginning, vending has grown to approximately a $42.9 billion food service industry with most vending machines making thousands of transactions each year.

Current State of Affairs

For years and years, food-related vending enjoyed unbridled growth as factories and offices sprang up across North America. Even today, food remains the largest vending segment at about 93 percent of the industry, according to the trade news journal *Vending Times*.

Vending Times editor-in-chief Tim Sanford elaborates: "This is true if you define food very broadly as anything people metabolize, such as beverages, candy and snacks, ice cream, hot and cold sandwiches, platters, and so forth. In terms of dollars, the packaged cold drink category is the largest by far, because the major soft drink companies have large bottling organizations that place their own vending machines, often in locations that would not be profitable for a vending company (a 'third-party operator' in bottler terminology). Bottlers also lease equipment to those vending companies, and the vending companies often buy their own equipment, so they can stock the machines with beverages from a variety of suppliers.

"In 2009, the last complete year for which we have totals, more than 3 million machines had combined dollar sales of $23.3 billion," Sanford says. "Confections and snacks represented the second-largest category, with 1,240,000 machines enjoying dollar sales of $9.7 billion. The disparity in unit sales is not as great; candy and snack items usually sell for less than packaged cold drinks do. It certainly is true that vending in the United States primarily is a food-and-refreshments business, although limited deployments of machines selling things like iPods always get a lot of publicity.

"At the moment, vending is in somewhat of a decline and yet the demand for vending has never been greater. It's not that vending is selling less products, it's that the big accounts are harder to find," explains Sanford, who believes that you can still do very well in the business, but that you need to understand the business thoroughly before jumping in.

Sanford also believes the vending industry today confronts a challenge: the demand for vending services never has been greater, as companies downsize and move away from providing manual foodservice for their employees. However, there are fewer accounts large enough to justify the operating costs of providing "full-line" vending service. The modern vending business took shape between the mid-1950s and the mid-1970s because it could satisfy the demand by large enterprises (primarily factories) for food and beverage service that could be accessed quickly by large numbers of workers, and would be available to people working second and third shifts, and weekends if necessary. The need for 24/7 service still exists, often in acute form, but it is much more difficult to meet it with traditional vending service when there are 40 people in the location rather than 1,500.

"The problem is that the demand is exercised by smaller businesses because the old 1,500-man factories are fewer and fewer," says Sanford. "Many companies have downsized, so we don't have 120 employees at one office anymore. Instead you have maybe 60 people. They still want vending machines, but the location is not as attractive as it once was.

"The classical solution to this problem, which remains effective today, is the small vending operation," Sanford ponders. "An independent business in which the owners install, fill, collect, and service all the equipment does not have the overhead costs associated with buying several trucks, hiring drivers for them, and leasing or buying warehouse space. Many small operators do not wish to become larger, for that reason alone. Others start small in the expectation of growing over time."

The result, because of a combination of downsizing, telecommuting, and increasing satellite offices, is that the vending operator needs to place more machines in various locations to compensate for the smaller number of employees in one location. The demand is still there; it's simply more fragmented. The problem for the vending operator is that more machines and a larger route mean more time and money expended to make the same money that the old-time operators could make from a handful of very large locations.

Some of this problem, however, can be alleviated by planning differently from how the old-time operators worked. For some this may mean more smaller-sized machines and the use of software technology to allow the machine itself to communicate when it is running low on product. According to Sanford there are very experienced people in the industry from whom newcomers can (and should) learn a lot before starting out. However, there is nobody who can provide a foolproof method. You will need to create your own system and establish your own routes.

> ### Smart Tip
> Attaching additional services onto your vending business will get you through lulls in sales. Have you been in the business for a while? Could you save new operators some heartache with your knowledge? Consider being a vending mentor or consultant and charging a flat fee to go over business plans with newbies. It's also a great way to continue making money after you retire.

One of the keys to building any type of business today is understanding the wide diversity of tastes and product possibilities that the consumer has come to expect. There currently are 44 different types of soda under the Coca-Cola brand on the market today in the United States, not to mention new types of drinks being created daily by various manufacturers, including herbal teas, sweet teas, energy drinks with algae, and even clear sweet liquids with colored, gelatin balls afloat (Orbitz). Instead of simply buying orange juice, you'll find frozen, small containers, quarts, bottles, "pulp," "no pulp," and various combinations of orange and another juice. The point is that consumers, faced with such a range of products, have become particular in their selections. Therefore, you will need to embrace the various possibilities and determine what will work best in your demographic market and where you can sell specific products. Not unlike a detective solving a crime, the successful vending operator today is skillful at putting all of the components together to answer the questions:

1. What do I sell?
2. Who wants what I'll sell?
3. Where is my unfulfilled market?
4. How will I reach that market?
5. How will I keep customers' attention?

To make things more interesting, and provide the vending operator with more options to fit these smaller but still vending-conscious businesses, a variety of different-sized machines have appeared in recent years along with new products suited for vending machines, ranging from hair flattening irons and bicycle parts to frozen pizzas and digital cameras.

Although consumers in countries like Japan buy an ever-expanding array of vended products, vending is generally considered to be a "mature" industry in the United States. Unlike the youthful technology industry, where innovation makes millionaires overnight, today's keys to vending success are controlling costs, strategizing, aggressive marketing, exceptional management, and a lot of plain hard work. According to Elliot Maras, editor of *Automatic Merchandiser* magazine (www.vendingmarketwatch.com), "Vending is not a simple or easy business.

Fun Fact

The 2010 "State of the Vending Industry Report" reveals that the most notable change in the industry is "the increase in nutritional snacks, which include breakfast bars, cereal, fruit snacks, functional bars, nutritional pretzels, granola bars, rice cakes, and trail mix." This continued a trend from 2009, but in 2010 the gain was much larger (7.7 points in revenue sales and 4.4 points in unit sales).

Anyone who says so is a fantastic liar. If you are going to get into this business, commit yourself to a lot of studying and hard work. Shortcuts don't exist."

A Fresh, New Outlook

In addition to hurdles posed by tangible economic forces, in the past vending also had to combat negative perceptions. Alas, despite the blatant need for more attention to customer preferences, there are still some vending operators who do things as they have been doing them for years. When it comes to changing with the times and perhaps exploring new innovations, Tim Sanford sums it up well: "You'll hear the phrase 'that's not the business we're in' by some of the veterans. Vending operators in general—like many other small-business owners—are mindful of Bert Lance's famous advice: 'If it ain't broke, don't fix it.' The trick is to recognize when something is broken, and to know what tools are available for correcting the problem."

Today, evidence suggests a whole new game for those ready to market to a specific group—Gen Y. As reported in a recent *Vending Times* article, the National Automatic Merchandising Association's executive vice president and chief operating officer Dan Mathews presented multiple points at the 2011 OneShow supporting why Gen Y is the new golden opportunity market for vendors. A NAMA commissioned study with indepth interviews with operators and consumers accumulated findings that are causing the vending association to "embark on a groundbreaking image-building campaign primarily targeted at Generation Y."

Old opinions about consumer attitudes regarding vending as a last resort were strongly contradicted, with 80 percent of them now rating it "positively" or "very positively." Additionally, those ages 18 to 27 (Gen Y) held the highest regard for vending. Because Gen Y is the trendsetter for Gen X and the baby boomers, appealing to them will eventually gain ground with the other groups.

New technology is addressing negative interactions with the introduction of cashless payment and troubleshooting alert systems that operators add to their repertoires to combat the common complaints of lost money and products not dropping down into the grab area.

Here are just a few of many reasons, revealed from the study, to market to Gen Y:

- They really like vending, and in fact choose it predominantly over shopping at convenience, grocery, and drugstores.
- They consume lots of snacks and drinks.
- They prefer the cashless payment, which can lead to spending more money per transaction.

▲

- They like interacting with machines and are not intimidated by the idea that the machines may malfunction.

They set the trends that older groups follow.

During vending's heyday of growth and prosperity, attending to customer satisfaction was irrelevant to making a profit. Today, consumers are in the position to demand top-notch customer service, especially after the recent struggles of the challenged economy. Though the economy is softening, it's clear that the emphasis on old-fashioned attention to customer needs has allowed certain businesses to withstand and even rise above the storm. This is apparent to the extent that many books on the "new" model of old-fashioned customer service hold top rank on the bestseller list, promoting not only top-notch products and services, but also a lasting social engagement. You'll read more about this in Chapter 14.

Another factor contributing to a negative perception of vending will be discussed in more detail in Chapter 3. To summarize briefly, scams in vending are so prevalent that hundreds, if not thousands, of innocent individuals are sold vending machines every year under false but convincing pretenses. Often, the victims of such schemes, called "Blue Sky schemes," place machines at various locations, slowly go bankrupt, and then simply abandon the equipment, leaving consumers frustrated and without recourse. A few of our operators started off behind that eight ball and learned its painful lesson. Their advice can help you make better decisions.

Back to the Future

Before you close this book and give up your dream in despair, we want you to know the picture isn't entirely black. The Hudson Report shows that various technological, economic, demographic, and other forces are opening doors to new ways of doing business and new markets to explore. For example, cell phones and pagers reduce vending businesses' overhead by decreasing the need for secretarial support. Laptops, notebooks, and wireless handheld devices like a BlackBerry phone allow for inputting information directly at the site with the latest in software, rather than scribbling down machine data and crunching numbers later by hand. Cashless vending systems allow detailed monitoring of sales and encourage people to spend more per transaction. Cash recycling enables customers to make more purchases without needing change. Apps help identify where people are and what they want.

Generations X and Y have been profoundly affected by technology and the increasingly fast pace of the world around them. They are becoming more self-reliant at a younger age than their parents, and often start making their own purchasing decisions early in life. Students are juggling classes, workloads, and extracurricular activities. The idea of buying an item without waiting in line is more and more appealing. In business and industries, many companies have gone from 35 to 40 hours up to 45 to 55 hours, creating the need for quick, easily accessible food. In most businesses today, time is of the essence, so vending machines are welcomed for that quick snack or cup of coffee.

As the world gets faster and more technologically oriented, the need for vending machines increases. To get a picture of where vending fits in the overall market, see the "Market Share of Vended Products" chart below.

Market Share of Vended Products

Packaged cold beverages[1]	54.2%
Snacks, confections, pastries[2]	22.5%
Hot drinks	8.4%
Vended food[3]	6.7%
Ice cream	2.0%
Milk	1.9%
Bulk vending	1.0%
Cold drinks (cups)	1.0%
Cigarettes and cigars	0.7%
All other	1.6%
Total	**100.0%**

[1] Includes nonperishable cold beverages (such as soft drinks, juice, water, tea, and isotonic) in cans and bottles.

[2] Includes shelf-stable packaged, single-serve snack and candy items both "wide" and "narrow" and pastry sold through nonrefrigerated vendors.

[3] Includes refrigerated, frozen, canned, bowl-pack, and other shelf-stable main meal items.

Source: *Vending Times'* 2010 Census of the Industry

▲

What Does It All Mean?

Admittedly, the swiftly changing landscape is making the process of doing business particularly difficult for established vending organizations that are accustomed to doing everything "the old way." In addition to the Hudson Report, articles in *Automatic Merchandiser*, reports in *Vending Times*, and statements by organizations like NAMA repeatedly admonish vending companies to pay more attention to merchandising, customer service, computerization, and related efficiencies.

In other words, just filling machines, and being on your way, isn't good enough anymore.

For entrepreneurs like you, the current and future trends of the industry offer as many opportunities as roadblocks. Unfettered by "the way we've always done it," you can turn the challenges of the rapidly changing marketplace to your advantage faster than can an established organization, where old habits often die hard.

Our Focus

To help you become a successful operator, this book draws on the insights of entrepreneurs who took advantage of opportunities by entering relatively new vending fields or embracing the forces of innovation and change. It also provides insights from those who watched countless wannabes and savvy survivors.

Because consumable products dominate the profit potential in the vending industry and offer you the best opportunities, we'll focus on this segment. We'll also introduce you to issues faced by entrepreneurs who identify an unexplored vending market and strike off to conquer the unknown.

Additional Opportunities

What's not addressed in depth here is amusement vending—arcade games, jukeboxes, etc.—and street vending. Bulk vending—stickers, toys, and gumballs—and office coffee service (OCS) are also underrepresented.

In the case of amusement and street vending, many of the basics of vending consumables apply. Even more information will apply to bulk vending and OCS, but their segments also face issues beyond the scope of this work.

For those interested in those varieties, we recommend using this business guide to acquaint yourself with the fundamentals and as a valuable source for worksheets and checklists. In addition, you will find references to more specific assistance listed in the Appendix.

Testing, Testing, 1-2-3

Want to ease into the vending lifestyle? Try tending to a small set of candy and gumball bulk machines before sinking the bigger bucks into larger, electronic machines. Try it as a six-month or year experiment to see if you're suited for bigger ventures. It can leave you feeling more confident when you do start playing with the big boys, and could pave the way for some easier machine placement; your bulk customers may say yes to an upgrade to electronic machines.

As Antoine Cameron points out in *How to Start a Vending Business, Volume 1*, smaller, bulk machines are easy to transport in a car or truck, require low maintenance, and are easier to place than larger vendors. While you'll need to own more machines to make the same money you would from a soda and snack machine, bulk candy machines require less of your time. Used bulk machines can be found on www.craigslist.org and www.freecycle.org for just $50 and up. Bring lots of quarters when you check out these pre-owned machines and insist on a run through of loading them with product, inserting change, and dispensing product at least ten times, and then emptying the change with the seller. Get ready to eat a lot of M&M's.

Meet Our Operators

Vending business owners most often refer to themselves as "operators," a term we've wholeheartedly adopted. We'll supply you with all the jargon you'll need to navigate the industry in the next chapter and in our Glossary, but for now, we'd like to introduce you to the voices you'll hear throughout this book.

Jennifer Berdoll Wammack grew up working on her parents' pecan farm, learning the business inside and out, including running the attached retail pie and candy shop that makes use of the fresh harvest and family recipes. Berdoll Pecan Candy and Gift Company began 32 years ago when her family started to grow and harvest pecans on an orchard that is now 15,000 trees strong.

When Jennifer and her husband, Jared, purchased the business from her parents, they had only one problem: keeping the doors to their shop open long enough to satisfy all the people with never-ending appetites who kept pulling up in their cars in the parking lot. This was what inspired Jennifer and Jared's unique vendor concept.

Jennifer couldn't stand the fact that even though she worked long hours to satisfy the constant stream of customers, she'd always miss selling to the hungry people pulling up to the store just as she was leaving for the day. She stayed later and later, pushing her limits to capture sales opportunities, until one day she had an idea. What if people could buy Berdoll's homemade pecan pies and candies from a vending machine that was available all the time? The success of her pie vending machine is famous now, but the road to success was blocked with a few challenges. You'll soon learn how this niche marketer's persistence paid off.

Fun Fact

According to the United States Department of Labor, most individuals working in the vending business learn their skills on the job. New workers are trained informally on the job to fill and fix machines by observing, working with, and receiving instruction from those with experience.

Wayne D. of Burnsville, Minnesota, a suburb of Minneapolis, is our most veteran entrepreneur. He started his business part time in 1978 while still working as a full-time cigarette vending sales representative for the tobacco company R.J. Reynolds. "I was nearing 40 and knew I wasn't going to be retiring with Reynolds," says Wayne.

Wayne chose vending because his Reynolds job gave him a bird's-eye view of what worked and what didn't. "I had a distinct advantage because I saw how two or three hundred companies operated," he explains. "So my wife and I started our company with 14 candy, snack, and cigarette machines in five different locations." Five years and a number of smaller acquisitions later, Wayne purchased a larger operation and traded his Reynolds position for working in vending full time.

Erik A. Borger started Kansas City's Originally Organic Vending as a response to his childhood and young adult battle with a love of eating and his frustration with the lack of available healthy, delicious choices. The idea for his company germinated when he was in high school, years before he ever knew a thing about health or nutrition. Erik reflects, "I was overweight as far back as I can remember, but my school's vending machines were essential in my eyes. By the time I hit 20 I was a heavy smoker and drinker, tipping the scales at almost 300 pounds. At one point I finally saw the light and a major life's change occurred."

From the young age of 14 Borger worked as a chef, and as the years went by, he also held positions in sales, delivery, and retail management, and even rode on the side of a garbage truck for a winter. Through it all, his annoyance with the unhealthy food offered in vending machines persisted. "No matter if I was in school, at the gym, or a local art gallery, my vending choices were always the same," he says. "There was never anything I could purchase that did not make me feel guilty, sick, or both."

His passion for health and nutrition finally led him to pursue both undergraduate and graduate degrees in exercise science, and this was when the idea for Originally Organic Vending started coming to life.

Janice M. of Baltimore, Maryland, represents entrepreneurship in its truest sense. "In May of 1995, I had a job interview at 8:30 A.M.," says the 30-ish, single mother of three. "After dropping off my children, I arrived for the interview at 12 minutes after 8:00, and I suddenly noticed I had a hole the size of Seattle in my pantyhose."

Although the receptionist directed her to the company canteen, by the time she found the hosiery, selected between beige, gray, or black, negotiated the checkout counter, and returned to the waiting area, time had run out. "I was told I didn't have time to put them on," Janice recalls. "Well, this was my first real corporate job and I wanted to make a good impression, so I didn't want to be late."

Janice figures her boss must have noticed the gaping crevasse, but he never uttered a word and offered her the administrative assistant position anyway. For the next year she revisited the incident several times. "I remember I just kept thinking about it—I don't know why. But I kept thinking it would have been really great if there had been a machine in the bathroom so I didn't have to go running around."

While she worked as an administrative assistant, Janice ran an event-planning business on the side and enrolled in a business training class offered by a local economic development organization: Women Entrepreneurs of Baltimore. She mentioned the idea to a fellow classmate, and he suggested she go to the library and research the subject in *Vending Times*.

"*Vending Times* didn't have anything listed that was solely pantyhose [although, editor-in-chief Tim Sanford recalls some pantyhose vending attempts as far back as 30 years ago], so I called vending companies to see if anyone had heard of it," Janice recollects. But no one had. So Janice decided to give the idea a go, and by midsummer 1996, her business was born.

Because she's not only pitching vending but trying a fairly new and innovative concept, pantyhose dispensing, Janice still works in the corporate world part time. But she remains optimistic and focused on her dream of someday making her business full time and even franchising her patented idea. "I just want to make a lasting impression for years to come," she asserts, "so that my children can grow up and say, 'This is something Mommy did, and we can do it, too.'"

Becky P. of Northridge, California, launched into vending full time in 1984

Fun Fact

As of the end of 2009, there were 462,000 offices and office complexes, 456,000 public locations, and 139,500 plants and factories served by vending operators. Statistics courtesy of the *Vending Times* 2010 Census of the Industry.

when she and her husband "became partners in life." Although he brought 30 years of vending experience to their union, he'd left vending when some family members suggested he become an investor in one of their projects.

"So it really was like we were starting from scratch," says the former human resources manager, who also counts restaurant and fast-food work as part of her background.

"But I had three jobs when we met, so he knew I was perfect for this industry because I was already putting in 100 hours per week."

While most food vendors begin with snacks and sodas, Becky P. and her husband formed their Southern California operation as a full-line service. This means they bucked conventional wisdom and offered fresh, refrigerated food from the start.

"If you go into cold food with a defeatist attitude, you will be defeated," Becky stresses. Full-line vending is for people who appreciate good food and fine dining. "Don't go into cold food if you're not willing to work it like a restaurant. If you want to work six hours a day or five days a week, forget it."

B.J. S. of Hendersonville, Tennessee, a Nashville suburb, got into vending after owning a construction company in Spain. A native of Sweden, he met his American wife while at school in the United States. The pair lived abroad until 1995, when they moved back to be near her aging parents.

For B.J., owning a vending company was a happenstance. "My father-in-law started the business, and he wanted to retire. I was looking for something to do, so I bought the business from him in July of 1995."

When he took over the business, gross sales just grazed a million per year. Trucks and equipment were antiquated and all the accounting was done by hand. "We bought a lot of trucks," he recalls. "The average age of the fleet was 10 years old. We bought ten vehicles in three years, which we financed at a cost of a quarter-million dollars."

Since then, B.J. has tested all the latest technology, plumped up his employee base, and expanded service to cover all five surrounding counties. Gross sales today top $3.5 million.

A Few More Experts

To assist with big-picture issues, you'll also hear from four experts, all with years of experience helping startup entrepreneurs just like you. For Randall Sutherland of St. Petersburg, Florida, becoming a dad at midlife was a delightful surprise. But when he saw evidence of his young son's burgeoning high IQ, it set him in motion with a whole new goal: to financially plan for an education in the finest private schools that would challenge young Ryan. Both Randall and his wife, Joyce, already worked full time at the post office as they had for more than 20 years, but Randall also chose to create a second income flow with vending because it would let him set his own hours and

I'll Buy That

The vending industry breaks down into seven distinct segments. To help you keep score, here are the terms you'll encounter and what each one means.

1. *4C's*: an abbreviation that stands for the basics of vending as it evolved (coffee, cup soda, candy, and cigarettes). Today, this segment is most often referred to as "snacks and soda."

2. *Full line*: the incorporation of fresh refrigerated items, such as sandwiches and frozen foods, to operators' offerings.

3. *OCS*: the commonly used abbreviation for office coffee service, where operators provide equipment and "kits" containing coffee and related items such as sweeteners, creamers, stir sticks, etc. Full-line vending operators often migrate into OCS and vice versa to meet the needs of their clients.

4. *Specialty*: refers to a particular line of products, such as french fries, pizza, or pantyhose, among many others.

5. *Bulk*: the vending of gumballs, toys, stickers, novelties, etc., in loose form. Crossover between full-line and bulk operators in both directions is common but not as frequent as the full-line–OCS connection.

6. *Amusements or music/game*: began on the jukebox/pool table side of the business but now includes music machines, video, and arcade games of all sorts. This is another area of crossover with full line, but most often in the form of a separate operation within a larger company due to the specific needs of this market.

7. *Street*: most often used to describe mobile operations located in public areas, such as sidewalks and shopping malls. Street vending is generally viewed as a subset or a combination of specialty, full-line, and amusement vending.

control how much he worked and profited. Vending seemed the perfect choice for years ahead, funding exposure to culture through the venues of school, sailing, and saxophone lessons, and trips abroad for Ryan.

Randall Sutherland's background in customer service served him well in dealing with accounts and customers, but it took him a long time to recover from the way his business started, because he lost a lot of

Smart Tip

To locate industry experts willing to provide you with assistance and advice, contact the National Automatic Merchandising Association or the industry organization for your vending specialty.

necessary capital due to lack of research. After he rose above those initial challenges his business thrived and paid for his son's higher education through college. He now serves as a consultant to operators just starting up.

Vince Gumma is co-owner of American Vending Sales Inc. (AVS) in Chicago. Established in 1971, AVS distributes vending machines, jukeboxes, video games, and pinball and redemption games as well as maintaining an inventory of tens of thousands of parts. Gumma joined AVS in 1986 after working in the printing ink industry and currently serves as an officer in the Illinois Automatic Merchandising Council (IAMC), a state affiliate of NAMA. He plays an active role in efforts to improve the image of the industry both by assisting with NAMA publicity efforts and helping startups understand the realities of owning a vending business. He has received numerous awards from the IAMC and, most recently, the NAMA Chairman's Award for his participation in helping the Illinois vending industry achieve favorable sales tax legislation.

John Ochi is vice president of Five Star Distributors Inc. in Vernon Hills, Illinois. Headquartered in suburban Chicago, the consumables distributor also maintains a location in Atlanta and was purchased by its current owners in 1975. In addition to delivering products, Five Star permits small operators to access its extensive line on a cash-and-carry basis. Ochi began as a warehouse worker in the vending distribution industry in 1974. He came up through the ranks, joining Five Star as partner and vice president in 1994. Serving as a member of vending's front lines from the fast-growth 1970s through the consolidations of the 1990s exposed Ochi to every aspect of the industry. His efforts to improve the industry earned Ochi Automatic Merchandising's Distributor of the Year Award.

Jim Patterson is principal of Patterson Co. Inc. in Kenilworth, Illinois. The 60-year-old product brokerage firm serves the upper Midwest from its Chicago-area headquarters and is dedicated to matching the right product with the right vending operation. A third-generation member of the family business, Patterson came to the company after finishing college in 1980. Like all our experts, Patterson has experienced both runaway prosperity and the more recent lean years. He brings an affinity for technology as well as an eye for customer service to his active involvement in the improvement of the vending industry, and is a recipient of Automatic Merchandising's Broker of the Year Award.

Ready, Set, Go

Because no human activity exists in a vacuum, those who prosper in the shark-infested waters we call "The American Way" know it's vital to get out of the trenches and look at the big picture. By arming yourself with the knowledge in this chapter, you, too, have taken an important step toward running a successful business.

Now that you've surveyed the landscape, it's time to learn what you really want to know: How do I start and run a vending business? To find out, all you have to do is turn the page.

A Day in the Life

Now that you've gotten your feet wet, let's talk about what life as a vending business owner is all about. In this chapter we provide a look at what a typical day in the vending business may entail. Throughout the book, we discuss many of the aspects of the business in detail, including the selection of products and equipment. However, it's always nice to see what the

▲

job will be like on a daily basis prior to jumping into all of the "behind the scenes" details.

First of all, you will get wet feet. Even cold feet. You may even get blisters. This is part of the beauty of vending—every day you spend time outdoors, getting a healthy dose of fresh air and sunshine year-round as you go from place to place. Because there's a lot of walking involved, you should get yourself a pair of high-quality walking shoes with good arch support. Sanita, Dansko, Alegria, and P.G. Lite are specifically made for occupations that require lots of standing and walking, and can be found at www.zappos.com. There is also a discount retailer of some of those brands, which are considered seconds, but are still perfectly spiffy and supportive for hours on your feet: www.clogoutlet.com. While you're at it, pick yourself up some cushioned, seamless socks like Wigwam Dri-Release Ironman Pro Thunders (www.footsmart.com) to prevent blisters and keep your feet dry and comfortable.

Of course, this is the business as it starts out for those entering the vending field as well as for many who have chosen to maintain a hands-on business. If you become a major player in the industry, you may find yourself behind a desk most of the time, with other people handling the duties outside the office. It's not a matter of "moving up," but how you choose to run your business. Many vending operators are successful with just a couple of people handling everything themselves, while others are run with many employees.

Rise and Shine

Vending is a flexible business when it comes to daily routine. Many operators run part-time businesses, filling or "servicing" machines during the evenings or on weekends.

However, if you want to earn a full-time income, traffic becomes a make-or-break proposition. While travel time and distance are important factors to any operator's success, full-timers must adjust their schedules to take advantage of off-peak hours.

In addition, your type of operation will play a part. If you go into cold food, you'll be up before the crack of dawn. "We get up between 3:00 and 4:00 in the morning," says Northridge, California, full-line operator Becky P., "because we need to be finished servicing machines by 11:30 A.M. for the lunch break."

Making a List

Not surprisingly, your first task of the day is taking stock. Grab your route cards (machine inventory record sheets—more on this in Chapter 13) and notebook with clipboard to record customer feedback, and head for your vehicle. Your route cards provide inventory information to help you determine where to go first and how to set up your day. Then check what you have and decide what you need so you can pull the inventory from storage. As you load your machines you'll get feedback from passersby and will want to record their requests in your notebook.

Randall Sutherland suggests encouraging customers to email you directly as well as connecting with their office manager for a collected, group request email because then you'll have a written account of what you need to order. This is also much easier than calling to find out what people want, though you may occasionally wind up doing that, too. Post a friendly, attractive sign on your machine that includes your website URL (and blog if you have one), name, and email address so people know how to reach you when they get sudden cravings.

Sutherland advises developing the habit of recording all your notes in a central database when you get home so you can follow the course of each location, list its preferences, and track whether or not the requests actually sell, and to what extent. "Women tend to request a lot of diet snacks and drinks but don't actually buy them," Randall laughs. "It's not that they never buy them, but really, when break time comes, they tend to satisfy themselves with something with a lot of taste, not a low-cal granola bar. They'll walk by the machine admiring all of the new diet snacks they requested—they just don't eat them. Every operator I know says the same thing, yet the requests keep piling in."

Depending on your type of vending, organize items by location for quick transport from your wheels to your machines. Remember, walking back and forth between your vehicle and your machines is as much wasted time as idling in traffic.

Now load your vehicle, grab your cell phone and laptop, and head out.

At a Vendor

Unless you're Jesse "The Body" Ventura, or your inventory is small and light, plan to make at least a couple of trips from vehicle to machine. If you vend cold and frozen items, rotate and fill them first to minimize the minutes they're not on ice. Pull cold items from the chiller and put them in a cooler. Load your dolly appropriately and head to where your machines await.

When you walk into the break room or wherever your machines are located, first survey the scene. "A footprint on a machine or one that's been pushed back or rocked isn't the sign of a jerk," says Becky P. "It means you should check the coin mechanism and bill changer to see if they're working, and look around for a jam, such as a soda that's hanging up."

Even in the absence of foul play, test the coin and bill mechanisms. Then check and refill the money as needed to ensure your customers get the proper change. If you haven't already done so, remove the footprint and wipe down the front of the machine. As necessary, clean inside as well.

If you're dealing with a cashless machine, bring your credit card and test a couple of purchases to ensure everything is working correctly.

Ready to load? Not yet! Before you put anything in, unless you have software telling you in advance the amount of product purchased/left in the machine, you'll want to write, or enter onto your laptop, what has been purchased. That's what route cards are all about. Along with telling you where to head on your route, they provide an opportunity to list the data as you go. (Route cards are also called delivery receipts or machine cards. See Chapter 13 for an example.) Pay attention to what's hot and what's not. Make notes as necessary to help remind yourself later, when you're back at the office.

OK, now load the machine, and move on to the next one.

> ### Bright Idea
> Randall Sutherland suggests that when you start an account and install a machine, there's something you can do to set the tone for a warm relationship and show that you'll be giving "above and beyond" customer service. Create a gift basket comprised of one of each of the products in the machine so your customers can sample the merchandise. If you have 35 products in the machine, you should have 35 samples in the basket. Add a pretty card to the basket that says something like, "Thank you so much for choosing Highlander Vending as your snack service. It's an honor to serve you. We'll do everything we can to make you happy!"

Customers Count

When you run into people at your locations, greet them with a smile and cheery hello. Being social opens the door for requests and feedback and helps people make the connection that a real human being is behind the machines they use. "I always make the initiative to greet people," asserts Becky P. "The conversation may just be general—how are you, how's the family, the kids, how's work."

While you're servicing, you'll doubtless get special requests. Do everything you possibly can to honor those requests, says Becky. "Right then and there, you've taken a cold inanimate machine and given it a personality," says Becky. "They're going to think of your smiling face when they make that purchase the next time."

And you must honor complaints. "It's very important to listen," she continues. "There have been tons of articles written on this—as long as the complainer knows you will handle and respond to a complaint or problem right away, 98 percent of them will be satisfied and come back. If you blow them off, you've lost that customer."

Upon leaving the room, Becky and her employees also thank everyone present. This goes a long way toward building customer loyalty.

Courtesy Calls

Before you move on, pay a visit to the decision maker and perform a ritual similar to the one in the break room. In addition to general inquiries about the person and their family, show an interest in their business situation and build a rapport with the people in charge and their support staff. It never hurts to drop a sample of a new product you're considering or have started stocking.

Trouble Calls

Once you've finished with the machines and humans at your first location, you are off to your next stops. Invariably your cell phone will ring, your pager will buzz, or you will call into your answering machine and find trouble at the other end of the line.

Finessing trouble calls puts your customer-service, time-management, and problem-solving skills to the test. Each call requires balancing client expectations, revenue loss potential, and the impact on the rest of the route. Whatever you decide, you'll follow up by giving the client your best estimate of when you'll get to the scene of the crime. This is one situation where even the staunch old-timers are beginning to acknowledge the benefit of the latest in computer technology, in which machines can indicate electronically (via software) that something is about to go wrong mechanically. Such advance warning allows you to schedule a stop along your route.

When you do arrive at the offending machine, you may find the problem goes beyond a stuck coin or bill, or a botched cashless transaction. Here's where the quality of your machine manufacturer and distributor comes into play. The better

Bright Idea

Vending Market Watch editor Elliot Maras reported on a unique idea one college used to increase its sales by making things easier for its hungry customers. When students were asked how they felt about the current vending system at Northwest Missouri State University in Maryville, Missouri, they said they wanted to be able to use their student ID cards to buy snacks. The school enabled their machines for that ability so that the student ID cards could be used like cash cards. After the change, students could not only use their cards on campus for books and meals, but could also buy vended snacks on a whim. The school more than doubled its vending sales by honoring this request. Listen to what your customers want. "Cashless" is where it's at!

manufacturers offer telephone technical assistance and can navigate you safely through the emergency. If you need a part, a good distributor will quickly have one on its way.

Sales Stops

In between servicing machines and fixing jams, you'll also make courtesy calls. Unlike businesses that attract clients through advertising, vending success depends on developing relationships, which we'll talk more about cultivating through networking and with social media tools in Chapter 14. It also depends on keeping the faith, no matter how long it takes.

Who's Who

Every industry has its chain of command and specialized terms to describe the players. To help demystify the vending industry, here's a brief who's who.

○ *Broker*: another term for "independent sales representative." Brokers represent manufacturers that are too small or choose not to maintain their own internal sales forces. Although they don't actually sell you products, they're an important source of information and leads for purchasing products at competitive prices.

○ *Distributor*: companies that sell equipment and consumables directly to operators. Distributors carry the products of a wide variety of manufacturers.

○ *Manufacturer*: a company that produces vending equipment or consumables. Some manufacturers sell to operators directly, but most sell through distributors.

○ *Operator*: someone who owns and services vending machines. If you're reading this book, you're interested in becoming an operator. Sometimes the term vendor (see "Learning the Lingo," later in this chapter) is used to mean operator, but in this book we keep the terms strictly separate.

○ *Purchasing cooperative*: an association of operators, usually small businesses, that join together for purchasing purposes. By soliciting distributors as a group, cooperatives assure a certain annual volume and therefore command a lower price.

"Sales is like playing golf," says Hendersonville, Tennessee, full-line operator B.J. S. "You just keep on doing it. I pitched my service to one of my customers for five years until he finally gave in. You have to be stubborn and refuse to take 'No' for an answer. 'No' is for right now; tomorrow the person's mind might change."

Back at the Office

When you finish your route and return to the office, your day is not done. The load of coins and wad of bills require counting, sorting, and logging in your bookkeeping system.

Sound boring? You wouldn't be the first person to think so. "Don't fall into the trap of thinking, 'Oh, wow, look at all this money I have' and go out and buy a Corvette," says Becky P. "You have to be very, very disciplined in a cash business because, at the end of the month, you have your equipment loans, insurance payments, merchandise invoices, rent, gasoline bills, and sales taxes. Vending is a real business—you have to take care of your bookwork. You have to know where you are."

After you've finished with your paperwork, your other chores include merchandising, marketing, ordering, and various other administrative duties.

For example, you may have noticed while on your route that tortilla chips are hot at Location A, but at Location B you can't keep enough microwave popcorn in stock. In retail, proper merchandising translates directly to profits, so you take out your planograms (diagrams of where merchandise goes in your machines) for each location and figure out an arrangement that boosts space for the movers without impacting other strong sellers. You may study your data and realize a location is no longer profitable. Then you'll need to make a plan: Do you pull out immediately or try some other strategies?

When you're through with merchandising, turn to marketing. Return inquiry calls and initiate some of your own.

A vending business is, in many ways, like running a store where each part of your store is in a different location. Therefore, you need to stay on top of your sales figures, your inventory, and your marketing. The advantage you have over a store owner is that you are not dependent on one location, but on several. If a store were doing poorly, the owner would have to pick up and relocate.

> **⚠ Beware!**
> Never treat a customer's complaint as minor league. "It's not the $2 sandwich that you'll lose," Northridge, California, full-line operator Becky P. warns. "It's the fact that they're spending anywhere from $1 to $6 a day. If you lose that day in and day out, five, six days a week, what does that add up to at the end of the year?"

▲

For you, on the other hand, if one location is doing poorly, another may be doing great. You can find various high-traffic locations for your merchandise without having to relocate your entire business.

For Tomorrow

Depending on the kind of products you're selling, your next step is either packaging or ordering, and stocking product.

How you choose to package determines your profit. Jennifer Berdoll Wammack was discouraged from trying to load and drop a 9-inch, 3-pound pie with the prototype machine she and the team at Precision Vending were trying to create. She wouldn't take "No" for an answer, though, knowing a larger pie would bring in more money per transaction. She kept coming back with the exact same pie size each time she was asked to reduce it. Her candy is also packaged in 1-pound parcels, which as Berdoll Wammack underscores, "is much bigger than a Snickers or bag of chips, which really tried the team's patience at Precision."

Taking advantage of cashless vending attributes was key to capitalizing on pie sales from a machine; it's easy for people to go past their normal spending limits when they're using a credit card, and homemade pie priced at $18.50 is no cheap, mass-produced snack.

Baltimore pantyhose operator Janice M. buys bulk pantyhose and repackages them into smaller boxes.

Food operators use this time to stock up. "Those who start out without much working capital literally make collections during the day and use the funds to buy their product that night for the next day," Becky P. notes. "If you're big enough, or have space to warehouse products, then you can have things delivered and reload with items you have in stock."

Dump Your Cash

Always take deposits immediately to your financial institution. Sitting on cash is

> ### Smart Tip
> *Tip...*
>
> Today's vending machines can phone home, transmitting inventory levels, sales figures, out-of-service information, and other data directly to a desktop PC. Of course, you need to buy machines that are compatible. Most modern vending machines over the past several years have been set up to work with the right plug-in equipment. They conform to the vending industry transfer status known as DEX, short for "digital exchange." Ask before purchasing an older machine, whether or not it is able to transfer such data. Here is a company that stocks DEX-compatible machines and accessories, replete with detailed attributes: www.asavending.com/technology.htm. To understand how DEX works in conjunction with telemetry, go to www.telemetrytalk.com.

Learning the Lingo

You'll find lots of vending lingo explained in the Glossary, but here are the bare-bones terms you need to know to navigate the industry like a pro.

○ *Client.* The person or company who contracts with you to place vendors at their location.

○ *Customer.* A person who makes purchases from a vending machine. Often, a customer is an employee at your client's business.

○ *Planogram.* A diagram of an individual vendor with a specific product assigned to each spiral. As vendor capacity grew (most machines now include 40 or more spirals), more sophisticated selection and placement of products (aka merchandising) became necessary for profitability, and the planogram was born.

○ *Route.* The territory covered when servicing machines. The exact definition of this term is nonspecific. Sometimes it means the locations you visit in a given day. Sometimes it means the number of people who service locations for your company. For example, if you have 15 machines and you service seven one day and eight another, you'd have two routes. However, you'd also have two routes if you hired an employee and you serviced 50 machines a week and your employee serviced 15 machines a week.

○ *Servicing machines.* The process of cleaning, maintaining, repairing, and, most important, filling vendors. In other words, servicing machines is what you do every day on a route.

○ *Spiral.* The space allotted for a type of product in a food vendor. Because snack machines move products forward via a metal spiral mechanism, the term has been adopted to mean any individual offering—snack, sandwich, soda, etc. However, use of the term varies within the industry. For example, in a telecard machine, a spiral is called a bin.

○ *Vendor.* The abbreviated term for "vending machine." In the industry, vendor sometimes means operator, but in this book we keep the two terms strictly separate.

typically an invitation for theft. Ask how the bank will accept your cash, which may need to be bundled a certain way, or in the case of coins, rolled. Establish a good

▲

A Spoonful of Motivation

Although you'll certainly bring a variety of skills to the table, there are a few personality traits you'll want to have in your repertoire, which include being:

○ *Cash-wise.* Because you receive cash immediately, rather than billing your customers and receiving payment later, attention to basic bookkeeping is a must. "If you can't balance a checkbook, don't get into this business," stresses consumables distributor John Ochi of Five Star Distributors in Vernon Hills, Illinois. Maintaining a strong awareness of how much cash is coming in and what expenses you will need to set that cash aside for is a major factor in having a successful vending business.

○ *Persistent and organized.* Gone are the days of servicing machines without a plan. Today, convenience stores, company cafes, and telecommuting all contribute to fierce competition for vending dollars. The reason customers drive ten miles out of their way to Berdoll Pecan Farm during off hours is to get homemade-quality bakery goods and candy. It took Jennifer Berdoll Wammack about 90 days of tweaking her machines to perfection to make sure the heavy sweets came through the coils fully, and without disrupting the product or machine function in the process. With no one at the shop after hours (when people really took advantage of the vending service), it was essential that the vendor functioned perfectly. "The first time we did a trial run with our new equipment we showed up in the morning to empty the machine and the air conditioner had gone out, leaving us with a whole bunch of melted candy, but we just kept at it until it worked right," Berdoll Wammack remembers.

○ *Gregarious.* Vending may seem like the perfect occupation for an introvert—it's all about inanimate objects and machines, right? Wrong! Your success in vending will be heavily influenced by your ability to network, use existing connections for growth, and attract new clients by using above-average interpersonal skills. Don't worry. It's never too late to develop those traits. Pick up a copy of *PeopleSmart: Developing Your Interpersonal Intelligence* by Melvin L. Silberman and Freda Hansburg.

○ *Self-motivated.* Although the need for this trait practically goes without saying, the amount of literature on the topic belies its mystery. "People

---

A Spoonful of Motivation, continued

don't realize how hard we work," says Becky P. "Vending's not much different than running a restaurant—it's evenings, holidays, Saturdays, and Sundays. You have to be passionate and love it." Self-motivation comes from keeping a goal to succeed in front of you and continually telling yourself that you can reach that goal if you resist those urges to take time off from your route. It takes tenacity for all business owners to maintain their focus and stay motivated.

---

rapport with your bank and use the ATM for deposits if you can't make it to the bank before they close.

What's My Take?

What you make in vending depends on how many machines you service and the net profit of each. "Income? It's very hard to say," says *Vending Times* editor-in-chief Tim Sanford. "You get the right locations and you can do well. It's a very local and personality-oriented business. Two things vending operators need to cultivate are the skills to scope out good locations and the ability to make a reasonable forecast regarding how much money they can make at a given location," adds Sanford, who has seen guys who can look at the cars in the parking lot and determine why or why not a location will be good. Honing these skills and learning from the experience of others are two key ways to make a good living in vending.

"Vending's like every other retail business—on average, you have to work on volume," says Becky P. Although all of our experts stressed that vending requires hard work for relatively small per-machine

Tip...

Smart Tip

Like most operators, Randall Sutherland hates vandalism. Here's one of his tips for prevention: "Make sure to install the vandal guard that comes with your machine immediately. Little kids have tiny arms that can go way up inside the machine and steal merchandise, as well as get stuck and hurt. When a kid (or someone with a small arm) gets in there and steals, you pretty much can kiss the next customer goodbye; they'll put their money in and not get the product because the front of the spiral will be empty."

profits, they also emphasize that those who do it right are prosperous. If what we've said in these first two chapters leaves you cold, maybe it's time to consider a different industry. On the other hand, perhaps you're pumped because your skills fit the profile: People-oriented; good with numbers, logistics, and sales; and a tenacious work ethic.

If so, read on and we'll tell you exactly what you need to know.

Buy a Business or Start from Scratch

Everything you need to build a vending operation from the ground up is right in front of you. But for whatever reason, you may be wondering if there's a way to jump-start the process.

Indeed, there is. There are also hundreds of individuals who fall victim to vending business opportunity scams every

▲

year. To avoid being one of them, read this chapter, which presents some valuable dos and don'ts, then goes into the question of whether to start the business from scratch or buy an existing business.

One Operator's Story

So pervasive is the business opportunity scam in vending that the industry has its own term for the scam: Blue Sky. Although we learned much about Blue Skies from everyone we spoke to, the best way to tell you about them is through one operator's story.

In 2008, Erik A. Borger was working long hours in retail when his father was diagnosed with cancer. Borger recalls having barely any time for himself, not to mention for a sick father. Months went by while he spread himself so thin that between his job and father's hospital bedside, he only saw his wife for ten minutes each night. With the intention of helping his dad and finally starting the business that had been developing in his head for years, he gave his employer a two-week notice. "I slowly began doing my homework, browsing machines and different manufacturers online until I stumbled across a company who sold machines with healthy product graphics, location placement, and even a credit card reader," Borger says. "I was very interested in what they might provide. They informed me that their machines were custom made, I would be guaranteed an exclusive territory, and be taught all I needed to know about the vending business," Borger grimaces. "Being a naive 27-year-old, I bought their pitch hook, line, and sinker. Sixty-four thousand dollars later I had my five machines and a giant loan payment to go with it. Fortunately, actually unfortunately, after our local bank decided to deny me the loan I applied for, my mother stepped in and helped me out. Shortly after my payment went through I found after some digging around that the owners had gotten in trouble with the law over mass spamming and a vending scam operation, of all things. Disheartened, yet determined to succeed, I prayed to God for grace and awaited my fate."

Borger recounts the many disappointments: "The company certainly lived up to its owners' tarnished past with a two-month delay on machine placement. When the machines finally arrived, it quickly became apparent that the 'custom made' machines were just standard AMS 39s ($4,600 each, new) with fancy graphics on them. It didn't take me long to figure out that I was in trouble. After all five machines were placed, it became clear to me that the location finder took anything they could. My first month in a local school produced $30 in sales. Buying those machines was the worst mistake of my life, but I had to move on and focus on how to salvage my mistake. Quickly, I called the company and had some machines moved to better locations where I would at least earn more than $30 a month. I also began scouting out food and drink sources which would allow me to make more than 9 cents off of each product, and after loads of investigatory shopping I developed a planogram that would somewhat succeed."

> **! Beware!**
> Advertisements promising big bucks for part-time or minimal work are scam-alerts. Typically, in all business, if something appears too good to be true, it usually is a scam.

Is There Anyone You Can Trust?

Fortunately, this tragic tale has a happy ending, and, as you know, Borger went on to have success as an operator. But it does beg the question: "Is there anyone you can trust?"

The answer is many people. First of all, you should always check with the attorney general's office both in the state where you are living as well as the state in which the company making the business offer is located. Then you have the Better Business Bureau, Federal Trade Commission, and National Fraud Information Center to call on for help and information. Next, turn to industry associations. For vending, that's NAMA, but there may be other helpful organizations. If industry associations haven't heard of the company in question, be wary. Even if the company is not a member of the association, the organization probably knows about them if they're legitimate.

Search the internet or visit a library and ask the librarian to help you search business databases to locate the outfit in question. If the party in question does not turn up or appears to be in a different business, that is a red flag. Also, contact references—if a business won't provide you with the names or numbers of any satisfied clients, they may not have any. Even if they do, ask to tour one or two of their routes and see how open they are to it. A good operator should want you to see their work ethic and style, hoping you'd continue in the same vein. After all, they're trying to make a sale, so it behooves them to sell you on various elements of the business so you don't call later, disgruntled and befuddled. Randall Sutherland says if you offer to sign a non-disclosure agreement stating you'll not pursue any of their clients (if you don't wind up buying the route), or sell the route information to others, there's no reason they shouldn't comply.

As a veteran operator consultant, Sutherland is paid either a half or full-day rate to go over information with new operators. They want to know what kind of truck to buy, which distributors or supply sources to use, which products are big sellers in the area, and how long it will take for a machine to pay for itself, factoring in things such as depreciation. "To find someone locally who will do this for you, check the bulletin boards at places like Merchant's Mart (www.vistar.com) or Vending Services of America to find someone successful who's been in the business for a long time," says Sutherland. "Most guys will do that to help out newcomers, even if they currently don't advertise consulting as a service. They're not that competitive."

If the veterans you ask feel threatened and you don't get anywhere, ask industry associations to put you in touch with veteran operators outside your area of competition. As we mentioned in the first chapter, many operators dabble in more than one vending category, and they're a reservoir of information waiting to be tapped.

You can also call the offices of industry publications *Automatic Merchandiser* and *Vending Times*. Both magazines produce annual listings of everyone in the business.

Reputable Opportunities

Although we've painted a scary picture, don't reject the vending industry, a business opportunity, or a franchise out of hand. There are plenty of reputable companies to help you get started. Your job is separating the wheat from the chaff. See the "Burn Protection Checklist on page 35."

Fortunately, vending is a close-knit industry. While there are a lot of very small operators who don't participate in associations like NAMA, most everyone who hires an employee gets into the loop. And because they've all been where you are, you'll quickly find out how happy they are to lend newcomers a hand.

Even equipment distributors urge newcomers to call upfront. "Honestly, I get people on the phone in tears," says Vince Gumma of Chicago's American Vending Sales. "They've already spent $40,000 or $50,000 in retirement savings, and I can't help them."

Again, the key is to network before you buy. Regardless whether your specialty is new or old, vending trade magazines, NAMA, and veterans like those interviewed in this book offer a big-picture vantage point they're eager to share. Take advantage of their knowledge and experience.

If you do encounter less than savory sellers, please do your part in helping your community of vendors to avoid them by contacting the organizations on this list, supplied by The Vending Connection (www.vendingconnection.com), an educational guidance center for new vending professionals:

- FTC toll free hotline: (877) FTC-HELP (382-4357)
- FTC online complaint form (www.ftc.gov)
- Canadian PhoneBusters hotline: (888) 495-8501
- Internet Fraud Complaint Center (www.ic3.gov)
- Software Piracy (www.siia.net/piracy/report.asp)
- Nonemergency number for your local police department
- Better Business Bureau (www.bbb.org)

Burn Protection Checklist

The New York Better Business Bureau published on its website an excellent guide to avoiding scams. The Council of Better Business Bureaus suggests you ask the following questions before deciding on a purchase of any vending equipment or route offers or packages:

1. If the advertisement indicates any connection with a distributing company or manufacturer, have you seen satisfactory evidence, in writing, from the distributing company or manufacturer authorizing and backing up the advertisement?   ❏ No ❏ Yes

2. If the advertisement refers to specific earnings from vending machines, is there proof that those earnings are factual?   ❏ No ❏ Yes

3. Does the advertisement clearly state that it is an offer to sell vending machines?   ❏ No ❏ Yes

4. Does the contract you are asked to sign plainly state all terms or conditions?
❏ No ❏ Yes

5. If reference is made to locations or routes, have you seen proof that the locations have been secured by contract and are available for inspection?   ❏ No ❏ Yes

6. If familiar brand names are used, have you seen proof that their manufacturers have given permission for the products to be mentioned?   ❏ No ❏ Yes

7. If the promoter claims or implies sponsorship of civic, charitable, religious, or fraternal organizations, have you seen proof of that sponsorship? ❏ No   ❏ Yes

The Company

1. How long has the firm been in business? _____

2. What is its past record of accomplishment? _____

3. Are its principals well regarded and experienced? _____

4. What is the financial strength? _____

5. What are its plans for future development? _____

6. What is its record at your Better Business Bureau? _____

7. How selective is it in choosing potential operators? _____

Burn Protection Checklist, continued

The Product to be Vended

1. What is the product's quality? _____

2. Is it a staple, a fad, or a luxury item? _____

3. Is it seasonal? _____

4. How well is it selling now, and has it sold through vending machines in the past? _____

5. Would you buy it on its merits? _____

6. Is it priced competitively? _____

7. Is it packaged attractively? _____

The Machine

1. Is this machine of the quality customarily purchased by experienced operators?

   _____

2. Is the cost in line with that of comparable machines? _____

3. Have you seen and operated the actual machine you plan to buy? _____

4. Is the machine large enough to handle the suggested or promised volume?

   _____

5. What is the machine's frequency of repair record? _____

6. What are the terms of the manufacturer's written guarantee on the machine?

   _____

Location and Placement

1. How much will the location owner get on each item sold through your machines? _____

2. Is the distributor obliged by the contract to find locations for you or do you have to find your own? _____

Burn Protection Checklist, continued

3. Is the territory well defined? _____

4. Is it exclusive? _____

5. Is it large enough to offer good sales potential? _____

6. What is the income level in the area? _____

7. What is the nature of your competition? _____

8. What is the experience of other vending operators in your area who have done business with this franchising organization? _____

    _____

The Contract

1. Does the contract cover all aspects of the agreement? _____

2. Can it be renewed, terminated, transferred, and if so, under what conditions?

    _____

3. Must a certain amount of merchandise be purchased? From whom? _____

    _____

4. Can you return merchandise for credit? _____

5. Under what conditions is the contract invalid? _____

The rest of this helpful guide can be viewed at www.newyork.bbb.org/SitePage. aspx?site=24&id=1face262-86c5-4fd3-81e0-3871b77bc2cc.

Starting from Scratch

When you start a new business from scratch, the upside is that you can plan it as you wish and run the business in a manner that is best suited to meet your goals and objectives. To do this, however, you need to be prepared to do plenty of research and find the products and locations that would best draw business. You will need to carefully select distributors and establish relationships. Just as Janice M. did research and forged her own path in the pantyhose business, you could do the same with a product that you have not seen readily distributed (although finding such a product is increasingly more difficult) or you could look at existing products, distributors who handle them, and potential locations, and crunch the numbers to see if such a business would be profitable. Some vending operators have literally gone from location to location doing their research. They have then read up on how the business works and after several months of planning, put together a plan and a route that could start them off—typically as a part-time business before jumping in with both feet.

Tim Sanford, editor-in-chief of *Vending Times*, says, "There is no one right way to start in this business. There are two ways people traditionally get into the vending business. One is that they work for a large vending company like Canteen or Aramark, the two biggest vending companies in the United States. They work as a route driver, route supervisor, or maybe they become a route manager. If you work for someone for a while, you get to know the business. Then you can find someone who wants to work with you and put in ten machines, and you'll be able to hit the ground running. You'll have experience and know how to talk to accounts."

Obviously, this is a manner in which you learn the business while being employed by someone else before going out on your own. It means investing some time, but also means a much better chance of having the background knowledge once you are ready to open your own business.

"The other way many guys get into this field is by attending a trade show and being seduced by one of these attractive young ladies in a bathing suit handing out four-color brochures about how to make money in vending. They buy ten machines which cost way too much, go out to get locations, and find out that they can't make any money at those locations. Suddenly they realize that they've just paid for an education and go back and attend NAMA conventions, start reading the literature and subscribe to *Vending Times*, and work their way out of a hole into a successful business," explains

---

Dollar Stretcher

Here are three tips from *AARP* magazine's "99 Great Ways to Save" bulletin to help new business owners keep costs down:

1. *Consumer Reports* studies show cars and trucks with stick shifts typically get two to five more miles to the gallon than automatic transmissions.

2. The best time to buy a car from a dealership is at the end of the month when salespeople are scrambling to meet their quotas.

3. Check www.gasbuddy.com for the lowest local gas prices. You can even download its free app compatible with certain brands of cell phones.

SCORE

SCORE is a free mentorship program run by the SBA that offers coaching in every occupation, by every kind of professional veteran you can imagine. There are chapters all over the United States with kind-hearted sorts who just want to see you do well. They'll go over your business plans and offer goal-setting objectives, counseling on customer conflicts, and insider tips on the local vending community. It's best to choose someone local, though it's not mandatory, so you can meet face-to-face, and possibly go on a few practice route runs. Wouldn't it be great to learn from someone else's mistakes rather than your own? Look for your future mentor at www.score.org.

Sanford of the Blue Sky schemes that draw in many people who later turn their losses around. Of course doing the research first, attending the NAMA conventions, and reading the literature before spending any money could save these people a lot of heartaches.

Starting a business does not mean doing it entirely yourself or trying to learn everything about it. Today, you can start the business yourself and hire professionals as needed, such as a professional location company, to help you with the hardest part of the business—finding prime locations. Between the internet, NAMA, *Vending Times*, and numerous resources out there, you can find plenty of professionals to assist you and read plenty of valuable information about the industry.

Buying a Business

Unlike starting a business, which you could do slowly by just operating three machines at first, buying an entire business means jumping right in with both feet. If you are 100 percent ready to go and knowledgeable about how to run the business, this is one way to have an "instant business."

The benefits of buying an existing business are that you have machines, distributors, and locations all ready to hit the ground running. You can step in and continue where the previous owner leaves off without missing a step. You simply need to introduce yourself to everyone you'll be working with and establish a rapport. While you can certainly make changes as you go, you can do it at your own pace, changing some locations, replacing some lesser-selling items with some new ones, and so on.

Starting from Endings

Some of our operators agree that capitalizing on an existing operation is a better value for the money, comparing apples to apples. If the proprietor has taken excellent care of all aspects of the business, you'll be much farther ahead with connections in the community and credibility with banks for expansion. The going rate for an established operation is 25 to 45 percent of the company's gross sales.

By purchasing his business from his retiring father-in-law, B.J. S. dodged some bullets. However, he stresses caution. "Look at the equipment—not so much age as the appearance. If it's clean and old, then someone's taken care of it. You can see pretty quickly if the equipment's been abused or it's been refurbished or whatever."

In addition, B.J. emphatically recommends retaining a knowledgeable attorney to steer you through the process. "Unfortunately, in this industry, I think the income statement only tells part of the truth," he warns.

"As a prudent businessperson, I wouldn't take somebody's word for it," B.J. continues. "Make up some type of contract where you have a safeguard. Put the excess in escrow or allow for a 10 percent fluctuation or whatever it is. You'll see in the first week if the income statement is accurate. But you're not going to see it until you own it."

The big questions when buying any business are who's selling the business and why? Ask probing questions and do some research. Is the seller trying to dump an existing route that is not very profitable, or is he or she simply tired of the daily routine and looking to retire to Florida or Arizona? You need concrete numbers to evaluate the business for the last few years and you need to talk with distributors. You can always check with the associations and see if the seller is someone they have a relationship with or someone they've never heard of. You'll also need to talk with your accountant and attorney to make sure all numbers and documents are accounted for and that everything adds up to success. Associations, vending publications, and experts in the field can tell you if you're getting a good value for your dollar, or if the business is overvalued.

As we mentioned before, you also want an owner who agrees to stay on for a short time to teach you the routes and the ropes of the business. Any owner who wants to just drop a business in your lap and run away is likely not completely on the up and up.

When buying a business, you will typically have to make some compromises. Unlike starting everything on your own, there will be certain aspects that won't be to your liking. However, you are much farther along the road if you buy a good business—and evaluating the potential of the business you are thinking of buying is the key.

A Matter of Personality

How adaptable are you? Do you like to start things from the beginning or jump into a project that's already started? Are you the type of person who enjoys building furniture or buying it fully constructed? These are the kinds of questions you need to ask yourself before deciding between starting your own business and buying an existing one. There are growing pains when you start from scratch. There are mistakes that entrepreneurs learn the hard way. The location you thought would be marvelous may not turn out to be very profitable, or the product you thought would be a surefire hit may disappoint. This is more likely to occur when forging your own path. If, however, you start your own vending business well aware of the potential pitfalls that come with the "learning curve," and you are ready to accept that it will take time to perfect the system, find the best distributors, and build the routes that optimize sales, then you will be starting off with the right mindset.

However, if you know that you will be impatient and may become frustrated and disenchanted if the business does not start out as you had hoped, you may be better off buying a business to limit the hard lessons and (with the right business) increase the possibilities of having a fairly stable business from the onset.

Keep in mind that you will pay a price for buying a ready-made business—literally. Depending on the size and scope of the business, and the types of products sold and number of routes, you will pay much more than if you start from scratch, since, as mentioned earlier, you can start off very small and grow as you see fit. Again, it's all a matter of your personal choice and how much money you have available. Certainly, for someone who wants to jump in and start a full-time business, buying the right vending operation is a good option, while for the person who is looking to test out the field, starting small with your own business is the more obvious option.

Finding Your Niche

While not as glamorous as, say, becoming a jungle guide, the life of a vending operator sounds perfect to you. Knowing this much means your cup is half full. Topping it off requires determining what type of vending you'd like to do and whether there's a demand for you to supply.

The business lingo for these activities is targeting your market and conducting market research. Think of these steps akin to feeding yourself—you have to know what kind of food you like and where to find it. The more you know, the more satisfied you'll be. Similarly, the more thorough your research, the more satisfied (profitable) your business will become.

Do some business owners skip, or shortchange, the process of evaluating their market's potential? You bet. But they're the ones who flounder or fail.

Since you're reading this book to succeed, use the handy tools provided in this chapter for startup work, and come back to it for guidance as your business grows.

Tried-and-True or Trailblazing?

To narrow your vending options, first decide whether you're a trailblazer or path follower. Trailblazers enter new markets, or define their own market, like pantyhose. Path followers prefer tried-and-true markets such as snacks and soda. Which one should you choose? Either is completely appropriate, and both have their pluses and minuses.

Where No One's Gone Before

The main advantages to trailblazing are obvious: There's little or no competition and lots of room for growth. This means you're first in line rather than just another voice in the crowd. You won't be looking over your shoulder very much because there are plenty of clients to go around.

The principal downside is lack of familiarity and support. Not only must you convince a prospect your company is best for the job; you have to sell them on the concept as well. There is also less of a network for you to lean on for information and advice. In Jennifer Berdoll Wammack's case, she needed to be more creative than her machine creators in order to accomplish her mission: to make three-pound pies and one-pound bags of candy vend from her machine. Told "No" time after time, she kept coming up with reasons why the team should keep looking for an answer, which first came in the form of an experimental welding of two coils together. "We had to not only weld two coils together to manage the weight and balance of the pie, but we also had to add additional motors to the machine, because each coil is supposed to function by its own motor," she says. "Oh, and then we had to design a way for the coil turns to synchronize. A pair of coils welded to one another had to turn identically and they aren't designed for that. It wasn't easy." What she and her team have now, however, is a wildly successful selling machine.

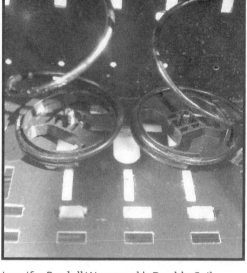

Jennifer Berdoll Wammack's Double Coil, Double Motor Modification for Pie Drop

Jennifer Berdoll Wammack's Pie Vendor

"A lot of people don't want to hear about something new," says Baltimore pantyhose vending innovator Janice M. "The attitude is 'I don't care; go away' unless you've been around for 30 years and they recognize the name. In addition, corporate procurement officers are often men, and they simply don't understand the challenges faced by pantyhose wearers."

Niche Markets and Trends

Trends and niche markets burst onto the playing field when a need is noticed and its panacea is invented. An individual invents a solution to a problem or need and begins to share it with others, and the success of that marketing either rages or sinks largely as a result of how accurately the entrepreneur gauged placement of the product.

Sometimes existing niche markets are busy gobbling up a wonderful product and someone comes along and creates something that fills similar needs but is slightly different or a little bit better than the original idea.

With so many ways to be a player in the retail market, it can be hard to choose what your first venture will be. A creative way to unearth possible markets in need is to make a four-column chart to serve as a study (see the "Niche Products and Services Study Sheet" on page 46). The four topics you'll examine in this chart are current trends, the markets that flock toward them, the need the trend product satisfies, and new product ideas that would satisfy similar needs for that audience. Ask yourself what else that

▲

Niche Products and Services Study Sheet

Current trends	Markets that flock to them	The need that was satisfied	New product ideas for similar needs

audience may want. Before you challenge yourself with this exercise, take a look at the unique vending businesses profiled in the sidebar on page 47 and the needs they filled. It should get you thinking like a true innovator.

Someone Needs to Market This!

Now that you've already done some brainstorming on your own, we'd like to give you some ideas for vending markets that are not yet saturated.

- *Hospital DVD Use and Re-use.* Hospitals are filled with captive audiences needing entertainment to fill the hours before their (or their loved ones') discharge. Most rooms have DVD players in them, so what about a DVD machine that dispenses movies? Users could get a 50 percent refund once they returned the movie to the machine. There are lots of people giving away DVDs at www.craigslist.org and www.freecycle.org, so you could stock your collection for free.

- *Craft Supply.* In assisted living homes residents often make crafts. A vendor that dispensed markers, glitter, scrapbooking supplies, and make-your-own greeting card kits (or any other craft kits) might be a hit.

They Found a Need and Filled It

Bike Fixation, LLC, http://bikefixation.com

Chad and Alex of Bike Fixation decided that the high number of cyclists in the Minneapolis/St. Paul, Minnesota, area needed to be able to repair their bikes in a jiffy at a vending station open from 6:00 A.M. to midnight, 365 days a year. Voted the number-one bike-friendly city in America by *Bicycle* magazine in 2010, Minneapolis/St. Paul offered an active, hungry market for Chad and Alex to tap into. Their first vending machine is positioned smack-dab along the Midtown Greenway, a superhighway built just for cyclists.

Trendy Vend, www.trendyvend.co.uk

Sisters Talia and Kayleigh Baccino thought up Trendy Vend one night when they were out on the town. It's the one-stop fancy pants shop that offers anything night clubbers could want as they party for hours and hours. The machines advertise the latest fashion items as well as dispense gel inserts for those tired dancing feet and offer invisible deodorant, lip gloss, hair wax, gum, aftershave, and antacids.

Pop N Go™, www.popngo.com/#!products

California-based Pop N Go answers the call for healthy snacks by providing hot-air popped corn, by the order, in single-serve, entertaining preparations while you watch. Everyone loves popcorn, but health-conscious snackers are concerned about the saturated fats and chemicals involved. This company appeals to that gap in the market by offering what people want.

Grave Candle Vending Machines

These machines are available in several countries and appeal to those attending church services or visiting loved ones in cemeteries. They attract one of the most captive audiences of all, other than visitors to prisons, by focusing on what worshippers and mourners want. Here are a few examples: http://commons.wikimedia.org/wiki/Category:Grave_candle_vending_machines.

- *Gay Wedding Accoutrements.* Gay weddings, commitment ceremonies, and civil unions have been in the media a lot lately. Within the states that grant marriage licenses to same-sex couples there are many wedding accoutrement services available. Wedding accoutrement kits have long been available in the Las

▲

Vegas one-stop wedding shop state, but what about in states that perform many same-sex ceremonies? A classy looking machine dispensing birdseed to throw, bride-and-bride or groom-and-groom mini wedding cakes (cupcakes), garter belts, and silk boutonnière flowers positioned next to a kitschy ceremony spot might fill your pockets.

- *Sports Hydration Refill.* Shoppers can refill large bottles with filtered water at many grocery stores. At sports arenas, gyms, and parks where people run it might be nice to have a vendor that refills reusable bottles with either water or electrolyte-rich sports drinks now that consumers are more conscientious about not wasting plastic.

- *Business Card Maker.* If you can make your companion animal an ID tag inside a large store such as PetSmart, why can't you make your own business cards at a vendor? If you had your own card vendor you could offer many styles at a touch screen interface for serious, professional styles and also "just for fun" cards such as "Party Animal," "Super Mom," and "The King of Golf." Your machines might do well at office supply conventions and stores, nightclubs, and tourist attractions.

Familiar Turf

Not surprisingly, the flip side of trailblazing is path following where advice, information, and support abound. For that reason, most operators follow proven paths. "If I were starting up, I'd contact the local or state chapter of NAMA and ask for references outside of my marketplace," says Wayne D., the full-line operator in Burnsville, Minnesota. "Most of us aren't too hung up about competitors. We would rather help new operators so they don't add to the stigma that vending machines never work."

Helping Each Other Out

Operators do help operators out. Most of the operators we interviewed agreed that in most cases they help one another, rather than try to hijack routes or take advantage of one another. Those types are out there but are generally not the kind of businesspeople who are highly visible in the community and successful.

Bright Idea

Join the community of operators online at the Vendors Exchange International Inc. forum (www.veii.com). It's a good way to learn about the preferred equipment, locators, and distributors of the vending community.

Some vending businesses let newcomers ride on a route to see what it's like and try to provide some guidance, since the vending community is a tight-knit group, all trying to forge a better impression of the industry.

Gaining a Competitive Edge

The key to establishing yourself in a competitive market is showing prospects you are head and shoulders above the rest. Economic, demographic, and technological changes offer entrepreneurs opportunities for success, even in today's crowded market. The key is having a plan.

If you can bring in a cost-effective product that a demographic group wants and can buy efficient machines that work far more often than not, you're ahead of the game. For example, students at a university may want the same popular drinks as other universities. If, however, you land the account to service the brand-new student center and can maintain a $1.00 cost for a bottle of water, rather than $1.25 or $1.50, and you have the popular favorite brand always well-stocked in a highly reliable machine, then you've done the job as well or better than the competition could do. Of course, you first need to calculate that you are making money on the deal.

A competitive edge may also mean offering variety. If, for example, the student center has a Coca-Cola machine but you can bring in a machine that offers something that reflects the current leading trends, such as healthy options, you may be met with a sigh of relief. If you stock fruit juice, smoothies, protein shakes, and sports drinks, you may find the customers at that location are ripe for such variety. Erik A. Borger's natural soda offerings, which make him 50 cents on the dollar (a higher return than a lot of other healthy snack kickbacks), are a big hit with youth. "The kids like the pictures on a lot of my healthy products," Borger says.

The key to being competitive is knowing what you can offer over your competition. Therefore, you need to get to know who else is in the area and offer something different, or better. Erik A. Borger says, "I'm the only healthy vending company here in Kansas City that I know of, so I am a niche." As the focus on better nutrition grows, so will the value of his position.

> ## Smart Tip Tip...
>
> Consider featuring your machines and products on social buying websites such as www.groupon.com, www.buy-withme.com, and www.livingsocial.com. These companies feature your service as a discounted offer in their mass-marketing blitz, then you get new customers, and the social buying websites get a cut, making everybody happy. Your offer can be a first-time customer deal or something temporary that you can afford to give up in the short term to get more business in the long term.

Waiting for your local audience to catch up with national trends is uncomfortable. When you're featuring products in a market that recognizes trends later than markets in other parts of the country (and before others), it's only a matter of time before your market will catch up. Think of tiny towns that start playing popular movies in their theaters two years after the films have been through major cities. To be the only supplier of a hot item when it becomes popular is exciting. Enjoy the process, because soon after you become popular you'll start to have competitors.

As mentioned earlier, the vending community is typically a tightly woven group, so very often the competition is not with operators who are established in a given location, but for a new location. "Vendors give each other some courtesy, rather than trying to take someone else's account, since they wouldn't want someone to do the same thing to them," explains Tim Sanford.

Stay in the Zone

Although trailblazing vs. path following is a philosophical dilemma, the recommended size of your market area is not. Since drive time and fuel costs are significant factors, it's wise to stay within a 30-mile radius of your office, 50 at most. This constraint alone may help determine your vending type. For example, if you are planning to serve a rural area that's already served by a local food vending operation, a nonfood operation might be a more viable choice. On the other hand, if the headquarters of the existing food operator is miles away, you may be able to offer a more cost-effective option. What this means is by knowing what the market already does and does not offer, you can plan accordingly.

Know Thy Options

We've already discussed which vending markets are currently the largest, but the success of a pioneering entrepreneur, such as Janice M., shows it's wise to look at the forest before focusing on a tree.

To find out about the many types of vending machines and products already available, check out the annual buyer's guides produced by *Automatic Merchandiser* and *Vending Times*. While there's plenty of overlap between the two, not all options appear in each publication. You can find *Automatic Merchandiser* at www.vendingmarketwatch.com and *Vending Times* at www.vendingtimes.com (more information is in the Appendix at the back of the book).

You can also keep reading to find out some of the other options now available—discussed later in the book—and can do your own research by simply studying the machines serviced by other operators.

Mission: Possible

A mission statement tells the world what your company is about. It generally also includes something about your goals and, sometimes, how you intend to achieve them. Writing a mission statement is a vital part of finding your niche because it helps you define your target market and stay focused on what's important. Use the "Mission Statement Worksheet" on page 52 and the examples below to come up with your own.

Although in many industries a long, detailed mission statement is de rigueur, vending operators generally prefer something succinct. Here are three real-life examples:

1. "To provide the highest-quality vending service in Nashville."

2. "Quality through integrity. To provide the very best customer satisfaction."

3. "To be a cut above. Good enough isn't enough; it has to be perfect."

Know Your Demographic Market

As you narrow the specialty options, include a market assessment as part of your market research. Know who will buy and what they will be more likely to purchase. For example, vending Tex-Mex is likely to be unsuccessful in a primarily Asian demographic region. Nor will targeting factories work if they're all headed south. Instead, cater to Asian tastes or target hospitals instead of factories. In general, look for areas of growth or market segmentation, such as a rising population of women aged 24 to 30 where pantyhose might be a very viable option. If, for example, you are in a region in which families are on the upswing, think about starting a toddler and child supply vending machine. Operators such as Celena Lentz of Nanny Caddy (www. nannycaddy.com) are cashing in on frazzled parents with an extension of the diaper machine—the "everything parents and kids" machine. Now parents can get baby wipes, nursing wraps, hand sanitizer, diaper cream, pacifiers, and more from the Nanny Caddies

Fun Fact

According to a recent news report by *Vending Market Watch*, bottled water companies have reduced the weight of PET resin plastic single-serve bottles by 32 percent over the past eight years, which is just like taking one out of three bottles out of our nation's waste stream.

▲

Mission Statement Worksheet

Use this worksheet to brainstorm a mission statement for your business. The components of a mission statement include:

○ Future goals: your vision of your company in a year, five years, and beyond

○ Client perceptions: your vision of how you want your clients to think of you

○ Industry perceptions: your vision of how you want the vending industry to think of you

Mission Statement for: _____(your business name)

_____

_____

_____

_____

_____

_____

_____

_____

_____

_____

_____

_____

_____

_____

_____

_____

stationed in shopping malls, airports, museums, and national tourist attractions all over the country.

Look at local websites and review the demographics at the town planning commission, where you can also look at the upcoming plans for the area. Get a feel for who will be moving into the community. Check out your city and surrounding areas by plugging them into www.city-data.com. This site contains everything about a geographic area from inches of rainfall per month to median home values. Look at www.yelp.com to see which services local residents frequent and prefer most by the

---

Who Is Searching for What and Where Are They Searching?

A way to get a feel for who is searching for what and where they are searching is to take advantage of Google Trends (www.google.com/trends).

The way Google Trends works is to tell you the place in the world where people search specific words most frequently. Search One below shows the cities that people searched the most with the following basic vending-related search word combinations at Google Trends.

Search One

"vending"
1. Cincinatti, OH
2. Charlotte, NC
3. Atlanta, GA

"vending machines"
1. Salt Lake City, UT
2. Las Vegas, NV
3. Miami, FL

"vending machines sale"
1. Houston, TX
2. Miami, FL
3. Atlanta, GA

"healthy vending"
1. San Diego, CA
2. Los Angeles, CA
3. Washington, DC

▲

Who Is Searching, continued

"vending company"
1. Richardson, TX
2. Atlanta, GA
3. Dallas, TX

A simple Google Beta search (https://encrypted.google.com/) with more specific word choices related to vending reveals the most commonly used word combinations around the country. They show up in the menu right below the search bar.

Search Two below shows a search for the following terms and the accompanying terms most used with them on Google Beta:

Search Two

"vending services"
1. "of richmond"
2. "Charlotte, NC"
3. "nj"
4. "of America"
5. "in Michigan"

"vending machine companies in"
1. "nj"
2. "florida"
3. "ny"
4. "utah"
5. "dallas, tx"
6. "ohio"

Think about how you would search for vending services online. What would your word choices be? The words you'd attach to "vending" would be "services" and "machine companies in (your town)." So Search Two shows the number of people looking to purchase operator services.

Now think about your differing choice of search words if you were a future operator looking to start a vending business. Search One shows what words you might attach to "vending" to find machines, or particular types of machines and routes for sale. To just look at the searches for "vending" and "vending machines" is not definitive because the searchers could be looking for either.

number of stars and flavor of reviews they rate with. Once you know the details of the population you'll be serving, study the trade papers and vending websites for the hottest items for that demographic group. You'll always find some standards such as soda, but you will likely discover some niche items that will have people returning to your machines often.

Except in the most depressed areas, a new niche or angle can almost always be found with the right amount of time put into researching what your community wants that people don't already have, or have enough of.

Evaluate an Innovation

If you're considering a vending specialty that is your own brainchild, or even one that's relatively new, conduct some direct consumer surveys. Surveys can be informal oral inquiries, formal written questionnaires, or a combination of both.

"One day, we were doing presentations during a Women Entrepreneurs of Baltimore class, and I started talking to a few of the women," Janice M. recalls. "I asked them how they would feel if they could purchase pantyhose through a vending machine. Everybody said, 'That's really cool. Who do you know that's doing that?' I said that I was. They all looked at me and said, 'That's great. Yeah, I'd purchase them. I cannot tell you how many times I have been to a wedding or a funeral or job interview or church on Sunday when everything is closed—that would be great.' "

Spurred on by the enthusiastic response, Janice developed a written survey. "I actually have footage of me walking down the street with a clipboard asking people what they thought: Would you buy pantyhose from a vending machine? If you wouldn't then why not? They didn't know me from Eve, so they didn't have any reason to sugarcoat anything. People are brutally honest when you're doing research, which is fine because it helps."

Due to the success of her efforts, Janice continues to rely on them. "I still have that [survey] on file because I'm going to use it again. In fact, I used it when I went out to Baltimore/Washington International Airport

Fun Fact

The technology of telemetry saves invaluable time by communicating the following errors from machine to operator:

- Bill validator full or jammed
- Changer communication error
- Machine not cooling
- Temperature too hot
- Column jam
- Sold out
- Coin jam

Additionally, the "curbside polling" that telemetry provides helps save operators and their drivers time commuting from stop to stop by accessing data at each of their remote machines to create the most efficient travel.

because they didn't see the need [for pantyhose vending]. So I told them about the survey and all the women who'd checked 'yes' beside 'Would you purchase this from a vending machine?' Then my contact said, 'Send me a package.' " You'll see the "Market Research Survey" Janice used on page 57. You can tailor it to your own specific vending niche.

Site Surveys

For traditional vending specialties, spend time surveying your operating radius from the ground. Take a few exploratory road trips and observe the mix of businesses, schools, hospitals, and high-rises. No matter how long you have been living in the area, you'll see things differently when you are looking with an entrepreneur's eye.

Stop in at potential locations and see what is already vended. Is there room for more variety or a more targeted product mix? Are the machines clean and well maintained? Are they new and attractive or old and shabby?

Follow Janice's lead and survey people using the machines. What do they think of the service and product mix? What would they like more or less of? Are they generally satisfied or dissatisfied? Why? Listen carefully and take good notes.

Other Survey Methods

"Obviously, you can cover a lot more over the phone," says B.J. S., the full-line vendor from Hendersonville, Tennessee. "I called Dun & Bradstreet and bought a database listing all Nashville companies including contact names and phone numbers. It cost $100 and came on diskette, so it was easy to break down and sort."

Although it's important to do some driving around, surveying by telephone can be cost-effective if you can get respondents to take the survey rather than hanging up. In a society that has been inundated by telemarketers, it can be frustrating to get people to take telephone surveys, so you need to promise them that it will only take a couple of minutes and then have very short, pointed questions about vending machines that only require short answers—don't forget you need to tabulate all of the responses.

> ### Dollar Stretcher
> Survey Monkey (www.surveymonkey. com) is a free online survey and response tabulator for up to 10 questions and 100 responses. The service includes customer support and pre-designed question styles. Their unlimited questions survey is $19.95 per month and lets you gather 1,000 responses per month, along with lots of extras. Don't forget to add some humor and gratitude to your survey, and a free snack from one of your machines wouldn't hurt either.

Market Research Survey

Dear Consumer,

   We need your help. Please tell us how we can better improve our services and products for you.

1. Would you purchase pantyhose from a vending machine if available at your location? Why or why not? _____

   _____

2. What price would you expect to pay for them? _____

   _____

3. What colors would you choose (white, black, gray, navy, etc.)? What sizes (small, medium, tall, full-figure, etc.)? _____

   _____

4. Would you purchase products from our catalog through the mail? Why or why not? _____

   _____

5. What age range are you in? 18–24, 25–36, 37–45, 46 and up? _____

   _____

   Any additional comments: _____

   _____

   _____

   _____

   _____

We would like to take this time to say thank you.

For a free sample of our products, please send your request to:

A-1 Vending Machines
P.O. Box 0101
Baltimore, MD 21205
Or call us at: (123) 456-7890

Source: McLean Machines and Co. Inc.

▲

More Competition than You Think

New vending operators often define their competition only in terms of other vending businesses. However, this assumption is far too narrow.

"We are a retail business," emphasizes John Ochi of Five Star Distributors in Vernon Hills, Illinois. "The machines are a form of retailing; there just isn't a human being sitting inside the box handing the stuff out."

This means any retailer who carries similar products is vying for your customer's dollars. "Too many operators think they have a captive audience," observes 20-year vending veteran Wayne D., a full-line operator in Burnsville, Minnesota. "But you don't. I like to say the only captive audience we have is the women's prison."

Another hindrance to vending is that you're competing against a stigma that's firmly entrenched. "The biggest problem the vending industry has is there's a public perception that it's the last resort," Ochi asserts. "Everybody's had bad experiences buying through a vending machine because some operator didn't make sure the machine gave good service."

The moral of the story: When you're conducting market research, look around the neighborhood for other retail options. If you're going into food, ask how long lunch hours last and if employees generally leave the premises. Include a visual or qualitative survey of potential locations to determine attitudes toward the current operator.

Above all, remember that once you hang out your shingle, the spotlight will shine on you just as hard as you're shining it on others. Be prepared to go the extra mile, and your business will thrive.

You might opt to go online with a web page that has your survey. Of course, you'll need to draw people to the site, which will mean marketing the name and web address to your demographic group. This is easier to do with a web-savvy population, such as college students. Run an ad in the college paper and offer a free download or something that you can give away that is cost-effective for the first 100 people that take the survey. The web survey should be concise and to the point, as was the survey set up by Janice.

A more costly, but effective means of doing market research is the focus group. This is where you gather a number of people in one place and ask them more detailed questions about the vending possibilities. For this you will need to give something away. Many advertising companies give away $50 or a free dinner (as worked out with a client) to get people to participate. In one hour you can get exactly what people would and would not buy from a vending machine and why. Be selective in whom you ask—have your demographic group narrowed down prior to a focus group.

Bulldozer Chasing

Those lucky enough to live where office or industrial buildings seemingly inflate overnight have one of the best markets around. "Whenever a new building would go up we'd literally drive around and count cars in the parking lot," says Becky P. of her tactics during startup. "Then we'd go back at night to see who had night shifts because those employees are a captive audience."

Build It Slowly

Once you've completed your market research, keep it handy. The data you gather is as useful for sales leads as it is for diagnosis. And it can even help you evaluate the viability of routes that become available as you begin to grow.

The year after he started, Wayne D. and his wife began following just such a strategy. "In 1979, we bought another small route that was a spin-off of a larger vending company's routes. We worked out a plan of what we were trying to accomplish so that we'd build [the operation] up to where I could leave R.J. Reynolds." It took another five years, but Wayne stayed focused and eventually reached his goal.

Continue to Do Market Research

One of the reasons why there are operators selling products that were outdated in the late 1990s is because they are not doing their homework . . . or in this case, updating their market research. Trends change, neighborhoods change, and demographics change. What was popular three years ago may not be in vogue at all today. For example, telecards are no longer the major seller they were in the late '90s because everyone and their mom has a cell phone today. Likewise, people are drinking Odwalla Smoothies and other products in increasing numbers, so soda may not be the only item selling in your demographic area. Stroll through the neighborhood supermarkets and see the size and placement of some of the displays.

You need to keep data current on what people are buying. See if the area that once sported young families now is dominated by senior housing and if the ethnicity has changed. The operator who goes in every day with blinders and routinely refills the machine with the same old thing year after year but cannot figure out why sales figures are declining is not doing his or her homework.

Structural Strategies

You've done your homework. You know your mission. You're ready to hang out your shingle.

Whoa! What'll you put on that shingle? Who needs to be notified? And what exactly do they want to know? What's your M.O.?

▲

Requirements and Defining Your Business

By this point you probably know if you're going it alone or bringing others on board. Either way, local, state, and federal agencies, including the omnipresent IRS, want to know your modus operandi: Are you a sole proprietorship, partnership, or corporation?

Most vending operators stick with the least complicated version, the sole proprietorship. Even spousal teams, pervasive in the industry, usually select this option.

Despite the fact that her husband brought all the vending experience to their relationship, on paper it's Northridge, California, Becky P.'s business. "When we started, it was highly beneficial to be a woman or minority business owner because it opened accounts to us." Financing also came easier, says Becky, due to programs targeting women and minority business owners.

Sole proprietorship is, by all accounts, the easiest structure under which to run a business. You get a business license and file whatever necessary business forms are applicable within your state and you are in business. There is very little paperwork and few formalities, other than paying taxes, of course. Income is reported on your personal or jointly filed tax returns.

Incorporating, however, is also a popular choice for vending entrepreneurs. When you're incorporated, the corporation carries the liability instead of you personally. You can also use it when negotiating with banks by reminding them the corporation guarantees the note. Even though the bank will probably still ask you for a personal guarantee, you can use your corporate status during negotiations. The biggest plus for incorporating is that the company stands as a separate entity, meaning that you are not personally liable if your machine falls over on someone while they are kicking it because they lost a dollar bill.

That extra protection helps many entrepreneurs sleep more securely at night. That is, once they finish the paperwork. Incorporating does include plenty of paperwork and has various requirements that you must fulfill as set forth by the state in which you incorporate. There is also the possibility of double taxation when you form a corporation, meaning you pay corporate taxes and then when you take money out of the corporation, you pay taxes again on your personal assets. You need to sit down with a business attorney or your accountant and weigh the pluses and minuses of incorporating as well as how to avoid double taxation as much as possible.

A Limited Liability Corporation (LLC) is another, newer option, which serves, to some degree, as a hybrid between incorporating and going solo. The advantages of forming an LLC are that the members are afforded limited liability and have pass-through taxes similar to a partnership. By forming an LLC, rather than a corporation, you receive all of the benefits of forming a corporation but avoid some of the drawbacks, such as double taxation and excessive paperwork. Of course, LLCs are not offered in all states, so you will need to inquire in your state. Additionally, some investors, because LLCs are new, may not be as forthcoming when it comes to lending you money since they are not familiar with how an LLC operates. Of course with an attorney by your side, you can overcome some of these concerns.

As for partnerships, operators who attempt this should proceed with caution. "In vending, a partnership is a marriage getting ready to fail," says Burnsville, Minnesota, full-line operator Wayne D., who experimented with forming nonfamily partnerships early on. The three- to five-year ramp-up most vending startups require is what makes partnerships a difficult choice. "Over the course of time, people's ambitions change," he says. "Generally, the entrepreneur's motivations and skills far outweigh those of the people he takes in for the partnership."

A Name of Your Own

Once you've committed to a business structure, it's time to give your enterprise a name.

If you consult the Yellow Pages and search online, you'll quickly discover many vending company names are simply variations on their owners' names, such as "A.J. Vending" for "Al Jones." While a similar title for your firm is perfectly acceptable, today's fiercely competitive vending industry demands an identity with an edge.

Additional Google searches for "vending" and your city name will reveal some of the names that are already taken in your area.

Vending operators emphasize that being successful means viewing your business as retail sales delivered by a machine. Consider synonyms and alliterations of product and business names that you like in similar industries. For example, if you'll be vending food and like the name of a snack called Crispy Bits, jot down "Crackle Bites Vending." If you're vending small toys and like the name of a children's toy store called The Treasure Chest, jot down "Tiny Treasures Vending" or "Prize Closet Vending."

Cover All Your Bases

Before you check your brainstormed, fabulous name against the resource list on page 64, scribble down several options in

> ### Smart Tip
> *Tip...*
>
> Try Wordlab's free Business Name Generator widget (www.wordlab.com). Punchy words are shaken up into random mixes to make unique, often catchy business names.

case you discover the one you want is already taken, and don't choose a name that will irritate your competitors because it is too similar to theirs. Avoid naming your company something that sounds confusingly similar to a related industry name. Why annoy hardworking entrepreneurs when there are so many unique options to be had? It's best to be supportive of the business crowd in your region—they're your community, after all, and you never know when you'll need their support. To boot, they worked hard to create their business, just like you are right now.

Before you pick up the phone and fire up your computer to verify name availability, choose at least three names you'd like in case one or two aren't available.

Remember How Consumers Search

Now that you've got some ideas for catchy names that describe your great products, you should consider attaching the name of your city to your business

---

Search Your Names

Check your name ideas against these resources:

○ Hardcopy Yellow and White Pages

○ The virtual pages (www.yellowpages.com and www.whitepages.com)

○ Yelp (www.yelp.com, a consumer-driven, locally oriented business review site)

○ Network Solutions (www.networksolutions.com, a domain registry)

○ The Thomas Register (www.thomasnet.com)

○ www.google.com. If you find businesses on Google with the same or very similar names, look at their website names to make sure the domain you choose will not be mistyped or confused with theirs. It's smart to choose a business name that will translate easily to a domain with the name of your city included. This way when people are looking for a vending service in Houston, Texas and search "vending Texas" on Google, your cleverly named service, Texas Vending Treats, will show up, as will your domain. We know how smart you were to make sure that www.texasvendingtreats. com was available before you chose and registered it!

○ The United States Patent and Trademark Office (www.uspto.gov/main/ trademarks.htm)

---

name for the sole reason that it can be found more easily with internet searches that way. Consumers usually search first with the name of the product or service they're looking for, and second with the name of the area they're searching in. Type the word "vending" into the Google Beta search box and you'll see that the intuitive current list (programmed based on current searches going on all over the world) that drops down below gives suggestions for what it thinks you're looking for. These suggestions are based on what the highest numbers of consumers are searching for in that search box related to the first word you type. For example, after you type in "vending" you'll see a number of combinations with the word "vending" pop up below the box. The search engine is trying to guess what you're looking for based on the most popular things that other people are looking for. This should serve as some insight for clever name choices.

While it's impossible to be 100 percent sure that your name is unique, this will at least let you know who has officially registered theirs and avoid competition in your area. Don't forget to check with your county clerk's office to see if your name is already registered as a fictitious or assumed business name in your area. Sites such as www.yelp.com and www.whitepages.com will aid in the search for like-sounding names. A similar name is out if it's in the same industry and is less effective if there are a number of them across industries. When you check www.networksolutions.com and www.domains.com to see if the name in question has been turned into a web address yet, don't fret; many .coms are taken but other extensions are available.

One of the operators we interviewed wanted her customers to know she viewed them as unique individuals with sophisticated palates and named her business A Matter of Taste. "Like life, it's very much a matter of taste; what one person loves, another person cannot stand. Over the years, we've gotten great response to our name," she says.

While her creative process was less complex, another of our entrepreneurs knew she needed a memorable name to introduce herself and her concept. "I thought, well, it's a vending machine, how about McLean Machines? I started to like it and everyone I talked to about it said, 'You know, that's a catchy little name.' "

Those who purchase an existing operation should let the company's current standing be their guide if the moniker has a positive association. If not, then rename the company. Even though Van Vending isn't exactly bedazzling, one of our operators acknowledges retaining it "because it had a good reputation."

To start your own list of name possibilities, jot down some simple ideas such as those based on your region's name (example: New Mexico Vending). As your

Smart Tip

A free online resource for legal information, Nolo. com (www.nolo.com) offers business naming and trademark registration advice to cover all bases.

Tip...

list grows, practice answering test phone calls with the possible choices. No matter how clearly you enunciate, a name like A&J Vending will always sound like "ANJ Vending."

Although your name should be a reflection of you, you can certainly jump-start your brainstorming by checking out the names of successful vending operators online with the most professional sites. Then use the "Name Brainstorming Worksheet" on page 67 to narrow down your choices.

Make It Official

With your favored moniker option in hand, it's time to get it in writing. Basically, this means contacting the appropriate government entity, checking to see if the name is available, and registering the name as your own, generally for a fee. Don't be alarmed by the terms "fictitious" or "assumed." This simply means the name you're using to do business.

Regardless of the law, registering now prevents misery later. Why? Because the longer you're in business, the more valuable your good name will be to you. If you've registered it, there are no worries when a squatter (a squatter is someone who registers numerous domain names that he or she does not intend to use at present or possibly ever) comes along. If you haven't registered, even the best attorney may not charm the court.

In addition, financial institutions in some states require proof of business name registration before opening a simple business checking account. Because the IRS insists on separate personal and business accounts, save yourself some time by registering your business name before going to the bank.

In states where you're required to register (since a few do not require it) you'll likely find variations on how to get the forms. You can call the secretary of state's office and request the appropriate forms or search online under "business license" for your state and you'll find whom to contact. The Small Business Administration (www.sba.gov) is also a place to find out about small-business licensing. Before you hang up, you may ask the status of up to three name options.

One way to speed up this process is by using the fax-back or internet services many state governments now offer for obtaining forms and checking name availability. Using these services reduces the time it takes to lock in your favored business name.

Bright Idea

Although not required, sole proprietors without employees may obtain a Federal Employer Identification Number. Applying for and using this number on your tax returns and all official documents (such as business checking accounts and contracts with clients) is an excellent way to differentiate you and your business in the eyes of the IRS.

Name Brainstorming Worksheet

List three ideas based on the type of vending you plan to provide (e.g., food, tele-cards, personal products):

1. _____

2. _____

3. _____

List three ideas based on descriptive adjectives (e.g., speedy, zesty, reliable):

1. _____

2. _____

3. _____

List three ideas based on your geographic location (e.g., neighborhood, county, region):

1. _____

2. _____

3. _____

List three ideas based on a well-known local feature (e.g., terrain, historical reference, native plants or animals):

1. _____

2. _____

3. _____

❑ Contact your local business name authority to see if your favorite names are available.

❑ Try your favorite out loud and over the phone to make sure it's easy to pronounce and understand. Get feedback from family, friends, and others, such as contacts within the industry.

It's a go? Excellent! Now register it and make it your own.

▲

After your name registration forms are processed, you'll receive an official certificate in the mail. Then, in many states, you have a specified period of time during which you must advertise your business name in a local newspaper and document the ad to the state. If you don't take out an ad immediately, you'll likely be contacted by a company that places such ads and provides the necessary paperwork to the government, for a nominal fee.

Framing your dba ("doing business as") certificate and hanging it on the wall is a nice way to make your new business seem more real, especially if you're like most vending startups and operate out of a home office.

Homebased Zone

Speaking of home offices, your next encounter with the government should be your local zoning authority. Although the tradition of homebased businesses is older than the Liberty Bell, residential neighborhoods value child-friendly streets, prompting municipalities to restrict business activities accordingly.

Generally, residential zoning regulations ban enterprises that generate considerable customer and employee traffic. But since customers visit your machines and not your business, the former isn't an issue. The latter only becomes a problem when you are having other employees working from your home or you are using your home to store large amounts of inventory. Many cities are not very strict with home business laws, since working from home has become far more commonplace in recent years.

In fact, it is typically not until there is a complaint that you face a problem. Neighbors will get suspicious and become uncomfortable if eighteen-wheelers are backing in and out of your driveway every day. While we are not suggesting that you "break the law," we're basically advising good judgment in your decision to work from home, and if you do so, to maintain a low profile—no neon sign out front. If you are concerned, talk to your immediate neighbors and address their concerns. This can go a long way, particularly if you're one

Smart Tip

Tip...

When choosing a name for your business, think of the terms that the "mostly females over the age of 35" dominant demographic of Facebook use to search with. Because Facebook is currently the largest social media site, it would be smart to register for pay-per-click ads on this site featuring key words pertinent to its largest demographic. Consider naming your Facebook fan page using popular search terms cohesive with your business name as well. To learn popular Facebook search terms, create an account (this is extremely easy) and begin searching for things related to your business. Watch as the search box anticipates what you're looking for, offering popular suggestions.

of the many vending businesses that doesn't require deliveries from large semis. On the other hand, if you live next door to the Grinch, it's not worth pushing the envelope.

But don't get discouraged before checking the facts. For nine years, Becky P. operated her ever-growing operation out of her home and 700-square-foot RV garage. By the time she moved into a commercial location, she had six employees, in addition to herself and her husband.

More on homebased offices in Chapter 7.

Permits and Such

While you're at city hall, ask about permits and licenses. Some municipalities require a general business license while others require registration of each vendor. In the latter case, you may be provided with stickers to affix to the machines. If so, don't cut corners. Failing to affix the stickers can invalidate insurance or open cans of things far worse than worms.

For food vending, you'll need a food handling license either from the U.S. Department of Agriculture or the municipality where your vendors are placed. Generally, you need one or the other but not both, according to NAMA. To be certain, ask each city (or, in rural areas, county) where your machines will be located.

When you've finished with local agencies, you're almost through with officialdom. Only sales taxes remain. Because vending is an automated retail transaction, it's subject to sales taxes, if your state collects them. After you've obtained your name registration certificate, contact your state's department of revenue and ask for sales tax permit application forms. You may be able to find them on the IRS website at www.irs.gov.

Covering Yourself: Insurance

It's no secret that our society is very litigious. It's also no secret that the cost of guarding against a lawsuit is very important in business today. If someone can sue a college because one of its students was "mooning" a friend and fell out of his dorm window (true story), then someone can sue you for an injury they claim occurred because of one of your vending machines, even if the person was actually sticking his or her arm inside trying to steal candy. Therefore, you need protection, or you need to practice "safe vending" so to speak.

> **Tip...**
>
> ## Smart Tip
> Check with your state's vending association to find out about sales tax savings strategies. For example, Hendersonville, Tennessee, full-line operator B.J. S. reports his business is paying a tax of 1.5 percent on gross receipts rather than the regular 8.25 percent sales tax. "To be eligible, all we have to do is purchase a $1 sticker for each machine."

This sage advice also applies to other types of vending, according to operators. However, in nonfood vending, slightly less coverage may do. "I carry $1 million in commercial vending machine liability insurance," says Baltimore entrepreneur Janice M. "That's $1 million per incident, per person, per machine."

In some regions, purchasing liability coverage is more than wise: It's required to get your foot in the door. "Here in California, any business of any consequence requires $1 to $2 million in liability insurance before you can do business on their premises," says Becky P. "That's not just for vending operators, but for any outside vendor."

In some cases if your vendors are on your property, as at the Berdoll Pecan Farm, your property insurance may cover your machine. This is how Jennifer Berdoll Wammack insures her custom pie vendor where it sits outside her store.

Successful operators also suggest commercial vehicle insurance, which generally goes well beyond personal policies. Regardless of your location, building and contents insurance is a must.

"Within my building insurance, I have a business interruption rider to prevent downtime," comments Becky. "For example, if this place burned to the ground, I would immediately get a $20,000 check to go buy more merchandise and keep the vehicles running. I wouldn't have to go through the investigation and all that stuff before I'd get any money. My insurance company will just instantly keep me up and running."

While operators are quick to value insurance for themselves, mention workers' compensation and the gripe-fest begins. Regardless of vending type, those with employees are subject to this much-maligned coverage.

But industry associations and publications point out that high workers' comp premiums are as much the fault of employers as employees. According to *Automatic Merchandiser* magazine, vending industry premiums soared for years in part because employers failed to teach and enforce simple safety practices. More recently, employers have become hip to the "experience modification" discount (legalese for establishing and following an employee safety plan), which has improved overall safety dramatically and lowered industry premiums. The publication also notes that successful operators involve their employees in safety policy making and evangelizing. After all, reduced comp costs translate into higher profits, which means more profit sharing.

Another Take On Risk Management

A recent article on www.vendingmarketwatch.com by Bill Werber lends a new perspective on insurance for operators. Werber defines risk management as "the practice of protecting an organization from financial loss by identifying, analyzing, and controlling risk at the lowest possible cost" and brings several tips to the table on how to do this.

He urges operators to first concern themselves with disability insurance in the event that they are injured or sick so that their families are taken care of. He suggests that managing the risk of damaged vending machines by treating "vandalism and damage as a cost of doing business as opposed to trading premium dollars to and claims dollars from your insurance company" may be the best approach rather than "transferring the risk of financial loss to your insurance company."

> ## Bright Idea
> Do you know which candies keep best in summer heat? How about a trick to keep that hot summer candy from sticking together or instructions on drilling out a vending machine lock? Try www.candymachines. com/blog/ for helpful technical tips and facts about all things candy.

For more on this alternate perspective read the rest of the article here: www. vendingmarketwatch.com/article/10273442/do-you-have-the-right-business-insurance.

Be certain you know all there is to know about insurance. Then use the "Startup Checklist" on page 76 to make sure you've covered all your bases in the areas of business structure, naming your business, licensing requirements, zoning regulations, buying insurance, and hiring advisors.

Here is a list of providers that offer vending operator insurance for your comparison shopping:

- www.allstate.com/business-insurance/wholesale-distribution.aspx
- www.safeco.com/
- www.zurichna.com/zna/home/welcome.htm

Protecting Your Inspiration: Patent It

As you know from Chapter 1, women's hosiery entrepreneur Janice M. hit on a new vending concept and took off with her new idea. As part of her discovery process, she learned no one else held a U.S. patent on the pantyhose vending concept. Realizing all her work could be in vain if someone swooped down and snapped up her idea, she applied for a patent.

All original inventions should be patented (and most are) so that you maintain ownership of the rights to that product. Some people have several patents covering a variety of inventions (Thomas Edison had more than 1,000!). There are three basic types of patents that cover designs, plants, and utilities. The third one, "utilities," covers inventions and processes, which is where your new invention will likely fall. In the case of Janice, her patent was not for inventing pantyhose, since the product already existed, but for the process of selling them via vending machine. Therefore, she does not own the rights to selling pantyhose, but to selling them through a vending machine.

If you have an original product or an original manner of selling something that is not sold by vending machine (as far as you know), you can apply for a patent. You first need to contact the United States Patent and Trademark Office (its website is www.uspto.gov) and do a patent search to make sure someone else does not already hold the patent on your product or process. The USPTO offers a free search option. If the search turns up no similar patent, you can then apply for a provisional patent, which will protect your invention or process for one year while you determine whether there is a market for the product. Within that year you can then apply for a regular patent. The USPTO will provide you with all of the specific information on exactly how to apply. Essentially, to get a provisional patent, you need to have a cover page, description of the invention, a technical drawing that shows how the invention works or the process, and a $165 fee (possibly lower if you prove that you are a really small business—like one person). The application for a full patent should be filled out very carefully as you are required to provide a more detailed explanation of your product and what makes it unique—review your wording carefully with an attorney before filing. If you are granted a patent, it is good for 20 years and you can then sell the rights to use your invention to others.

Getting Good Advice

By now you're probably wondering where to turn for help with all these matters. Here's where the cost of hiring an expert pays dividends in the long run.

Successful operators look to professionals for accounting, legal, and insurance advice. For some, this means consulting such gurus directly. For others, it's through the services of industry-specific organizations like NAMA. Still others use general business associations such as their local chamber of commerce or a government-sponsored organization such as the Small Business Administration (SBA).

NAMA offers sample client contracts and accounting practices booklets. To customize such items, NAMA members may utilize advisors affiliated with the organization. Or you can hire a local professional to review your situation.

Of course, you might want to consider a combination of one or more of these avenues and ask veterans in the business if they can guide or mentor you as long as you are not competing with them—you might also look to hire consultants in the field to help you get off the ground.

Turn to Nolo (www.nolo.com) again, this time for free legal advice. It offers wisdom in the categories of licensing, accounting, bookkeeping, finances, litigation bankruptcy, contracts, marketing and e-commerce, buying, and selling. It even has a lawyer directory with tips on how to choose the right one for your needs. All lawyers listed in the Nolo directory take the Nolo Pledge, agreeing to adhere to its high standards.

Even more creative is Janice M.'s solution. She surrounds herself with not only advisors but also mentors. The pantyhose vending trailblazer began by tapping into the tax, legal, and accounting assistance offered by the Women Entrepreneurs of Baltimore, one of the organizations she belongs to. Later, she consulted the SBA for financing, the National Association for the Advancement of Colored People for business development assistance, and a brokerage firm about taking her business public. Today she has an accountant, an attorney, an insurance agent, and a website designer and counts the editor of *Black Enterprise* magazine as a significant mentor.

Successful professionals in your community may be able to recommend quality advisors.

With your structural strategies under control, you are now ready to take the next steps. The issues discussed here should be the only ones you need to address. However, the types of vending operations and laws regulating them are as diverse as the culture in which we are living. Seeking out specifics that apply to your situation will ensure that you get all your i's dotted and t's crossed.

A Business Plan

Before venturing into the next chapter, on gathering the cash necessary to start a business, it behooves you to have a business plan in place to help you get the funding you need and as a means of guiding you in your business. After all, how do you know you are doing well if you have no plan of action?

A business plan can be as simple or elaborate as you wish to make it. Essentially, it is a blueprint for your business. It can help you show lending institutions that you have thought out this plan from every angle and have a complete picture of the business you are planning to start, including the finances that will be needed, how the money will be spent, and what the projected return on the investment will be in one, three, five, and possibly even ten years down the road.

▲

The other primary reason for writing a business plan is that it serves as a living, breathing document that can keep you and your associates on track, allow you to measure progress, and help you determine whether or not there's potential for growth over time. You may look at your business plan and decide that everything is going better than anticipated, thus allowing you to expand, perhaps by adding a new profit center. Conversely, your numbers may be lagging behind your projections. This might lead you to determine how to improve upon the bottom line by making changes.

The Components of a Business Plan

Your business plan will include the following, plus other information as deemed necessary. These are, however, the key elements.

1. A *Table of Contents*. This makes the plan organized for the reader.

2. The *Executive Summary*. Although this comes first, it is often written last after you've thought out all of the various areas of your business. It is here where you provide an overall summary in a page or two of your vending business including the reasons why you are starting the business—your goals, plans, and objectives for the business, the industry and your place in the market, your target audience, marketing plans, and future expectations. This is, in fact, a summary that should entice potential investors to read further—it is the single most important aspect of a business plan and one that should provide a solid, factual basis for your vending business being a success. It should also not include a lot of hype.

3. *Industry Analysis*. Researching this section of the business plan is a marvelous way for you to bone up on the industry. It is also the place in which you describe the vending industry at present. You will need to use numerous sources, such as the NAMA, *Vending Times*, the Bureau of Labor Statistics (www.bls.gov), and various trade publications to put together a state of the industry page. You will then show where your vending business will fit in and what will put you on the cutting edge of the industry, or at least for the area in which you are setting up your route(s).

4. *Business or Operational Overview*. Here, you will provide a comprehensive overview of your plans for the business. How will the business operate? What kind of business structure will you have? What resources will you need? Where will you be based? For example, you "will operate the business from a home office in Stamford, Connecticut, and have a 3,200-square-foot warehouse in nearby Bristol."

Explain the vending machines you will use and types of products you will be selling. Discuss the distributors, the route(s), and explain how it will all fall into place. Provide the background logic for your plan of action—why vending machines in x and y locations? Why such and such products for your chosen route?

5. *Your Marketing Plan.* The marketing plan is an important aspect of your overall business and one that you will need to pay strict attention to. How will businesses know about you and your services? What type of research and consumer marketing will you be doing to determine your best areas for sales? All types of marketing between your business and potential clients, as well as customers, should be included here. Gather as much background information as possible to support your demographic research. Finally, explain your plan for reaching the audience. Are you planning to advertise? Will you use direct mail? The internet? Special promotions and coupons? If you have media contacts or know of publicists that will help you spread the word, also include that information in this section. Again, the mere process of writing this section will get you motivated to work on this important area—marketing.

6. *Competitive Analysis.* This is obviously a very important part of the business plan. As much as you'd like to "trash" your competitors, you need to take the high road—or have a professional approach. Discuss all of your direct and indirect competition (meaning other vending businesses as well as retail businesses that could draw business away from your machines). Provide information on their businesses, including their prices along with areas in which they do well and areas in which they are lacking. Finally, use the information you have gathered on your competitors to show what you can improve upon and what will bring customers to you. This is your competitive edge and what separates the successful entrepreneurs from the wannabes.

7. *Operations Plan.* How does your vending business work? Do you handle the route yourself? Do you have several people handling routes for you? When do you check inventory and where do you maintain your inventory? How do you repair broken equipment? All of the particulars of running the business should be spelled out here so that you have as foolproof a plan as possible to have a smooth running business.

8. *Management Team.* If you are all alone, then this is a brief overview of why you are the man or woman for the job. A few paragraphs should do it, recounting your applicable

Bright Idea

If you plan to expand into other product lines, such as pizza or pantyhose in the near future, mention your ideas in the Business Plan, including when you anticipate adding such products to your list. Don't make things up—have a realistic plan for expansion or don't include it.

business experiences. Lenders and investors do not really care about the bake sale you ran in middle school—they want to see that you have some business background, particularly in dealing with clients and customers, since vending is a business in which you will have many interpersonal relationships.

9. *Financial Plan.* Another biggie, this is where you "show them the money" so to speak. Here, you will include all the financial information from starting up the vending business to the projected profits. Use any charts and graphs necessary to

Startup Checklist

Use this handy checklist to help you cover all the regulatory, insurance, and other structural issues.

Yes! I have:

❑ Decided on a business structure: sole proprietorship, partnership, or corporation

❑ Filed the necessary forms to become a partnership or corporation, if I chose either of those structures

❑ Registered my business name

❑ Applied for business licenses in the municipalities where I'll be placing vendors

❑ Investigated zoning regulations

❑ Consulted with a business insurance agent about liability, building, equipment, workers' compensation, and other necessary insurance

❑ Complied with the following special circumstances:

_____

_____

_____

_____

❑ Considered establishing a relationship with an accountant and an attorney

❑ Started outlining and even writing a business plan

show how money will come in, expenses will be handled, and profit will ensue. Let your accountant help you with this part and try not to exaggerate or get carried away. Projecting finances inaccurately is one of the reasons many businesses fail. Be cautious, conservative if necessary, and show estimates of how you will build your business. You may also include supporting material at the end of the business plan along with your resume and any additional financial documents that support the business plan. Some sources to help make your point are the NAMA State of the Vending Industry Reports (www.vending.org) for showing growth, trends, and anticipated consumption, and City Data (www.city-data.com) for showing proof of your targeted demographic.

Before showing anyone your business plan, review it very carefully and rewrite it often. You want the plan to answer all of the questions anyone could ask about the future of your business. So as to not reinvent the wheel, look to one of the many sage resources on business startups, such as *Entrepreneur* magazine (www.entrepreneur.com/businessplan/), for a step-by-step, free downloadable guide. Try Enloop's (www.enloop.com) free plan writing app or pay $9.95 and submit up to three coached plans to be analyzed for chances of success with financial backing and the SBA (www.sba.gov), where you will also find business plans, templates, and coaching. There is also business plan software available with templates to make life easier, such as Palo Alto's Business Plan Pro (www.paloalto.com), among others. The Bplans website (www.bplans.com) has a marvelous sample of a complex business plan for a vending business.

While your business plan may be more or less elaborate than others, it is important for all businesses to have a written plan to define where the business is going. Once you are done reviewing and proofreading your business plan, have it printed on high-quality paper and bound. It can be the most important document in procuring the funding you need and for keeping you on track with your business over the startup period and beyond.

6

You'll Need Cash

Although you know going into business isn't going to be free, perhaps you aren't so sure when to begin crunching numbers or what numbers you need to crunch. So before we delve any deeper into the details of starting a vending operation, let's take a look at how you're going to figure out what it's all going to cost, and more important, how you're going to pay for it.

Startup Costs

Startup costs refer to all the necessities for starting your business. A number of factors will determine what these costs will be, including how big a business you are planning to open, where your business will be located, and whether or not you will be hiring employees.

An attractive reason to go into the vending business in the first place is that one of these expenses, your office, doesn't have to cost any more than you're already paying right now. Why? Because you can operate right out of your home.

Another reason why the vending business is attractive is because you can start small and grow, unlike some businesses, where you will need to pay huge sums upfront just to get started.

Of course, you'll need to invest in vending machines and products to put in them. "You can start up for as little as $1,000," says 20-year veteran Wayne D., who points out that bottlers provide machines for free but take a significant cut. "It depends on the magnitude of the business," continues the Burnsville, Minnesota, full-line operator. "That's what makes vending unique."

To give some food vending examples, Wayne throws out some common scenarios. "Let's say I have a friend with a manufacturing business with 300 people. That could be an excellent location for a small startup, and for that many people, the vending equipment would be about $25,000. Or let's say my friend has 20 apartment buildings instead. Then I could probably get by with $15,000 in equipment. It all depends on how well you research the locations and how well you could do there."

But realistically, most operators say launching a viable food vending business requires a bit more. "For a snack and soda business, I'd say $100,000 working capital," advises Becky P., who bucked conventional wisdom by immediately offering sandwiches and other full-line cold food items. "And $250,000 if you're going into full-line. To keep the business running you've got to have a year's worth of money for living expenses in the bank in addition to what you need for your business."

If you're growing slow and sure, proving profit before you expand, you're like Jennifer Berdoll Wammack, who spent $5,000 on

Smart Tip

Tip...

Shop around for a lender early on, and select one you feel comfortable chatting with. Then schedule a review of your personal finances. This allows you to make necessary adjustments to improve what's referred to as your "net worth" before you lay out your finances for a loan review committee. Also, have a business plan.

her base machine, then added some equipment to it, such as the dual motors and coils we mentioned. The extras made the cost of her first and only machine to date around $7,000, and it has been well worth it.

The Berdoll candies sell for $14.50 per bag and the pies for $18.50 each, and the machine has to be filled daily to keep up with demand. With profits Berdoll Wammack will be setting up more of the same vendors, but hasn't decided on the right location for the next one. In her case, the first location was the biggest impetus for sales, so she learned how important the right location is.

The Bigger Picture

On top of equipment and inventory, you'll also have expenses related to setting up your home office. Then there are other operating costs, such as insurance, phone bills, and sales taxes. We'll discuss more about figuring all of these costs and provide you with some concrete examples in subsequent chapters. See also the "Startup Expenses Worksheet" on page 82.

For now, let's introduce you to a hypothetical startup vending operation that we're going to follow throughout the rest of this book. Giving you this concrete example should significantly demystify the startup process and clarify all those bookkeeping and accounting terms we'll run into as we go along. It'll also give you confidence with these matters, which helps as much with winning new customers as it does with romancing the bank.

Quality Snacks

Quality Snacks is a homebased vending business with 15 snack vendors. It is operated out of the owner's spare bedroom. The garage has also been pressed into service as a storage location for vendors when they're between accounts as well as a work space for minor repairs. The garage also houses excess inventory, although almost all inventory fits in the owner's van and is replenished every day, as needed. The total square footage of space used for the business (spare bedroom and garage) is about one-sixth of the total square footage of home and garage combined, or approximately 16 percent. This is important to know for tax purposes. Because the owner of Quality Snacks has a family, a van has been leased and dedicated to the business and a second telephone line goes only to the office space to keep youngsters from answering important calls. Quality Snacks' owner does not draw a salary, instead taking a portion of the net as income. As a startup, the business is part time, with machine servicing limited to evenings and weekends to accommodate the owner's full-time job. See the "Quality Snacks Startup Expenses" statement on page 83.

Startup Expenses Worksheet

Here's a handy guide for figuring the startup costs for your business. For a ready-made worksheet, photocopy this page before you begin. To make your calculating even easier, come back to this form after you've completed the supporting worksheets in the related chapters and reviewed the helpful tips in the book sections covering line items such as marketing, insurance, and the like. For startup purposes, you can estimate at least a couple of months for monthly expenses to make sure you are covered.

Expense	Cost
Advertising/marketing	
Freight & shipping costs	
Insurance	
Internet service	
Inventory (from Chapter 9)	
Licenses and fees	
Office equipment and supplies (from Chapter 7)	
Postage and mailing	
Professional fees (accounting/attorney fees)	
*Rent or mortgage payments	
Subscriptions/dues	
*Telephone	
*Utilities	
Vehicle lease	
Vending equipment (from Chapter 8)	
Subtotal	
Other miscellaneous expenses (add roughly 10 percent of the subtotal)	
Total Startup Costs	
Owner's contribution	
Financing required	

Use a percentage of your home payment if using a home office.

Quality Snacks Startup Expenses

Below is the startup expenses statement for our hypothetical snack food operator, Quality Snacks.

Expense	Cost
Advertising/marketing	$1,200.00
Freight/shipping costs	$949.00
Insurance	$1,100.00
Internet service (first two months, plus installation)	$150.00
Inventory	$6,200.00
Licenses and fees	$300.00
Office equipment/supplies	$3,041.00
Postage and mailing	$90.00
Professional fees: accounting/attorney	$700.00
*Rent or mortgage payment (first two months' 15% of total mortgage payment)	$360.00
Subscriptions/dues	$100.00
Telephone (first two months' phone bills + installation)	$365.00
*Utilities (first two months' utilities)	$50.00
Vehicle lease	$500.00
Vending equipment	$73,960.00
Subtotal	**$89,065.00**
Other miscellaneous expenses	$8,907.00
Total Startup Costs	**$97,972.00**
Owner's contribution	$62,065.00
Financing required	$35,907.00

Indicates a percentage of the overall home expense for these areas, as used for business.

What About the Long Haul?

In addition to calculating what you need to start, you'll want to figure out what you can expect to take in from month to month and year to year. This is referred to as your "operating income and expenses." Put more plainly, it's what your operation brings in, what it pays out, and what's left at the end. You will want to have these projections for your business plan, particularly to show your banker or potential investors.

First, however, before showing anyone your projected profits, you'll want to see whether all the effort you're about to put into the business will be worth the return. For each new entrepreneur, the definition of a successful business will be slightly different.

However, you start a business with the intent of making money—for one person that's enough money to support a family, while for another, it's part-time additional income. It all depends on your goals and wishes. Some entrepreneurs are determined to make big money by expanding and become a major corporation; others are more than happy with a small, well-run family business.

Bright Idea

Do you have a vending idea that could help the world in an innovative way? Are you willing to move to another country to get it started? Start Up Chile is a program that funds approved startups with $40,000 of equity-free seed capital, provides a temporary one-year visa for people to develop their projects for six months in Chile, and offers access to the most potent social and capital networks in the country. First you've got to pass the admission process conducted by Silicon Valley experts and a Chilean Innovation board that focuses on global mindsets and worldwide potential. Read more about this exciting program at www.startupchile.org.

Lease, Borrow, or Buy?

Once you have added all your expenses, the next step is deciding whether or not you can afford the bottom line. If the numbers look too large for what you've saved or think you can borrow, consider starting smaller or saving a bit longer before you begin.

According to industry statistics, your average rate of return (the percentage you have left over as a profit) will likely be less than 4 percent. Some of the successful operators we interviewed say their average is between .5 percent and 2 percent. Therefore, be careful before you assume you'll simply get a loan.

Starting a business typically requires borrowing money from a lending source, whether it is a bank, credit union, angel investor, or a personal loan. A line of credit is also an option, but usually used for remodeling, expansion plans, cash flow, or other ongoing expenses once a business is up and running. You use a line of credit much as you would use a credit card.

Typically a larger sum of money in the form of a loan is the way to start your vending business. Vending is risky for banks because their collateral (your vendors) can be removed and stashed out of sight to keep them from being repossessed. "You have to have an excellent credit rating," stresses Becky P., who had borrowed and repaid several bank loans before going into vending. "With my business background, I never had a problem going into my bank and selling myself. In fact, when banks started giving lines of credit, the manager came over [to my office] and said, 'I want you to have this because you run your business properly.' "

In the case of a business such as Quality Snacks, the owner is putting up a large percentage of the money himself. Not unlike buying a home, the more you can put up yourself, the easier it is to secure a loan. Lenders see that you are also taking a financial risk.

The Small Business Administration is a great place to go for business loans. They do not actually provide the money, but can secure the business loan.

Some vending business owners start small with the express purpose of taking smaller loans and paying them back promptly. Such a record of paying on time can help build your credit rating. Prior to seeking a loan, you should check with the major credit bureaus:

- Equifax. (800) 685-1111, P.O. Box 740241, Atlanta, GA 30374, www.equifax.com

- Experian. (888) 397-3742, P.O. Box 2002, Allen, TX 75013, www.experian.com

- TransUnion. (800) 888-4213, 2 Baldwin Place, P.O. Box 1000, Chester, PA 19022, www.transunion.com

Do this only once, since the loan officers will also inquire, and the more your credit ratings are checked, the more suspicious it can appear to lenders.

Your Distributor Can Help

If you can't get financing from your bank, don't assume that you're out of luck. Instead, talk to your equipment distributor.

"Typically, a piece of equipment will be financed for two years," notes Vince Gumma of American Vending Sales in Chicago. "The average payment is $165 a month." If you're lacking capital to make a down payment but your business plan looks viable, you may be granted financing with a large final payment at the end of the financing period. In such cases, the last payment is often 10 to 20 percent of the total amount you're borrowing.

Of course, your best bet for winning the approval of your distributor's financing company is still to have collateral of your own to offer, such as equity in your home.

By making regular payments to distributors and showing that you are running the business on a small scale, you can also enhance your credit rating—make sure the distributor reports your prompt payments to the credit bureaus.

Personal Loans

If you are lucky, you might find an angel investor, someone who is wealthy, believes in your business plan (and your ability to run the business), and is willing to take a chance on you. Of course, as is the case with any loan, you'll need everything in writing, with an attorney to look over the agreement. It's important for any type of individual investor to determine what he or she is looking for from the investment. When do they expect to see some returns on their investment? Do they want to be involved in the business or are they silent investors? Make sure all stipulations are ironed out in advance—this includes borrowing from friends and family. Many personal relationships have been strained or obliterated because of business

---

There's More Than One Way to Finance Your Dream

Here is a list of creative financing resources that may help you:

○ Accion, www.accion.org—a nonprofit, micro-finance network

○ Coalition of Community Development Financial Institutions, http://cdfi. org—financial institution loans for small-business startups

○ Prosper, www.prosper.com—a community of private lenders wishing to help finance projects they believe in

○ Raise Capital, www.raisecapital.com—a connection site for entrepreneurs and investors

○ Woman Owned, www.womanowned.com—loans for woman-owned businesses

○ On Deck, www.ondeckcapital.com—a short-term, commercial lending source for those with less than perfect credit, but a strong cash flow

dealings—know with whom you are dealing, especially when money becomes involved. Be forewarned.

Underfunding Undertow

Regardless of your source of cash, the most important thing when it comes to financing a business is having enough (see the "Quality Snacks Projected Operating Budget" statement on page 88 and the "Projected Operating Budget Worksheet" on page 90). Many a former business owner would be a successful entrepreneur today if he or she had not underestimated and underfinanced.

Those who do make it, despite being underfunded, generally would avoid making the same mistake twice. "Before [I went out and raised funds] I was using my own money," recounts Baltimore pantyhose operator Janice M. In addition to income from her administrative assistant position, the single mother of three was also maxing out her credit cards. "I was going through getting my gas and my electricity shut off. But I just tried to stay focused to get done what I wanted to do."

Soon after her finances hit bottom, Janice began looking for private investors. "Most of them were working people," says Janice, some of whom generously gave as little as $25. "One man saw me making something happen and gave me $5,000." In all, the vending innovator raised $14,000, which helped carry her through her business' second and third years. "Later I also went to the Women Entrepreneurs of Baltimore [a nonprofit business development group she belonged to] and they gave me $1,000."

While it worked for Janice, it is typically not advisable to take money from all sorts of people unless you keep very good records of where you are getting personal loans. You open yourself up to too many cooks telling you how to run your business and too many

Dollar Stretcher

Taking advantage of those incessant credit card solicitations you receive in the mail can provide you with some financing flexibility, but don't go hog wild. Banks and other financing sources often shy away from people with the potential to run up excessive credit card debt. Limit yourself to four or five credit cards and stay out of debt if you want to maintain a good credit rating.

people complaining if you do not follow their advice, which equals many headaches.

Quality Snacks Projected Operating Budget

Below is the projected operating budget for the first year of operation of our snack food operator, Quality Snacks.

Income	
Machine sales	$126,200.00
Other income	0
Total Annual Income	**$126,200.00**
Expenses	
Advertising/marketing	$3,000.00
Commissions	$11,520.00
CPA/accounting	$2,000.00
Depreciation	
Office equipment/furnishings	$4,200.00
Vehicles	0
Vending machines	$4,608.00
Insurance	$2,200.00
Licenses and fees	$600.00
Rent	$2,160.00
Repairs/maintenance	$640.00
Telephone	$1,400.00
Utilities	$300.00
Internet service	$150.00
Payroll	0
Product expenses	
Cost of goods sold	$57,600.00
Product loss	$2,400.00

Quality Snacks Projected Operating Budget, continued

Income	
Professional services (including contract)	$800.00
Sales/use taxes	$9,216.00
Subscriptions/dues	$270.00
Travel, meals, and entertainment	$200.00
Vehicle expenses	
Lease payments	$6,000.00
Maintenance and repair	$3,000.00
Vending equipment expenses	
Machine loans (5 machines)	$9,900.00
Parts and repairs	$230.00
Storage	0
Delivery/moving/freight	$1,200.00
Other miscellaneous expenses	$309.00
Total Annual Expenses	**$121,994.00**
Net annual profit (loss) before taxes	$4,356.00
Income tax (estimated)	$388.48
Net Annual Profit (Loss) after Taxes (roughly 3.5% of your sales)	**$3,967.48**

Now, you may be wondering why you would want to work so hard for such small profit. Like any business, this business will take three to five years to grow. As you establish yourself in the marketplace, sales will (hopefully) increase at a faster rate than expenses. Some of your startup expenses, such as setting up your office, will not return every year—except for a new item here or there.

Projected Operating Budget Worksheet

Here's a handy guide for figuring your projected operating budget for your first year in business. The easiest way to crunch the numbers is to use the data entered on the one-month "Income and Expense Statement Worksheet" in Chapter 16 and multiply each line item by 12.

Income	
Machine sales	
Other income	
Total Annual Income	
Expenses	
Advertising/marketing	
Bank service charges	
Commissions	
CPA/accounting	
Depreciation	
Office equipment/furnishings	
Vehicles	
Vending machines	
Insurance	
Licenses and fees	
Office expenses	
Equipment/furnishings	
Office supplies	
Rent	
Repairs/maintenance	

Projected Operating Budget Worksheet, continued

Telephone	
Utilities	
Internet service	
Payroll	
Salaries/wages	
Benefits	
Payroll taxes	
Workers' compensation	
Product expenses	
Cost of goods sold	
Product loss	
Professional services (including contract)	
Sales/use taxes	
Subscriptions/dues	
Travel, meals, entertainment	
Vehicle expenses	
Vehicle purchases	
Lease payments	
Loan payments—principal	
Loan payments—interest	
Maintenance and repair	
Vending equipment expenses	
Machine purchases	

Projected Operating Budget Worksheet, continued

Lease payments	
Loan payments—principal	
Loan payments—interest	
Parts and repairs	
Storage	
Delivery/moving/freight	
Other miscellaneous expenses	
Total Annual Expenses	
Net annual profit (loss) before taxes	
Income tax (estimated)	
Net Annual Profit (Loss) after Taxes	

Office, Sweet Office

It's no secret—vending success requires being out and about. The more vendors you own, the more money you make. It's as simple as that.

Therefore, swanky digs are irrelevant because your customers visit your machines and not you. Most of the time you won't need an office to serve as a reflection of your business style.

▲

Even if you grow to be a multimillion-dollar operation, you'll rarely, if ever, entertain clients on-site. Thus, vending always has been, and probably always will be, a perfect business to start in your home.

The Home Front

Not only do most vending businesses begin as homebased, but successful entrepreneurs stress the cost advantages of an in-home location. "What people don't realize [about vending] is that all you get to keep is a half-cent of every dollar you make," says full-line operator Becky P. "If you're extremely successful, you might make one or two cents. Working out of the house was a godsend for us. When you're struggling, trying to cover overhead rent in addition to your mortgage or apartment payments is very difficult. Having a homebased business helps tremendously by keeping overhead down."

Of course, at some point, you may outgrow your in-home setup. In the event that you are getting into the vending industry by purchasing an existing outfit, maybe a home office is already out of the question. But no matter where your office is located, here are some tips on getting it appointed.

Homebased Basics

Since so few vending activities are desk-centric, you need not worry about devoting a great deal of space to your home office. A corner of your kitchen is typically just as viable as a finished room over your garage. However, the quiet room over the garage may be preferable.

> **Tip...**
>
> ### Smart Tip
> In the rare cases that you need to host a meeting with a potential client or use office services, virtual offices offer a handy package that can help you create presentations, handle documents, arrange meetings, rent board rooms, provide professional reception and answering services, have coffee served, and even get a fancy address for your reputation. Because a virtual office is a great combination of online services and actual office space, you can use it just like a regular office, but without the overhead. If you've got a snazzy portfolio or digital presentation on your laptop, it all works together to make you look sharp. See www.cornerofficeinc.com, www.davincivirtual.com, and www.virtualoffice.com to understand how virtual office features can work for you.

What is important is finding a location where you can make your administrative minutes count. Sharing the living room with your children's Nintendo game or *101*

Dalmatians video won't encourage productivity or produce sounds you want clients to hear in the background. If you have an active family, look for a quiet zone, like a corner of your bedroom, which allows you to step inside and shut the door.

"When I go in my office, my kids know I'm in there to work," says Baltimore operator Janice M., a single mother of three. "When I go in and close the door, I really feel like I've stepped into the office. When I leave it, I can go into another part of my house and really feel like I'm at home. I think that's really essential. You have to find a place to go that you consider your office space."

Decking It Out

Furnish your office with the basics—a desk and a chair. You're not impressing clients, and you won't spend hours on your fanny, so whatever's functional and comfortable will typically do. Functional means sturdy enough to support a computer and roomy enough so that you can do your paperwork. A secondhand desk may be easy to find. A few scratches or dents shouldn't matter, since this is for work purposes and not for clients to see.

One Westchester, New York, woman who does the accounting for operators found a desk in very good condition at a local garage sale for $10. Someone simply needed to get rid of it. While skimping on a chair seems like a good way to save money—using the folding chair in the garage, for example—you will spend enough time at your desk to feel the back and neck pains if you don't have a desk chair. Doctor bills will cost more than splurging for a decent office chair, so consider the repercussions of not having a chair that is at the right height for you or is not built for office use. Again, look for something secondhand since appearance doesn't matter.

Paperwork storage is next. Resurrecting a rusty file cabinet stashed in your basement or the corner of a pawn shop is one option. Using cardboard file boxes from the local

Dollar Stretcher

Freecycle (www.freecycle.org) is a community with a mission to keep usable goods out of landfills and has many free office goods posted for the taking. A recent search in Minneapolis, Minnesota, turned up a free cabinet full of office supplies, moveable cubicle walls, and an electric typewriter.

Craigslist (www.craigslist.org) has a section that in major cities is chock full of free goods. A recent search in Portland, Oregon, showed listings for these free items: inkjet printer/fax machine, desk, office chair, file cabinet, chair mats, scanner, and desk lamps. Are you willing to do a little driving? As you can see from this list it might be worth checking the Craigslist and Freecycle directories in neighboring cities, and even those a couple of hours away.

office superstore is another. You won't be drowning in paperwork, but you will need a home for client contracts, route cards, utility bills, inventory invoices, and the like.

For technology purchases such as your printer, fax, computer, and phone, search www.amazon.com. New equipment is competitively priced there with so many vendors competing for the great marketing that Amazon offers. The prices we'll show you below are all for new equipment, listed on Amazon, from a variety of retail vendors. See the "Office Equipment Expenses" list on page 105.

Cell Phone, Sole Phone?

A simple cell phone can serve as your primary phone if you're disciplined about answering it with your professional business greeting and paying attention to caller ID.

> ### Smart Tip *Tip...*
>
> When deciding between the many competing retailers on www.amazon.com (and similar sites), look for a five-star rating from as many buyers as possible. A five-star rating from only 15 buyers doesn't mean that much considering anyone could get 15 of their friends to order and give a rating online. But having a five-star rating from 225 users? Now that's someone you can expect to stand behind products and have pretty great customer service. Read the user comments. They can reveal more detail about the product than the retailer's description provides.

You can save a lot of money by opting for a separate, no-frills cell for your "home phone," which will allow you to make more long-distance calls for less than a traditional landline service with added long-distance fees. For example, a Straight Talk program phone by Tracfone can be purchased at Walmart in the range of $30 to $120, depending on the bells and whistles you prefer. The monthly charge for six hours of calls to any U.S. destination is $35. This way you've got your long distance, voice mail, texting capabilities, world time converter, and even a camera in one package, at one low price. For $45 a month you can be as chatty as you want and use unlimited minutes.

You will need a landline to receive faxes at your home, but there are other ways to get faxes. You can receive them at most libraries and FedEx Office locations, and make use of online fax services.

Why wireless? "I have to be the sales team and the marketing team and everything," explains Janice M. "Even though I have an office, I'm never really in one spot. I want people to be able to reach me."

Many high-end phones are close to free with the purchase of a two-year service agreement. You can expect to pay $200 to $300 for a smartphone such as a BlackBerry or Treo. The iPod and iPod Touch phones run about $300. These will allow you to use e-mail on your cell anywhere with wifi. Doing quick internet research, recording voice memos, taking photos, and even taking credit card payments are all possible with the right phone.

Cell phones can be an operator's best friend, minimizing the impact of mechanical malfunctions. "Today's machines are so computerized that the manufacturer's technicians ask you to punch in things to get a readout of what is wrong—motor error, solenoid error, etc.," says Becky P. "But you have to be standing at that machine with the capability to punch stuff in."

Cell phones are a must if you want to stay competitive in business today. If a competitor can be reached immediately to come and fix a malfunctioning machine, but you cannot be reached as easily, whom do you think the client is going to want to work with? Don't forget to charge that phone every night so it doesn't fail when you need it most.

POS Equipment

Knowing that cashless technology is one of the strongest trends in vending right now should be strong motivation to embrace like-minded concepts such as the Square, Apple's latest POS convenience. It works with iPod and iPod Touch phones (check for additional compatibility) and is a tiny, convenient plug-in for your phone with an interesting fee arrangement. The tiny Square card reader is postage-stamp-sized and plugs into any device with an audio input jack. There are no contracts or monthly fees beyond the per-card swipe rate of 2.75 percent, plus 15 cents. There are many additional convenience features in Square (www.squareup.com).

Even though we're just talking about outfitting your home office right now, it'll pay off to make sure your purchases, and the companies where you buy them, are compatible with features you'll probably want later, such as cashless vending transactions, accompanying software, web payment processing, and of course, the option to use mobile phones as payment terminals. The following companies offer a variety of these services to operators.

- Apriva (www.apriva.com/products/pos)
- Vivopay (www.vivotech.com/products/vivo_pay/index.asp)

Computers

There are very few people doing business today without a computer and an internet hookup. Unless you are running a very small part-time business, you need to stay up-to-date with technology if you want to succeed in a competitive industry like vending.

According to 20-year operating veteran Wayne D., getting a computer was the most important factor in his business' success. "At the time, we didn't really understand the impact it had or the ability it gave to manage your business so much better," he says.

▲

Janice M. agrees. "Before I started using a computer, I found myself constantly reordering things that weren't selling." In addition to straightening out her inventory, the computer also allowed Janice to produce her own stationery, market research surveys, contracts, customer feedback forms, and even colorful sales presentations.

In short, a computer will pay for itself in the long run. Internet service is inexpensive and will keep you in touch with the ever-growing and changing industry. You will find yourself ordering business forms,

Smart Tip

If your office is a portion of a room, it's still easy to document business-use square footage for the IRS. Place several yardsticks or tape measures on the floor to delineate the area. Be conservative. Then, take close-up photographs of the space with the yardsticks in view, as well as some 360-degree shots of the entire room.

finding distributors, discovering new innovations in machinery, and connecting with a very expansive vending universe once you start searching the vending industry on the internet.

Remember when you're trying to choose a type of internet service that many cities now have libraries and cafes with free wifi access. If you can't afford it now, then use one of those resources. You'll need a high-speed connection to coordinate jockeying back and forth between research, social media marketing, following up after networking events, and creating "gifts" for your growing online audience, which we'll cover in detail in Chapter 14. All this is deductible as a business expense, since you are using this for your company.

Both PCs and Macs come with software packages tailored to your needs. You could think of buying a computer as one of those bare-bones necessities that you don't want to purchase but have to—and then just use it minimally for word processing, e-mail, bill paying, and billing customers. Or you could realize that the right computer is a tool that makes the rest of your life easier, enables your highest potential for creativity, and gives you priceless opportunities to be a player in the most modern form of business communication, therefore standing apart from the "good enough" crowd.

Why be good enough when you can excel? We realize you're not made of money, but if you're excited about the prospect of using your computer to stay connected at any time and with any medium, because it's not only expected now, but also a lot of fun, then open your mind to a purchase that will pay for itself. See the "Computer System Checklist" on page 100.

PC or Mac?

People will never stop arguing about which is best, a PC or a Mac, and they both have their merits, but you will hear a deafening crowd of Apple users cheering the low numbers of viruses they get and the machine's intuitive user design. The PC users will argue that most of the business world uses PCs, therefore most business systems and software are designed for them, and they are priced more reasonably. The following articles discuss both sides:

- www.hongkiat.com/blog/mac-vs-pc-myth-busting-consumer-guide/
- www.apple.com/why-mac/better-hardware/
- www.popularmechanics.com/technology/gadgets/tests/4258725

Whichever side of the fence you wind up on, we highly recommend you get a laptop so you can do business anywhere, anytime. Of the many reasons to own a laptop, here are four to consider:

- Even if you have a smartphone, tackling a huge workload on a tiny phone while you're at a café eating dinner just doesn't cut it.
- If you decide to go on "vacation" and are lying on the beach when you receive an e-mail saying that a hot prospect would like to see a proposal, you'll be happy you purchased a laptop so you can race to a wifi connection at one of the local hotels or restaurants, whip something snazzy up with your photo, video editing and presentation software, and take care of business.
- After you've danced the cha-cha and are relaxing in your island hotel room you may remember that you pulled your phone out and snapped photos of a strange vending machine you saw that day. Wouldn't it be a perfect time to blog right now with no interruptions, inspired by your new vending ideas? Even from far away you can continue to deliver "gifts" to your social media audience, as they will come to expect, relying on you as a vending sage.
- Searching for unique vending merchandise as you travel across the United States just by pulling into any place with a wifi connection expands your shopping selection and possibly inventory.

You can usually buy last year's hottest new computer model for less money since dealers want to move them out to put the new ones in. A desktop with a monitor and keyboard

---

Bright Idea

The Max OS X comes with easy-to-use movie (iMovie) and soundtrack-making software (GarageBand) that you can use to throw sharp presentations together for showcasing vendors to clients, appealing to audiences in social media forums, and creating content for your website and blog. A recent check at www.bestbuy.com found it on sale for $899. It has enough storage to handle your accounting and spreadsheet software and prompts you to connect to whatever wifi signal you are closest to by name.

Computer System Checklist

Use this handy checklist when you go computer shopping.

Essential Hardware

What should you look for in a computer system? Here are some minimum requirements you should check for:

- ❏ Pentium IV-class processor
- ❏ Current version of Microsoft Windows
- ❏ 512MB RAM
- ❏ 80GB to 120GB hard drive
- ❏ CD-ROM drive (32X or faster)
- ❏ High-speed internet connection
- ❏ A 17" monitor
- ❏ CD-RW* drive

Essential Accessories

- ❏ Surge protector (protects you against a power outage wiping out the files you are working on). You can also opt for a UPS (uninterruptible power supply), which is better than a surge protector—it works like a short-term backup generator for the computer.
- ❏ Printer/copier
- ❏ Optional hardware (in order of importance)
  - ❏ Sound card (PCs have minimal sound built-in, but without a sound card, output is limited)
  - ❏ Speakers

Essential Software for Mac or PC

- ❏ Microsoft Word
- ❏ Microsoft Excel
- ❏ Adobe Acrobat
- ❏ QuickBooks (or similar novice-friendly accounting software)
- ❏ Antivirus (very, very important for PCs)
- ❏ Internet browser

Extra Software That Could Prove Helpful

- ❏ Microsoft Streets and Trips 2010
- ❏ Intuit Turbo Tax

CD-RW means "CD rewritable." This is a CD drive that allows you to make and reuse CDs. CD-RW goes beyond CD-ROM, which only reads premade disks. It also surpasses CD-R (for "writable"), which permits making a CD but not erasing and starting over.

A computer that meets the above standards should be able to handle anything you will be likely to need. Of course, you will also need a keyboard, mouse, and modem (preferably a cable modem).

can be had for under $500—shop around. It is a good idea, however, to buy a computer from a known entity (such as Best Buy, PC Richard, Comp USA, or directly from a manufacturer such as Dell or Apple) because you want the warranty and the technical support when things do not work as they are supposed to work. Just as you will be called upon to repair a machine in a hurry, you'll want to have someone to call to help you in a hurry with a computer repair need.

Peripherals

Peripherals are all of the other items around the computer. You will need a printer. For $60 or less you can buy a printer that will give you headaches. For $200, you can buy a printer and fax machine in one

Smart Tip

It's possible to look great while you're toting around everything you need. Instead of throwing all your items into your laptop case, consider a photo vest. It's smart looking with a pair of khakis and a crisp shirt and has tons of pockets for your cell phone and charger, digital camera, tool kit, car keys, wallet, and of course, coins galore. The vests come in tan, olive, and black and range from $25 to $75 at B & H Photo, Video, Pro Audio (www.bandh.com).

Industry-Specific Software

There are several vending software programs that can make your life easier. Most are very simple to learn. Among the possibilities are:

❍ *Vending Essentials Premiere*, from Soft Essentials Inc., is an all-in-one software package that includes accounting, inventory control, route scheduling, product rankings, sales taxes and commissions, and other features. You'll find more details at www.softessentials.com.

❍ *Super Route Manager*, from Premier Data Software, has an onscreen menu that allows you to easily select between Route Collection, Inventory Management, Route Management, and other possibilities. You can analyze sales data from each location and even print reports. For details, go to www.premierdatasoftware.com and go to Route Management Solutions.

❍ *Business Plan Pro*, from Palo Alto Software, is a sample business plan that you can use as a model, or template. The plan details all aspects of a business plan and provides you with the essentials for your business plan. See www.paloalto.com.

Back Up Your Data

Back up your data from your computer onto a CD or USB flash drive every single day. It only takes a few minutes, and should be part of your daily routine, like brushing your teeth. This way, the worst that can happen is you lose a day's worth of data. If your computer doesn't come with a CD burner in it, which is rare these days, you can pick one up for around $50. USB flash drives are tiny, are easy to transport, and cost from $10 for a 4GB drive to $135 for a 64 GB drive. Many business owners have spent numerous hours trying to salvage their business data after their computer system went awry. While computers are extremely useful for storing data, streamlining your business and connecting you to the internet, they can, and do, go down or get viruses and you can lose information. Backing up your data daily will prevent you from a disaster—it's very important. In fact, many businesses keep copies of their database off-site, meaning they store a copy in another location. Companies affected by Hurricane Katrina, for example, were able to resume their business transactions by having such data saved in other, remote locations away from the area. In some cases they emailed data to a secure server, while in other cases, they simply copied data to a CD and kept copies at a location away from their place of business.

that will handle your business needs until you outgrow your home office. Since nearly every business and household has a printer, ask friends, family, business associates, and others for a recommendation of a good printer. A laser printer is faster than an inkjet and since you are primarily printing out business forms quickly, you will probably opt for a laser. Again, ask around and look online for some good deals.

Rather than getting a separate fax line, you can also have your business line or your home line double as a fax line by leaving a message instructing people how to send a fax. By asking for fax transmissions only at certain times of day, you can keep

Beware!

For most of us, it's tempting to blow off establishing a filing system. Even a few folders grouped broadly by category, such as "income," "credit card bills," "equipment invoices," and "inventory expenses" save you from hours of productivity-robbing headaches at tax time. There are plenty of software programs available as well that can be easily used to provide you with electronic filing systems.

your business phone line open. Or check with your phone company as some offer something called "distinctive ring" where you have a separate fax number to hand out to people that rings differently from your normal line so you know not to answer it.

Stashing Your Stuff

But what about storage? After all, vending is an inventory-intensive business. What do you do with your products before you load them into your vehicle?

In the past, a homebased vending business required a garage or other significant warehousing space. However, vending today is increasingly a "just-in-time" industry.

"We have a cash-and-carry service where operators come in and shop just as in a grocery store," asserts John Ochi of Vernon Hills, Illinois-based Five Star Distributors. "Then you don't require a warehouse—you use our warehouse. A number of operators who use our cash-and-carry service are not only in vending full time, they even have one or two employees."

For compact products, such as pantyhose, a closet (or even part of one) is enough for inventory. Then your only issue is vendors. With life expectancies rising and more seniors staying in their homes, ferreting out storage space doesn't necessarily mean turning to a friend. Seniors on fixed incomes are often happy to rent space in their garages, basements, or spare bedrooms. Visit a luncheon at your senior center or post a notice through your neighborhood community center to find empty-nesters with room to share. A local self-storage facility—if it is inexpensive—is another option, since there are numerous facilities now available.

Tip...

Smart Tip

Coolers can keep ice for a week and beyond. Here's a rundown on some top-of-the-line coolers to keep your merchandise fresh:

Cabela's 56-quart Outfitter Ice Otter keeps ice solid for a week: $289

Coleman 58-quart Marine Cooler keeps ice solid five days when the temperature is 90°F: $70

Cabela's Exclusive 54-quart Steel Coleman keeps ice solid three days when the temperature is 100°F: $170

Yeti 65-quart has dry ice capabilities with legendary retention periods: $323

Find all these coolers at www.cabelas.com.

Taxing Advantages

Home offices also present operators with important tax advantages. Just as the IRS permits businesses to write off the cost of an office located in a commercial property, it also allows deductions for maintaining one at home. The amount you may deduct is based on what portion of your home you use as an income-generating office. Let's say you turn a 12-foot-by-12-foot spare bedroom into an office. That means that you are using 144 square feet of space for business purposes. If the total finished area of your home is 960 square feet, then your business portion is 15 percent. Thus, you may deduct 15 percent of your rent, utilities, repairs, maintenance (including cleaning!), and various other incidentals as business expenses.

What's the catch? The portion you deduct must be exclusively used for business. The same goes for a separate structure, such as a garage, and storage space, such as closets.

Stat Fact
The National Automatic Merchandising Association's recent study on how consumers feel about vending revealed cost and value as their first concerns and variety (or lack thereof) as their second concern when rating their experiences with vending. Consumers want good value for their money and a lot of variety.

The same holds true for your car or van. You can take off the percentage of miles that you drive your vehicle for business. Therefore, if you drive 10,000 miles in a year, and 3,000 of them are for business, you can claim 3,000 miles at whatever the current IRS mileage gas reimbursement rate is at that time.

Does this mean you can't deduct a nook in the kitchen or the closet full of inventory in the hall? Not exactly. You may not include any part of your kitchen (or the closet) used for nonbusiness activities (even if your dining table doubles as your coin counting area). However, if the nook is only used for your business, you may use its square footage to figure the portion of your home used exclusively as an office. Determine your home business usage carefully.

Counting Coins

Depending on the size of your operation and the type of products you vend, you may need a coin or currency counter. Typically, you can buy a good one for $500. Of course, as with most items today, the more features, the higher the price. You can find currency counters for $300 or $1,500. Since far more machines today are accepting dollar bills, you may also look to buy a bill counter, which will also run you a few hundred dollars.

If you are doing your own counting, it's advisable to get a calculator with a tape so that you can look back and find any discrepancies.

Going Commercial

Although it's likely your homebased office will fit perfectly for years and years, every rule has its exceptions. If you're one of them, you'll have to go commercial.

Office Equipment Expenses

To help you budget, here are furnishing, equipment, and supply costs for Quality Snacks, our fictitious vending company. Note that items with asterisks have been found used, for free and priced low on Craigslist and Freecycle, so you don't have to purchase them new if you're willing to do a little searching and driving.

Desk*	$80.00
Desk chair*	$120.00
File boxes*	$10.00
File cabinet*	$30.00
Phone*	$50.00
Answering machine*	$30.00
Cellular telephone	$30.00
Calculator with tape*	$25.00
Coin/currency counter	$950.00
Rolodex*	$10.00
Stapler*	$5.00
CD-RW disks (25)	$12.00
All-in-one printer/fax/copier/scanner*	$200.00
Computer (including monitor and keyboard)*	$920.00
UPS (backup power supply)	$90.00
Business/marketing software	$250.00
Coin wrappers	$10.00
Envelopes, plain #10 (box)	$5.00
Paper, computer/fax/copier (box)	$20.00
Stationery, blank (to create letterhead, etc.)	$20.00
Miscellaneous office supplies	$130.00
Total Expenditures	**$2,997.00**

A multiplex office/warehouse facility is a good choice. "We're very pleased here," says Becky P. "We have about 2,100 square feet, office and warehouse combined. We lease the space, and it costs us about $1,400 a month."

Of course, before leasing any space, look at the lease carefully and review it with your attorney. Consider the terms of the lease carefully and make sure you understand the fine print.

You may consider leasing a space larger than your current needs. This will allow you to sublease the additional space until the time comes that your business has grown and you have taken on employees to fill the additional square footage. Of course, your lease has to have the provision that you can sublease, so make sure it is in the lease or ask about having it included.

If you purchase an operation that is already in a building, there is still an overhead-abatement option, according to Hendersonville, Tennessee, full-line operator B.J. S. "I own the building, personally, and the business rents it from me," explains the operator. "That way, you can set the rent and hopefully build up some of your personal wealth."

No matter where you set up your office, remember the old saying about all work and no play. Eating doughnuts on Thursdays and playing your favorite CDs are great personal perks to motivate yourself whether you're in home or out.

8

Your Vendors and Your Wheels

Because of the unique nature of vending, you should think of your machines as your robotic representatives and your vehicle as their delivery system. These are the tools that allow you to present your services and that function as the two most important representatives of your company, after you.

This chapter will tell you what you need to know to help you assemble a winning team of vending machines and will talk about the kind of transportation you'll need to keep your vending business moving forward.

Automat Axioms

There are numerous types of vending machines available, some of which offer a wide variety of products, while others carry only a few. Some sport glass fronts, allowing you to see the products within, while others show logos or even simply display words like "coffee, black." The latest in vending machines now have digital LCD screens promoting products within.

Whether or not you can see what's inside, the "guts" of all machines work similarly. Products are all neatly compartmentalized with a button or a number that corresponds to the product's location. Once that location, or "column," is empty, nothing else will be dispensed from that compartment.

For example, inside a machine that carries cola, root beer, and lemonade, there's not a central area from which the unit grabs a root beer when the "root beer" button is pushed. Only the column(s) stocked with root beer dispense(s) that item. In addition, columns can have different capacities, which allow you to place the most popular items in the columns with greatest capacity.

Another important nuance is overall size. Two units standing next to each other may appear to hold the same amount of merchandise. However, one may actually contain half as much as the other machine.

Typically, when you think of vending machines, you initially start focusing on the big beverage and/or snack machines. As you know, there are also small gum machines, and little machines for stamps and tiny toys, and small- to mid-sized machines serving up espresso or cappuccino. From candy to DVDs, vending machines handle an enormous array of products and they come in all sizes.

> ## Smart Tip
> Tip...
>
> Just as there are classic cars, so too are there classic vending machines. A few of the operators we talked to agreed that the Dixie Narco is a solid, reliable classic, which can last a long time if cared for properly. One operator called it "the Cadillac of vending." Before buying used vendors call six or seven companies that have been in business for more than ten years and ask them what kind of machines they use. Read the NAMA equipment reports and browse *Automatic Merchandiser* and *Vending Times* for additional information.

New vs. Used

In addition to selecting vendor type and capacity, you'll have to decide on new or used equipment. The answer to "What's the best?" isn't cast in stone. This will depend on how many machines you are looking to buy, where you are purchasing them and where you will be placing them, and how much of a budget you have. The reality is that a $1.00 soda can be dispensed from a new or an older vending machine, but if you've spent only $1,500 on the used machine, rather than $3,000 on the new machine, you'll recoup your money more quickly and be on the road to profiting sooner.

While some newer machines have advantages, many of the older machines last a long time. You need to learn about what constitutes a good, quality machine, and this comes from talking with recognized professionals in the industry and reading trade papers.

Attracting and retaining accounts are two arguments for new. "We buy new equipment because you know what you're getting," says Hendersonville, Tennessee, full-line operator B.J. S. "The client is happy to get new equipment, too."

From his vantage point as a product distributor, John Ochi of Vernon Hills, Illinois-based Five Star Distributors observes, "Most people who enter the food businesses buy used. But if you're launching a business where you have an 'in' at a certain facility, such as a software company, you may need what new technology has to offer to satisfy your client and your customers."

Expect to shell out between $1,500 and $10,000 for new food-related machines. For purposes of calculating startup costs, the average is about $5,000.

One of the key factors is who will be seeing the machine. Remember, placement is important. In a warehouse factory lunchroom, the customers may not be at all concerned about the appearance of the soda machine—as long as it works. In a college student union building, however, you might want an eye-catching state-of-the-art machine since the students are used to the latest in high-tech gadgets.

Opting for Pre-owned

As many advantages as there are to new equipment, operators and experts say there are still plenty of reasons to invest in old.

Erik A. Borger had a lot of problems with the new machines he spent too much on with

> **Smart Tip** *Tip...*
>
> Andy Hayes, president of American Vending Machines and a 22-year operator, has some advice for those just starting out: "Keep overhead as low as you can for as long as you can." He started his pre-owned vendor business because he couldn't afford to buy new machines and keep growing. It was too capital-intense.

> ⚠ **Beware!**
>
> If you're purchasing used equipment, look for a small plaque with a serial number and date of manufacture. Without these items, it's impossible to tell just how old a machine is and, therefore, the difficulty of finding parts, likelihood for downtime, etc., warns full-line veteran Becky P. "If the plaque's not there, buyer beware."

that questionable company that sold him the shifty vendors and locations package. He lost at least $2,000 in sales over a two-year period just from motherboard malfunctions.

One of the things Borger did to dig himself out of the $65,000 mess he was in was to buy an additional fleet of used machines to expand his territory and bring in more profit. Using Craigslist he found several high quality vendors, none of them more than $500, and has only positive things to say about the experience. "On the new vendors I spent so much money on, to date I have changed each one of their motherboards out twice, some even requiring four changes," he says. "In fact tomorrow I have to drive out to each machine and do a computer update. Conversely, my 1980s National has given me no problems. In fact, I hardly have any trouble at all with any of my used machines, which are all Rowes, APs, and Nationals. In my opinion, never, ever buy new."

Practice in Your Own Space

Just as you don't start learning to play golf at a crowded country club with hordes of people waiting for you to take every shot, you don't start learning how to repair, or even fill, a vending machine, at a client's location. Instead, do this at home or in your garage.

Practice filling and emptying your machine quickly, as many times as it takes until you can do it and have a conversation at the same time. When customers see you tending to the machine they'll inevitably walk up and start chatting. You want your process to be so second nature that distractions won't get you flustered or cut into your speed or pattern. Besides, you want to look like an expert at what you're doing.

Most machines come with a manual. Practice with the manual in hand. When you get into the larger machines, their 800 number for technical support will prove helpful as someone walks you through the more challenging elements of the process.

"For a 50-person location, there are properly refurbished machines that are beautiful," comments food vendor Becky P. "But just like when you buy a used car and take it to a mechanic, I'd have someone come look at used machines first. I'd rather spend $50 or $75 to get a technician's opinion than spend $10,000 on vendors that don't work." If a machine is new enough, it won't even need to be refurbished. In this case, you can get deals by purchasing them from other operators. "Lots of times, you can get good deals on machines from people getting out of the business," Becky explains. "You can find fliers for them in your cash and carries, such as Costco, Sam's Club, or even a vending products distributor."

You also need to consider how skillful you are at repairs. If you have no clue how to repair a machine, you may want to get newer models complete with the manuals and tech support.

Borger learned some basic maintenance on his pre-owned vendors the hard way, and says, "I took things apart to see how they worked and did a lot of fiddling with levers and belts. I have been lucky so far. I have been burned a few times but after you are burned you know what to look for. Never, ever buy a machine that you have to turn by hand to receive your product!"

One way to use pre-owned food vendors effectively is in situations Vince Gumma of American Vending Sales in Chicago refers to as "overequipped." "For example, maybe you're putting a bank of machines in the break room, but the vice president wants a coffee machine outside his office. In this case, I'd recommend putting a used piece near the VP."

Another key is location profitability. "If the difference in making a location profitable is used instead of new, I'd say you shouldn't be in that location in the first place," asserts Gumma. "If you're that close to the margin, service costs and overhead can quickly make you unprofitable."

One of the positives of the rapid advancements in new technology is that some of the machines that are considered to be older really aren't that old. Just as new computers come out each year, or new cars for that matter (with new features), the previous models are still rather new and impressive. If you can buy used machines from a couple of years ago, you may be buying a barely used vendor with "low mileage" and perfectly working parts.

It is recommended that if you decide that pre-owned machines are right for you, insist on paying no more than 60 percent of what similar new models cost.

Taxes, Death, and Technology?

There are certain things you can't ignore because they affect all of us no matter what our post in life. Ever-changing technology is an element of the vending business that keeps evolving and determines more than just success or failure. It is the tone between the user, or buyer, and the machine, or seller, which represents you. The buyer has a dialogue of sorts with your machine when purchasing that tasty treat they've been craving, and technology determines how that conversation will go.

Consider the conversation that goes well between two humans, after which both parties walk away feeling they've gotten something they needed. They are apt to repeat that process over and over because they feel good when they do it. But what happens when one person wants something and it's a struggle to get it from the other? They either walk away or need to think of new ways to get what they want from the source.

It shouldn't ever be challenging or irritating to deal with a machine. All hands point to making buying easier as a way to capture maximum sales, and frequently, that involves implementing the latest technology.

Either Change or Lose Change

The vagaries of bill acceptors bring up an important point for the operators using cash machines. Of course, if your machines are cashless there seem to be different, though fewer challenges. For food operators planning to serve locations with more than 100 employees, or for any size location that includes refrigerated food, relying on a dollar bill acceptor isn't enough with conventional vendors.

"If you spend any time in a break room, at some point you'll see somebody with a dollar bill who keeps feeding it into the machine and it doesn't want to take it," states Becky P. "And after the third try they walk out to the door to the catering truck—what does that tell you?

"You don't ever want to lose a sale," she continues. "We do have dollar bill acceptors on everything, but if you have a nasty bill, the ones in the machines aren't as sophisticated as the ones in the free-standing changers." Therefore, Becky outfits her lunchroom machines with bill acceptors as well as bill and coin changer units that are free-standing.

Beware!

Beware of scammers such as the ones Hackers Homepage (www.hackershomepage.com) markets to. They specialize in selling products that hack into all kinds of machines and steal products. Some of their devices cause vending machines to free vend products, cheat slot machines, read credit card information, and "jackpot" bill changers. Hackers are everywhere and it's hard to prevent their insidious behavior, but having two security cameras pointed on your machines, one zoomed in on the user's hands and another on the face, will enable you to record suspicious programming behavior. Search "hackers" on www.vendingtimes.com to read about charges and criminal investigations involving the latest notorious thieves.

For food vending machines, a bill acceptor adds approximately $750 to the cost. Free-standing changers range from $425 to $3,000.

It's almost impossible today not to have a bill acceptor on a vending machine. You'll lose sales from everyone who is not carrying change, and many people carry minimal change in their pockets. A changer is an option, but presents a two-step process. It also costs more to have a change machine at every location. Therefore, accepting bills has become so commonplace that customers have come to expect that option. When buying previously owned machines, this is a major deal maker—or breaker. In some cases, this is the part of the machine that has been refurbished for that very reason—to work more effectively. Make sure you evaluate the bill acceptor, and that it works well.

Plentiful Cash Options

In a March 6, 2011, report, Chuck Reed at *Vending Market Watch* educates operators about "Making Buying Easier for Customers" and how updated technology can catch sales that may have otherwise been lost just because of the cash-carrying habits of most humans.

Reed points out that less than 50 percent of customers carry less than $3 in change and small bills combined, and that ATM machines usually pump out cash to their customers in $20 bills. He talks about how operators report 80 percent losses when their machines require exact change and experience changer starvation. This refers to when there is no more change left, which stops all sales that require change back. Most purchases do require change back, so a large number of sales are lost as a result of changer starvation. One of the problems is that bill changers are expensive and also require fronting hundreds of dollars for change.

A technology that is increasing sales for operators is called cash recycling. This enables customers to make many purchases from the same machine no matter what kind of change or bills they have (to a limit). Reed's research found that some operators using this technology report a 75 percent increase in sales. To read more of this article, go to www.vendingmarketwatch.com/article/10251806/.

Add the ability for those machines to accept credit cards, and your machines may capture the 77 percent of credit-card-carrying Americans out looking for snacks.

> **Bright Idea**
>
> Customers who acquire at least 25 cashless ePort vendors through the JumpStart program are eligible for U.S.A. Technologies' Business Deployment Planning program assistance, which advises on the best financial returns for their cashless machines. Visit www.usatech.com/eport/ for more information.

▲

Cashless Technology

Everyone is talking about it, ushering it in, and anticipating when and if cashless technology will become affordable for modest startup budgets. Forerunner U.S.A. Technologies' JumpStart cashless, swipecard vendors come with the bundled services of installation, merchant account setup, wireless SIM activation, business deployment planning, and 24/7 customer service. The company is also trying to help operators upgrade and change with the times by offering only a low monthly service fee instead of a large initial investment upfront.

Craig Kushner of Monumental Vending won the 2010 NAMA Vending Operator of the Year Award, partially due to his use of new technology. Kushner and his partner, David Gordon, have evolved their business together since 1991, each year incorporating technology to make them the most efficient in serving that they could be, beginning with being the first company in the U.S. to receive service alerts from vending machines in need of repair. "They were the first operation to have DEX handhelds on all their routes," Elliot Maras of *Vending Market Watch* reports in the article "Monumental Vending Raises the Performance Bar Using Technology in Greater D.C." Read the details of this entrepreneur's journey that began with a garage-based business here: www.vendingmarketwatch.com/article/10273923/.

Motion Sensors

Jennifer Berdoll Wammack's pie vendor has a sensor on the bottom that records whether or not the product has dropped, which is key to investigating any claims on sales that occur with midnight munchers. When someone shows up at midnight, swipes their card, and gets a malfunction instead of a pie, though this is rare, it's essential to be able to understand what happened. The USA Tech credit card processor in the vendor automatically first checks the card that is swiped to see if there are enough funds in the customer's account to cover the most expensive product in the machine. Then, when the purchase is made, the card is charged accordingly and the original higher charge is deleted. Finally, if the product does not drop down the card is not charged and Berdoll Wammack is able to go online during a customer complaint and see according to the sensor's data whether the pie dropped.

> **Bright Idea**
>
> A motion sensor can reduce lighting energy usage by up to 88 percent. How does it work? The sensor dims the lights when no one is in front of the machine, saving electricity and making the bulbs last longer. Find out more about the Vendors Exchange LED Motion Sensor Kit at www.veii.com/new_technology/led_lighting_kit.

Nutritional Touch Screens

Now consumers can just touch a button on a vending machine and a program will extract nutritional information from the central database, www.nutritionaldatabase. org, and present it to the snack buyer.

Vendors Exchange International offers a version of this called MIND, an acronym for "make informed nutritional decisions." Read more about it at www.veii.com/new_ technology/the_mind__nutritional_information_screen.

The Right Machine for the Right Location

Veterans in the business can tell you why a specific machine is better for a specific location—not from a product standpoint, but from strictly a machine standpoint.

You will need to consider:

- The size of the location
- The number of potential customers and the demographics of the customers
- How large or small a machine you should place in that area

A Sampling of Location Prices

Location prices vary depending on vendor type and how many machines you'll place together, but to give you an idea of the range, this list shows a variety of machine location prices:

4-head bulk candy	$60
8-head U-turn bulk vending	$75
4-head sticker/toy capsule	$75
7' gumball	$175
Full size soda	$350
Large soda and snack	$500
ATM machine	$900

Don't forget to ask, "Is this the best deal you can give me?" It may yield a discount.

- How often you can restock that machine
- The other available choices for customers, such as a Starbucks down the street or an employee cafeteria

Putting the right size machine in the right place is something that takes time to learn—in fact, professional location businesses can be a big help in solving what can be a dilemma. However, you need to make sure whomever you choose to help you find locations are trustworthy and experts in the field. There are some companies that will find you locations that are not worth having.

> ### Bright Idea
>
> Think about vending salads in smaller rotary cooler machines. Randall Sutherland believes there's a need for machines like these because sometimes an opportunity to sell a desired product is missed due to the size of the machine. "You'll spend $7,000 or $8,000 for the machine and will get a lot of requests because the bigger ones can't fit in most of the spaces," Sutherland predicts.

One vending startup consultant we talked to said combo machines run $250 to $300 per location and the big full-size snack machines may be $300 each. Most locators work on a 50 percent deposit to start looking for the locations and then once the location is found and people go out, talk, and they decide they're going to take it, they pay the locator at that time. Most locators work on a 50 percent deposit to start looking for locations. Once the location is found they bring you, the client to the site. If you decide to purchase the location you pay the locator at that time. As for the machines themselves, a large, well-stocked but underutilized machine is not helping your bottom line. Conversely, a small machine that runs out of items daily is great because you're seeing sales volume, but also not helping you because you are forced to reload too often.

From working for a vending operator or from talking with people in the industry, you can learn to gauge the best fit for machines at a location.

Getting the Goods

One place to buy goods is from a larger vending operator in your area, and you can land big discounts if you buy large quantities at a time. Purchasing in bulk and reselling to operators is another way to make a profit, but don't do it without letting your suppliers know in writing what you're doing. Not notifying them would be a big mistake you'd regret. You could not only lose your discount but also be blacklisted with other suppliers.

If you are not buying directly from another operator, the most common place to acquire new or used vending equipment is a distributor. Distributors can be thought of as a vending department store—they offer machines built by a variety of different manufacturers and for a wide array of specialties.

Like anything you buy, this added layer between you and the producer ultimately increases costs. However, there's also a significant benefit. Because they carry competing manufacturers' wares, distributors can assist you with deciding what is best for your needs. "You should expect your distributor to offer advice and assistance gained from dealing with successful operators," notes Vince Gumma of American Vending Sales in Chicago. They should also provide comprehensive training on how to use equipment, perform preventive maintenance, and do routine repairs.

Speaking of repairs, vendors are like cars—the question isn't if they'll malfunction, it's when. Although you will often trouble-shoot by phoning the manufacturer directly, sometimes you'll need hands-on help. "Manufacturers may have one field person for several states," notes distributor Gumma. "A good distributor will have a large inventory of parts and several field technicians devoted to your area."

> ### Bright Idea
>
> The Bureau of Labor Statistics *Occupational Outlook Handbook* for 2010-11 reports job opportunities through 2018 to be excellent for machine repairers who have training in electronics and are willing to travel and work at times outside regular business hours.
>
> Operators would do well to increase their area of expertise with some training offered by NAMA. Its Technician Training Program can be taken in-house, as can its certification exams. Imagine if during the slower times in your schedule you could get calls from operators needing your repair expertise and thus keep your income steady. Read more about NAMA's education offerings at www.vending.org/education/programs.php.

Other sources of repair people are the larger vending companies who can point you in the direction of people that they use. Again, network within the vending industry since most people are looking for the industry as a whole to prosper.

In addition, you should expect your distributor to assist you with obtaining financing. "They should interview you, collect your financial information, do the legwork required to assemble credit documents, and meet with the finance companies to obtain the best rates," Gumma says. "If an operator's credit is good, they should even be willing to go 'on recourse,' which means they agree to share in the risk of lending the money," he continues. "For example, the financing company may say to the distributor, 'We want you to take 50 percent of this application on recourse.' Although the operator may still have to offer collateral, such as the equity in their home, the distributor agrees to stand behind them."

To locate distributors offering equipment in your specialty area, you can consult the annual buyer's guides produced by Automatic Merchandiser and Vending Times. The National Automatic Merchandising Association also offers listings of distributors that are members, allowing you to cross-reference your findings and evaluate industry reputation. For contact information see the Appendix.

Borrowing from Bottlers

For snack and soda types, another way to obtain equipment is to partner with a bottler. Though this will sometimes provide the free use of machines, it can also limit your product line to one brand. While the pros and cons may seem apparent, there are hidden dangers. First, vending trends for the foreseeable future clearly indicate those who customize their offerings to their customers' tastes are the ones who will survive. Second, stories of bottlers literally swiping profitable accounts abound.

You'll find countless detailed discussions of the latter issue in both industry periodicals *Automatic Merchandiser* and *Vending Times*, but the important point for those who choose the partnering route is to be wary. Partnering remains a viable option at startup, but successful entrepreneurs move toward owning their own machines with earnest.

Starting from Scratch

If you are a vending innovator, your approach to obtaining machines may be as unique as the specialty you're pursuing. Baltimore pantyhose vending pioneer Janice M. tried following conventional wisdom for locating machines by calling area vending companies but none had what she needed. Then she consulted *Vending Times* at her local library. "But it didn't have anything listed," she says. It did have different kinds of machines that might have contained pantyhose in them, but nothing that was solely pantyhose vending machines." Undaunted, she tried a patent search. "I called the United States Patent and Trademark Office to ask if anybody had ever received a patent for pantyhose vending machines. They told me that no one had ever registered."

After doing more research, Janice decided her vision was truly an exception. Figuring she was onto something, she patented the idea herself.

Although the patent protected her brainchild, Janice still lacked the machines necessary to launch her business. So, she invented her own. "The father of a girlfriend of mine is a manufacturer," she explains. "He sat down and taught me how to make the machines, how much it would cost, and how long it would take. He helped me design the machines and make some."

For Janice, who describes her wall-mounted units as "slightly larger than a sanitary products machine," a two-column machine costs about $500, a three-column $650. Her largest units, those with four columns, run $750.

"I wish our machine would hold more product," Jennifer Berdoll Wammack sighs. "Each coil offers six sales opportunities. The machine has 12 pie positions and 21 candy bag positions, with six tries behind each one. This is because the large product and extra coils and motors take up a lot of room.

"We can keep up with refilling it once a day January through October, but in November and December we just can't fill it fast enough."

Guarding Your Assets

Regardless of your specialty, type of vendors, their age, or where you acquire them, security is always a concern. Protecting machines from vandalism takes various forms.

For food and beverage machines, distributor Gumma recommends adding new locks. "Machines are shipped to operators with a shipping lock that everyone in the country has a key for," he reveals. "Bottlers also lend people machines that have the same lock, which means ten different companies in your area could have keys. For about $10 per machine you can have your own lock with your own key.

"We also suggest people with employees use different locks on each route," continues Gumma. "For example, Route A would have a different key from Route B.

"Vendor placement also impacts their safety," says Gumma. "For example, if your machines are outside, they should be in view of a cashier, receptionist, or security guard."

Many operators avoid high-risk locations entirely. "I don't do nightclubs," Janice M. declares. "There's too much of a chance people will break into the machines."

The vendor at Berdoll Candy and Gift has an anti-tomfoolery setup. Berdoll Wammack explains: "When we first got the machine there was a long time that we didn't have it bolted down and I used to be afraid that we'd roll into the parking lot one day and find it gone. Customers sometimes didn't understand that it takes the motor a couple of seconds to turn out their product and would start shaking the machine, but we really haven't experienced very much real vandalism. We have security cameras on the machines and all over the property and gift shop, and when the machine got doused with graffiti it showed up on the camera. But it was just some young kids being silly and my husband removed the graffiti with Goof Off."

Berdoll Wammack speculates on the virtual lack of vandalism she's experienced. "The vendor is right outside of our store, which is well lit from the outside and our huge scrolling advertising sign," she says. "It's also right along a major highway and we have tons of surveillance lights on."

Chains, heavy weights, and, in some cases, cages fit around the machine that can be closed when the business is closed and no one will be around. There are also alarms made for vending machines, including tip alarms, which will set off an alarm if someone is tipping or rocking the machine. The Vending Connection Yellow Pages is one place to find such security devices.

To avoid costly legal battles, make sure your concern for machine safety goes beyond the impact of vandals on your profits. "We advise bolting machines to each other or to a wall," stresses Gumma. "Not so much to reduce damage to the machines, but to keep them from falling on people—which has happened. We show operators how to do this themselves, but many times we'll send a tech out to help."

Fun Fact

Marcus Webb at *Vending Times* reports on the new Currency Optimization, Innovation and National Savings Act, or COINS, in an October 2011 article. If COINS is passed, the U.S. will stop printing paper dollars and replace them with dollar coins. He cites the Government Accountability Office claim that COINS would save an average of $184 million a year, amounting to at least $5.5 billion over 30 years.

Good Migrations

Of course, you also need to plan for getting machines from your dock to your clients' locations. Vending machines can weigh several hundred pounds, and it is not worth risking injury to try to move one yourself—for $80 you can typically get someone to help and keep you from a back injury or a hernia.

To find professional movers, look in your Yellow Pages or ask other store owners whom they have used for moving display cases and other heavy equipment.

You can also go online to Craigslist (www.craigslist.org) and look for movers, or place an ad for movers in your area.

Maintain It Right

Let's face it: The world's a grimy place. Finger oil alone coats every coin and bill in a pocket, wallet, or purse. The air constantly deposits tiny particles on moving and stationary parts. You'll want to fight off your vendor's sworn enemies each week by taking these simple steps:

○ Clean the coin mechanism and bill acceptor.
- Pour rubbing alcohol on the coin rails, which also cleans the coin acceptor.
- Run a cleaning card through the bill acceptor.
- Swab off bill acceptor belts and sensors.

Maintain It Right, continued

○ Check the selection buttons.
  - Clean off dirt and check to see if the buttons are making good contact.
  - Look on the back side for broken parts or bad connections.

○ Inspect the selection trays, motors, and spirals.
  - Make sure selection trays or shelves sit in their "home" position in the shelf rails.
  - Examine all wires going to the motor, tightening any that have loosened.

○ Check circuit boards.
  - Blow dust off boards using a can of compressed air.
  - Examine all wires connecting to boards and tighten accordingly.
  - Call for support if you see signs of corrosion.
  - Reconnect wires properly if you remove any for cleaning or replacement. Improper connections can blow the whole machine.

○ Inspect the bucket.
  - Open the door using minimal force and determine if it's moving freely.
  - Examine the hinges and replace when worn.

○ Clean condenser coils/fins.
  - Vacuum off dust with a hand vacuum.
  - Remove grease or grime with mild cleanser.

○ Inspect the power cords.
  - Tighten connections between machine cord, extension cord, and wall socket.
  - Free pinched wires.
  - Replace any cord where the wire's been bared or casing gashed.

○ Polish the exterior.
  - It's a fact: Clean glass and exteriors attract more sales!

Source: Route and Service Driver, a quarterly companion publication to Automatic Merchandiser

▲

Maintenance Matters

Although your only upfront cost will be a basic tool kit and supplies that cost $70 to $110, maintenance and repair will become a routine part of your life as an operator. Therefore, the maintenance and repair training offered by your distributor, as well as the ongoing support policies offered by the manufacturer, bear consideration as you're deciding what to purchase and where to get it.

"I'm not very mechanically inclined, but I learned to be," admits 20-year full-line veteran Wayne D. "After you pay what it costs to have someone else fix your machines, you figure out pretty quickly how to repair it yourself." Most repairs you'll make will be as simple as clearing jams in the coin mechanism, bill acceptor, or the spirals inside. More serious malfunctions generally require dialing up a professional. The key is to establish a rapport with a qualified pro who can be there when you need him. Accessibility is very, very important.

You can also minimize budget-busting repairs to compressors and the like by following the preventive maintenance routine suggested by the manufacturer. Typically, each manufacturer will provide tips for maintaining the machine and a manual to follow as you go. If you follow specifications, how much maintenance will be required? "We go through preventive maintenance during our training courses and tell operators that high-volume locations will require more maintenance than lower-volume locations," Gumma says. "We also tell people that soda and coffee machines have to be adjusted more often."

Time to Accessorize

Depending on your vending specialty, you'll want to budget for miscellaneous items to add power to your vendors, protect electronics from power failures, and clean machines inside and out.

While power cords supplied with each machine may be adequate, sometimes they are just too short. Therefore, be prepared to use a heavy-duty extension cord when necessary. Even in the absence of an extension cord, avoid fusing your vendor's circuits by delivering clean, steady current. Find out how much current the machine uses and make sure that when you plug it in the lights in your client's office, warehouse, or cafeteria do not suddenly go off.

Other accessories include cleaning cards for cleaning bill acceptors, rubbing alcohol to cleanse coin rails and coin acceptors, glass or multipurpose surface cleaner to swab down fronts, and an appropriate disinfectant to wipe down insides of food and beverage vendors.

Which Ones Should I Buy?

Now that you have all the background info, perhaps you're wondering how to decide which machines to buy.

"A startup operator shouldn't buy equipment before [he or she knows] the location and the requirements of the location," advises Gumma. "Successful operators typically come to us with something already lined up or they've at least got some kind of verbal commitment."

We'll address this issue and much more in Chapter 13. So hold tight for now, and let's move on to another vital consideration—how you're going to get around.

Getting Around Town

For many startup operators, whatever they're currently driving becomes their first route vehicle. "At the time we started, we worked out of the trunk of the car," says Wayne D., who began with 14 snack, soda, and cigarette machines in five locations. "When we needed a bigger vehicle, we went with a small van."

Erik A. Borger does his route in a Prius. It costs him $3 to $7 per day. He happily adds, "On my worst day with over a thousand drinks in the back I still get 48.6 miles per gallon. This is not a long-term goal but it works great for now. Down the road I will consider biodiesel. Every penny counts and to be successful in this economy you have to think outside the box."

"I'm using the same car I had prior to starting the business," Janice M. says. "But I'm considering purchasing a small truck next year."

No matter what type of vehicle you choose, remember your insurance company won't cover a loss if you fail to inform them you're using your vehicle for business

> **Beware!**
> Acquiring vendors before clients puts the cart ahead of the horse. "Randomly buying machines and thinking you'll get the right ones is ludicrous," stresses Vince Gumma of American Vending Sales in Chicago. The number of potential customers, male/female mix, ethnicity, age, wages, competitors (convenience stores, superstores, etc.), and even regional preferences impact what is profitable at a given location. You should know what you are planning to sell, and where you will sell it, before buying your machines. Buying machines before you know what you are selling (and where) is tantamount to hiring salespeople before you've decided what your store will sell or where it will be located.

▲

purposes. Count on your rates increasing when you switch from pleasure to business, but you need look no further than NAMA statistics to know it's worth the investment. Recent vending industry statistics name auto liability the second largest area for both frequency and cost of claims. You should also remember that you can ease the sting by deducting insurance premiums and other vehicle-related expenses (including tolls and gas when driving for business) on your income tax return.

Stat Fact
The Ford E-Series cargo van has been one of the best selling vans in America since 1961. "It has maintained its position as the leader in full-size vans for personal and commercial applications with continuous design and engineering advancements building on a long tradition of Built Ford Tough capability," according to Ford.

Running on Empty

If your current vehicle won't make the miles, then you must purchase something reliable. Entrepreneurs intending to grow a snack business into a full-time pursuit should head straight for a cargo van. A new one with a sliding door, antilock brakes, air conditioning, and air bags will cost between $25,000 and $38,000. Like any vehicle, used cargo vans vary in price with age, but plan to pay about $15,000 for a reliable one. Operators of nonfood vending businesses say it's easy to stay with an automobile, although many people (with or without vending businesses) are opting for the roomier SUVs today, which can certainly come in handy for the smaller vending machines.

Buddying Up to Your Back

Lifting items into and out of your vehicle may seem like a no-brainer activity, but your back may disagree. Just as you'll end your vending career early by improperly moving a heavy machine, you can blow out your spine when bending, twisting, reaching, and lifting the products you unload at each location.

This is particularly true if you're operating out of a passenger vehicle because it's not designed for the job. Arguably, your personal mobility is your most important asset as an operator. The best machines in the world won't do you a bit of good if improper lifting lands you in a wheelchair.

Unless you have an uncle who's an orthopedist or your best friend's a chiropractor, a good source of information on proper back care is NAMA's Be a Buddy to Your Back. This short video explains the dos and don'ts and comes with a laminated card showing appropriate lifting techniques and six back exercises. For information on how to obtain the video, consult the Appendix.

Stepping Up to Step Vans

As you grow, or if you purchase an operation that's up and running, you'll quickly find yourself upgrading to step vans. A step van is like a bread delivery truck, or a scaled-down version of the ubiquitous brown UPS vehicles.

In addition to expanded capacity and the potential for adding a refrigerated compartment, step vans allow for standing upright inside. This makes them much easier on the back when it comes to lifting chores. Of course the downside is they're pricier than your average cargo van. "By the time we needed a step van, we were a pretty good-sized company," says Wayne D. "We were four or five years old and were grossing over $200,000 annually."

For moving the larger food machines, however, you'll want to inquire about renting trucks with hydraulic lifts. In fact, if you have a truck, there are companies like Anthony Lift Gates (www.anthonyliftgates. com) that sell hydraulic lifts for existing trucks. In addition, there are also devices made that will help you with lifting and even climbing stairs. For example, Monolift, a product that can lift up to 2,000 pounds, manufactured in Worland, Wyoming, can be a lifesaver for moving the larger machines. For a list of possibilities, start with Vending Connection's Vending Yellow Pages (look under Moving Equipment) or contact NAMA. Don't be pennywise and pound foolish (literally) when it comes to moving the heavier equipment around.

When you reach the point where a step van is the logical next vehicle for you, decide which is best to buy the same way you choose vendors, recommends Becky

---

Smart Tip ⚡ Tip...

Hand trucks and dollies help maintain the natural position your body should be in when lifting, pulling, and pushing. Here are three products to check out at B & H Photo, Video and Pro Audio (www.bhphotovideo.com):

1. Conair Travel Smart LadderKart Combination Stepladder & Hand Cart, $69.95
2. Wesco Maxi Mover Folding Handtruck, $99.95
3. Wesco Mega Mover Folding Handtruck, $234.95

Bright Idea

When investing in a safe for your vehicle, consider a punch board or biometeric fingerprint detecting type. It can slow down potential thefts. Electronic devices take more time to beat than mechanical ones, and no one can duplicate your fingerprint. The electronic Stack-On cabinet takes up to 28 fingerprints, can be drilled into a wall or floor, and includes a hidden, trouble key. It's also California Department of Justice approved. You can find it at www.cabelas.com ranging from $125 to $280.

▲

P. "We do research through Consumer Reports and get sales pitches from different places. We also go up to people driving certain vehicles and ask them what the pluses and minuses are."

To learn more about planning and budgeting for everything you'll need to equip your business, see the "Vending Equipment Expenses" statement for Quality Snacks below, and the "Vending Equipment Expenses Worksheet" on page 127.

Stop, Thief!

You already know vending is a cash-based business, which means you don't have to hire a receivables department in order to get paid. This means that you will be carrying untraceable cash and products around. Protecting these assets requires a pretty simple combination of inexpensive equipment and a little common sense.

Vending Equipment Expenses

To help you budget, here are furnishing, equipment, and supply costs for the fictional vending operation, Quality Snacks, that we introduced you to in Chapter 6.

	New/Used
Vendors	$52,500/$26,250
Vehicle (cargo van)	$25,000/$14,000
Labor (to move machines to locations)	$750
Security locks (for vendors)	$150
Surge protector (with noise filter)	N/A*
Extension cords (heavy-duty)	$100
Safe or lockbox (for vehicle, bolted to floor)	$280
Dolly (transport inventory/move vendors)	$60
Cash pouches (zippered, with locks)	$50
Maintenance and repair kit	$100
Total Expenditures	**$78,990/$41,740**

*N/A = Not applicable. In other words, this hypothetical operation doesn't own this item.

Vending Equipment Expenses Worksheet

Here's a handy shopping guide for equipping your business. Although it's designed with the homebased operation in mind, you'll need the same gear if you're in commercial quarters.

Vendors	$
Vehicle	$
Labor (to move machines to locations)	$
Security locks (for vendors)	$
Surge protector (with noise filter)	$
Extension cords (heavy-duty)	$
Safe or lockbox (for vehicle, bolted to floor)	$
Dolly (transport inventory/move vendors)	$
Cash pouches (zippered, with locks)	$
Maintenance and repair kit	$
Miscellaneous	$
Total Expenditures	$

Although robberies may be most feared, far more common are thefts due to complacency. We'll talk more about security when we discuss route structures in Chapter 11. A lockbox bolted within your vehicle is one way to stash money safely; of course you need to make sure you have a locked vehicle and a safety apparatus for the vehicle.

If you are in the process of considering your startup expenses, and you have read Chapter 6 in which we talked about funding, you should take a look at the application for credit on pages 128–129, which is like those you will see when trying to secure that all-important startup loan.

Application for Credit

AMERICAN VENDING SALES INC.

APPLICATION FOR CREDIT

FOR OFFICE USE ONLY
SLSM _____
Date
approved _____
Credit
limit _____

_____ , Applicant

Correct legal name	_____ corporation _____ partnership _____ individual yrs. In business	arcade	_____ yes _____ no

Location (street address)	Telephone # ( )

City	State	Zip Code	Federal Tax ID #

Own	Morgagee	Address	City/State/Zip Code	Mortgage balance $	since

Rent	Landlord	Address	City/State/Zip Code	Monthly payment $	since

TRADE REFERENCES

1)	Name	Address	City/State/Zip Code	Telephone # ( )

HI credit $	Amount owed $	Length of time doing business	Personal contact

2)	Name	Address	City/State/Zip Code	Telephone # ( )

HI credit $	Amount owed $	Length of time doing business	Personal contact

3)	Name	Address	City/State/Zip Code	Telephone # ( )

HI credit $	Amount owed $	Length of time doing business	Personal contact

BANK (checking___ Loan___) 1)	Address	City/State/Zip	Personal contact	Account #'s

BANK (checking___ Loan___) 2)	Address	City/State/Zip	Personal contact	Account #'s

INFORMATION ON OFFICERS, PARTNERS, OWNERS

Name	Address	City/State/Zip	S.S. #	Tel. #	Title
Name	Address	City/State/Zip	S.S. #	Tel. #	Title
Name	Address	City/State/Zip	S.S. #	Tel. #	Title

"The undersigned, individually and on behalf of Applicant (if signed as an officer or partner of the corporation or partnership) does hereby certify to the truth, correctness and completeness of the information set forth above and on the reverse side, and understands that American Vending Sales, Inc. will rely upon such information if it decides to extend credit to the undersigned and Applicant. The undersigned and Applicant hereby authorize American Vending Sales, Inc. to investigate all the information provided above, and understand that American Vending Sales, Inc. may contact any or all the parties names. Provided, however, any investigation or contact by American Vending Sales, Inc.shall not be deemed as a waiver of its reliance upon the accuracy of the information provided by the undersigned and Applicant of this Application.

In consideration for any extension of credit by American Vending Sales, Inc. to the undersigned and Applicant, the undersigned, individually and on behalf of Applicant, hereby agrees to the following terms and conditions which shall be deemed applicable to all sales by American Vending Sales, Inc. to the undersigned and/or Applicant.

a) The undersigned and Applicant agree to timely pay all amounts due in connection with any sales made by American Vending Sales, Inc. to the undersigned and/or Applicant;

b) The undersigned and Applicant agree to pay interest upon past due balances at the lesser of two percent per month, or the highest rate of interest permitted by law; and

c) The undersigned and Applicant agree to pay all costs and expenses incurred by American Vending Sales, Inc. in connection with the collection of any balances due from the undersigned and/or Applicant, including by way of description and not limitation, court costs and reasonable attorney's fees."

_____
Signature

_____
Signature

Application for Credit, continued

PLEASE COMPLETE THE FOLLOWING AS WELL AS ALL SCHEDULES BELOW:

ASSETS		LIABILITIES	
Cash on hand & in Banks	$ _____	Accts. Payable	$ _____
Accts. & Notes Rec.	_____	Notes payable (sched. B)	_____
Inventories	_____	Unpaid Taxes	_____
Real estate owned (sched. A)	_____	R.E. Mortg. pay (sched. A)	_____
Equipment (net of deprec.)	_____	Other liabilities (please itemize)	_____
Autos & Trucks (NET)	_____	_____	_____
Other assets: (please itemize)	_____	_____	_____
_____	_____	**Total Liabilities**	$ _____
_____	_____	**Net Worth**	$ _____
Total Assets _____	$ _____	**Total Liab. & Net Worth**	$ _____

Net Income–Prior Year Ending _____ /19 _____ $ _____
Mo.   Yr.

Estimated Annual Sales–Current Year Ending _____ /19 _____ $ _____
Mo.   Yr.

SCHEDULE A–REAL ESTATE OWNED

Property Location	Bank Name	Date Acquired	Original Cost	Original Mortg.	Mortg. Bal.
			$	$	$
			$	$	$
			$	$	$
			$	$	$

SCHEDULE B–NOTES PAYABLE (EQUIPMENT, IMPROVEMENTS, ETC.)

(Bank or Fin. Co.)	Type of Loan	Date of Loan	Amount	(Mo. Pmt.)	(Balance)
			$	$	$
			$	$	$
			$	$	$

In order to induce American Vending Sales, Inc. to enter into sales or extend credit to Applicant, _____ ("Debtor"), the undersigned, being an officer or shareholder of Debtor and/or being financially benefited by the accommodations made by American Vending Sales, Inc., guarantees the full and prompt performance of all of Debtor's present and future contracts, agreements and arrangements with American Vending Sales, Inc. and the full and prompt payment to American Vending Sales, Inc. of any and all sums which may be presently due or declared due and owing to American Vending Sales, Inc. by Debtor or which shall in the future become due or declared due and owing to American Vending Sales, Inc. by Debtor.

This is a continuing Guarantee, and American Vending Sales, Inc. is hereby authorized without notice or demand and without affecting the liability of the undersigned hereunder, from time to time, to (i) extend credit to Debtor, (ii) renew, extend, accelerate or otherwise change the terms of the Debtor's Liabilities, or any instrument, (iii) accept partial payments on Debtor's Liabilities, (iv) and take and hold Collateral for the payment of this Guaranty. American Vending Sales, Inc. may, without notice, assign this Guaranty in whole or in part.

The undersigned waives notice of acceptance of this Guaranty notice of extension of time of payment, notice of any amendments or modification of said agreement and all other notices to which the undersigned might otherwise be entitled by law, and agrees to pay all amounts owing thereafter, upon demand, without requiring any action or proceedings against the debtor.

The undersigned agrees to pay all costs, expenses and attorney's fees incurred in the collection thereof and the enforcement of this Guaranty.

Dated _____ 19 _____

_____

_____

9

Stocking Your Machines

Now that we've discussed your automated sales force, let's talk about filling those machines up. While clean, attractive machines invite purchasers to draw near, what's in the machine seals the deal.

As discussed earlier in the marketing section, it is important that you know the demographic market in which you will be setting up your machines. Additionally, you will hopefully have an idea of how busy each location will be. For this, you may hire location experts to help you find the prime areas to set up shop. Of course, no one can land the accounts for you; that part you have to do yourself.

If you find areas first, you can then tailor your inventory to fit those locations. Conversely, you can first decide on an item that you strongly believe in (such as Janice, who did marketing and decided to sell pantyhose) and then determine the prime locations for that product. In this section, we take a look at some of the numerous possibilities.

Product Mix 101

Does this mean you will stock as many different individual items as your total number of columns for all the vendors you own? Hardly. "Your mix will be different for each location," says John Ochi of Vernon Hills, Illinois-based product distributor Five Star Distributors. "But some types of products will be the same in every location."

In addition to determining individual items to stock, satisfying desires for certain product categories is equally important. According to *Vending Times*, research shows at least 20 percent of consumers will walk away from a machine if they don't find the kind of item they want.

In other words, demand does not transfer from one category to another. For example, a person looking for chewing gum won't buy potato chips, nor will a woman who needs pantyhose settle for knee-high stockings.

Surveying the Landscape

At any given movie theater you'll find tots in line for the animated show and teens queued up for the latest horror flick. Not surprisingly, in the theater called vending, demographics also plays a leading role. "We look at the top-selling products in each category and then evaluate the demographics at the location," explains operator Wayne D. Therefore, the items at a predominantly blue-collar male factory warehouse will differ from a predominantly female-run business. Items at a college will differ from items at an elementary school or at a senior center.

At closed locations, such as offices or factories, presurveying the population hones in on preferences even more precisely. "For example, we give our contact at a location a list of beverages and ask them to survey their people," adds Wayne. "Then we take the top 8, 10, or 16 items, depending on the size of the location, and put those in." But this process often requires some fine-tuning because some survey respondents may not purchase beverages as often as others. "Let's say Diet Coke didn't make the initial cut," illustrates Wayne. "But after we put in the initial inventory, two or three people request Diet Coke. If two or three people buy a Diet Coke every day, then we make a lot of money."

Open locations require a different approach. Agricultural areas may attract seasonal workers of one ethnic background, while naval bases may draw another. Observing convenience store customers may allow you to determine what is more likely going to be popular at that location. Of course, you also need to consider what else is available. Products that can be readily purchased at the same location, or next door, without a long wait, may not be as popular as something that isn't as easy to buy.

Learning the Product Possibilities

The choice of products could fill this book and a couple more, if we went into all of the brands and variations on a theme. Soda alone has hundreds of possibilities, when you consider brands, bottle sizes, cans, selling by the cup, and so on. The list below is simply to start you thinking about the options. Some vending businesses have a more narrow focus, such as only coffee and cappuccino or only sports drinks and bottled water. Other businesses have vendors featuring a wide range of products. Typically, it is easier to start with a narrow range and expand as you grow, since there is a learning curve associated with most products. You need to know the specifics regarding customer preference, and that comes from experience, research, and in some cases, trial and error. For example, which size candies sell the most? Do chips outsell pretzels? Which is the bestselling healthy snack alternative? If you are selling healthy snacks, you're best learning the answer to the last question before branching out into another product line. Grow as you learn and learn as you go.

Here are a few vending products to think about for the somewhat impulsive, captive foot traffic crowd who love convenience:

- diapers, pacifiers, sippy cups, and baby food
- aspirin, ibuprofen, antacids
- mini-tissue packets, hand lotion, Band-Aids, shavers
- feminine hygiene and contraceptive products
- auto air freshener, sunglasses, baseball caps, and sun hats
- cookies, crackers, chips, candy, and pastries
- coffee and cappuccino
- bottled smoothies, water, and performance sports drinks
- healthy, tasty snacks not labeled as "diet" items
- ice cream, frozen mini-pizzas
- DVDs, cell phone holders, jewelry

There are numerous variations within each of these categories (and various other categories). Many of these fall under the broader headings of "snacks" or "beverages." The point is, as you can see, many possibilities exist, and the better you can match the right products to the right potential market, the more likely it is that you will have vending business success.

One of the recent, successful trends in vending are the cappuccino and espresso machines. "This is what nobody knows about . . . the countertop espresso machine," says Tim Sanford. "One such brand has been marketed in this country for years by an Italian manufacturer called Saeco. It's huge in Europe and moved here to the Cleveland area," adds Sanford, who recalls a woman who had run into a woman from Saeco and stashed the information about the coffee machines away for future reference. Later, she ran into a friend who worked for a software company as a personnel manager of about 25 people, and complained how difficult it was to get an espresso machine. "My guys want espresso. Microsoft has about 150 espresso machines and we can't even get one machine," the personnel manager explained. She had talked with large vending companies who could not service such a small account. The woman who had stashed away the information on Saeco, however, told her that she might have just the solution.

Sanford explains, "Over the past couple of decades, the vending industry has begun to blur into other methods of providing workplace refreshments. One of these is 'office coffee service,' a concept developed in the early 1960s, in which the operator provides a coffee brewer and periodically delivers coffee, condiments, cups, and 'allied products' (teas, soups, hot chocolate, and a great many other things). For a variety of reasons, OCS has undergone substantial changes over the past two decades, and the big trend in the new century has been the single-cup brewer.

"The pioneering OCS operators tended to avoid things like that, since they are more complex than a small restaurant bottle brewer, and so require some technical expertise to maintain," says Sanford. "But vending companies are not daunted by single-cup brewers, because vending machines are even more complex. As locations have diminished in size, the idea of providing 'total refreshment service' has found favor: the operating company can provide whatever mix of vending, coffee service, and pure water service (increasingly, through point-of-use water treatment systems rented to the account under a service agreement that stipulates periodic filter changes and maintenance). Countertop espresso machines are easy to fit into this model."

She went out and purchased a couple of machines from Saeco, put them in, with cinnamon and all the trimmings, recalls Sanford. Sure enough, she started on the road to success, serving smaller businesses with the espresso machines that companies wanted.

The key is finding the next trend that you can get in on, especially one with a great markup. Smaller locations with a need for machines can be your niche. Yes,

Hot Beverages Are Still Hot, Some Getting Hotter

CHART 15A: HOT BEVERAGE MACHINES, 4-YEAR REVIEW

2007	2008	2009	2010
341,000	338,000	320,000	315,000

CHART 15B: HOT BEVERAGE SALES, 4-YEAR REVIEW*

% OF SALES

TYPE	2007	2008	2009	2010
Fresh-brew regular	47.08%	46%	53.16%	54.9%
Fresh-brew decaf	4.99	4.0	5.32	5.42
Fresh-brew specialty/flavored	10.17	10.5	8.2	7.9
Freeze-dried regular	4.99	4.15	5.5	3.1
Freeze-dried specialty	8.75	11.5	6.7	7.86
Tea	2.37	3.5	2.3	1.72
Hot chocolate	13.24	11.5	11.67	11.67
Soup	2.5	2.0	0.6	0.53
Other	5.88	6.75	6.45	6.75

CHART 15C: HOT BEVERAGE SALES, 4-YEAR REVIEW*

PROJECTED TOTALS

TYPE	2007	2008	2009	2010
Fresh-brew regular	$483.8M	$446.2M	$432.2M	$411.75M
Fresh-brew decaf	42.9	38.8	43.25	40.5
Fresh-brew specialty/flavored	110.5	101.85	66.66	59.25
Freeze-dried regular	43.3	40.2	44.72	23.25
Freeze-dried specialty	121.1	111.5	54.47	58.5
Tea	35.1	33.95	18.7	12.9
Hot chocolate	116.1	111.5	94.88	87.53
Soup	28.4	19.4	4.88	3.99
Other	64.7	65.46	52.44	50.63

Some 2009 numbers have been adjusted since last year's report.

CHART 15D: HOT BEVERAGE PRICES, 4-YEAR REVIEW

TYPE	2007	2008	2009	2010
Fresh-brew regular	53¢	57.4¢	59¢	59¢
Fresh-brew decaf	53	57	58	58
Fresh-brew specialty/flavored	63	66	64	65
Freeze-dried regular	52	57	59	59
Freeze-dried specialty	62	59	59	59
Tea	51	57	55	55
Hot chocolate	53	60	58	59
Soup	53	58	57	57

Source: Elliot Maras and *Automatic Merchandiser* magazine

▲

Is Instant Food Research Coming to Your Vending Machine?

PR Newswire reported this observation with data collected from Deloitte's 2011 Consumer Food and Product Insight Survey:

> Smartphones are playing a role in the entire shopping process: The proliferation of smartphones and a much savvier base of shoppers have spurred consumers to use mobile devices to assist with several aspects of their shopping routines, according to the survey. More than one-third (34 percent) of smartphone users research food prices or product information while in a store. More than two-fifths (43 percent) of smartphone users have managed a food shopping list on their device while not in a store.

you may need to restock them very often, but the money you will be making will make your trips worthwhile. As Tim Sanford says, "Remote monitoring is picking up acceptance in an industry that has, on occasion, been resistant to change (not the coin kind)."

Uncharted Waters

If you go the route of pantyhose operator Janice M. and vend a completely new product, trial and error will likely be your guide. "When I started, I only had a two-column machine, so I only had two selections. I did black and white because those are pretty generic colors. Eventually, people started asking if I had other colors. As they would ask me, I would do different selections. I'd think, maybe I'll do gray and see if that moves—and it did."

While the trial-and-error method may seem confined to new vending specialties, to some extent it's a fact of life in every specialty. "Although our top 10 or 12 snack items will basically be the same in every location, we watch the service frequency of each category, such as chips, candy, or pastry," Wayne D. says. "If the service frequency shows that the pastry isn't selling, then we reduce the pastry spirals at that location and add more chips. You can't just furnish doughnuts and cookies because your customers don't want them every day. And what about the afternoon? In the afternoon they want a cake or a pie."

Variety: The Spice of Life

No matter what you vend, plan to introduce new options often. "It's a penny, nickel, and dime business," stresses Wayne. "Two extra sales a day make a lot of money at the end of the year. That's what we try to instill in our route people—if you sell $100 more per week just by making changes, you'll take in more money and have a lot of satisfied customers as well."

Look for choices that complement those that you already have. If, for example, Pringles are selling very well, then perhaps a new flavor of Pringles or a similar product will provide another choice for snack buyers. Variety is a plus in the vending industry today.

Freshness Sells

For food-related operators, paying attention to dates is crucial. "Let's face it, freshness sells," asserts full-line operator B.J. S. "If there's someone cutting you a deal, you're probably getting close to the expiration date of the product. Most suppliers don't deal on items that are selling well. Nine times out of ten, it's an item that's been sitting around, and somebody's trying to get rid of it."

For full-line operators like B.J., this means the turnaround time between receiving deliveries and placing items in vendors is tight. "Before I purchased the company, we used to stockpile things because the previous owner felt he had to buy more to get a good deal. But if you stockpile, sooner or later your inventory goes bad. Now we turn inventory on a ten-day basis."

In addition to attending to expiration dates, snack and soda operators must compensate for the environment's effect on their chocolate. "You can store it for 48

Bright Idea

Antiques shops are often clustered together to profit from one another's road or mall traffic and are found in quaint, little tourist towns in the country, as well as in major cities. A vending machine that carries soda pop and candy unique to those bygone days would offer the perfect snack and wouldn't require store hours to operate. Old-time soda pop brands such as Green River and Grape Nehi and candy brands such as Velvet gum and Sen-Sen can be found on vintage candy sites such as www.hometownfavorites.com and www.nostalgiccandy.com. To add to the mix, try offering small, collectible, retro tchotchkes, which can be found en masse at www.etsy.com in the antiques and vintage sections at good prices.

hours at a time in weather up to 90 degrees without a problem," notes consumables distributor John Ochi. "But some people store it up to 95 degrees."

However, these guidelines mean air temperature—not the climate inside your truck when it's sitting on asphalt in the midsummer sun. For such situations, you can get a simple picnic cooler and pack it with lots of ice. A 64-gallon model with a pull handle and wheels will cost you approximately $50.

Food products require you to have a plan carefully worked out for buying, stocking your machines, reordering, and restocking—not to mention removing outdated

---

Social Media—Use It or Lose Out On It

The National Restaurant Association's 2011 Restaurant Industry Forecast considers users of at least one of the following to be social media savvy: Facebook, Twitter, mobile phone applications such as Foursquare or Urban Spoon, and online review sites such as Yelp.

- ○ 92 percent eat at sit-down restaurants at least once a month.

- ○ 87 percent order carry-out or snack-type quick-service foods at least once a month.

- ○ 51 percent of social media savvy individuals (versus the nonsocial media savvy types) say restaurants are an essential part of their lifestyle, and that same group also carries these habits:

  - – Much more likely to use in-store technology such as electronic ordering and payment systems at the table, self-service kiosks, online ordering, and mobile phone applications for placing orders.

  - – More likely to connect with restaurants on Facebook, MySpace, or YouTube (29 percent, compared with 16 percent of all consumers).

  - – More likely to post or read reviews on consumer-driven websites such as Yelp (30 percent, compared with 19 percent).

Future intentions derived from this study find that more than eight out of ten restaurant operators say social media (Facebook, online review sites such as Yelp, blogs, and Twitter) will become a more important marketing tool in the future.

To view more of the distilled findings go to www.deloitte.com/us/pr/foodsafety/2011survey-part2. Get with this program and rake in more cash!

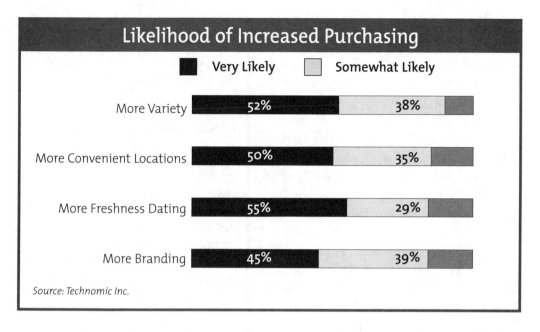

Likelihood of Increased Purchasing

■ Very Likely   ▢ Somewhat Likely

	Very Likely	Somewhat Likely
More Variety	52%	38%
More Convenient Locations	50%	35%
More Freshness Dating	55%	29%
More Branding	45%	39%

Source: Technomic Inc.

products that have not sold. Once you get a reputation for leaving products in a machine too long, you will lose business at that location—people don't want stale products. While the latest machines are made to meet various temperature requirements and you can buy or rent trucks designed to keep products cool, the most important factor in selling fresh products is your inventory control. Therefore, you must have a spreadsheet or computer program designed to let you know when your products may go bad. Pay strict attention to this aspect of your business.

Randall Sutherland points out an unpleasant aspect of supplying milk to your consumers: If or when the machine's cooling system fails, it stinks up the room the vendor is in. Are you prepared to deal with odor control? You should be responsible for any "damage" your company causes, including odor, which has the ability to turn people off to that particular food item for months. In addition to dealing with basic repairs to the machine, get ready to bring fans, antiseptic, and odor-neutralizing spray to deal with the problem swiftly and efficiently. This would be a good time to offer one of those perks, such as pizza, to make up for the inconvenience.

Going Cold Turkey

The rules for variety and freshness go double for those in cold food. "You cannot service cold food machines once a week," emphasizes Becky P. "We service the majority of our cold food machines six days a week, or at the very least, every other day. Even if a vendor only needs a few items, and we're just switching things around in the machine, we're working on the machine and we're there."

In addition, cold food sales hinge on eye appeal. "It's basic junior high home economics," says Becky. "Food is visual. Look at the food in the machine. If it doesn't look appealing, get it out of there. What you lose by discarding an item is minimal compared to the overall loss of people coming up and seeing a sandwich that looks nasty. You could have 40 other items that look gorgeous, but that one bad item will destroy the integrity of the entire machine."

Becky also recommends taking time to sit in break rooms. "Watch what people are bringing from home." You can then add some of those items to make it easier for people to simply buy lunch rather than making it at home, or you could offer the additional complementary products such as the snacks or dessert items they either don't remember, or need to round out their lunch.

Bright Idea

Can you think of any businesses or products that are so "hotcake" that they fly off the shelves? Think of Jennifer Berdoll Wammack's initial idea to substitute a vendor for a person to keep up with pie and candy sales. In some ways this is the way we think of robots, or machines designed to do what we want, but faster, better, and without human complications (such as needing sleep and sustenance). Do some online detective work and make a list of companies that can't fill their orders fast enough. Then start brainstorming about how vending machines could solve their shortcomings and how you might profit if you used the ideas for your own business.

With all the extra effort cold food requires, many in the industry will admonish you to avoid it at all costs. But Becky P. says if you're drawn to this specialty there are profits to be made. "You can make money on cold food, but it takes a tremendous amount of work and a tremendous amount of time," she stresses. "We have 1 percent and less waste, where the industry is 15 percent, because of the way we work it. We totally focus on the cold food, and the rest of the operation takes care of itself—we keep our customers in the room instead of going for the $2.99 fast-food value meal."

Name Brand or Off Brand?

When you begin investigating product options, you will quickly discover most every vending specialty offers a wealth of options. Do you go with recognizable names or less expensive unknowns? The answer depends on your vending line.

A good distributor should be coaching you on current product trends in your area because this pads the bottom line for both of you. What you choose to feature will vary with the clientele demographic from machine to machine. Are you placing vendors in locations that are more economically depressed or are you placing them in an office where executives think nothing of $300 client lunches?

Of course, there's also the "trend" factor. Students, for example, are more likely to look for brands they see advertised on TV, while someone waiting at a bus or train station may be more concerned with getting a quick snack or drink than worrying about having the latest brand. Consider the value of brand advertising at your locations.

Jennifer Berdoll Wammack's pecan pie and candied nuts vendor creates its own audience just by virtue of being placed next to a windfall of unfilled customer orders—that is, the customers who can't get into the store to get the delicacies they want turn to the machine for the same freshness and quality during nonstore hours.

While there are certainly some very familiar name brands that everyone expects to see, you can also gauge what other products may sell in a certain area that are perhaps not as universally known. Again, know your demographic group.

When Seasons Change

Once you've focused in on your product mix, factor in seasonality before you buy. "When it's hot outside, no one wants to buy pantyhose," remarks Janice. "Instead, they want knee-highs. But from November to March, it's cold, so women switch from knee-highs back to hose."

Food operators report variations throughout the year, but gross sales tend to even out overall. "I don't care if it's a transient location or a factory; machines sell the same, week in and week out," comments Wayne D. "If you have a snowstorm, then, yes, it's going to drop. If Christmas falls on a Monday, we'll do more business than if it falls on a Wednesday. And we know that between Thanksgiving and Christmas is one of our lowest points of the year in candy and snacks." But, he says, by studying your business overall, you'll anticipate the anomalies.

Of course, you might sell more hot chocolate in the winter months and more cold beverages in the summer—depending on the locations.

B.J. S. concurs. "We have some school business that shuts down in the summer, but we sell more drinks in the summer. In the winter it's more snacks, so it pretty much evens out." He also suggests location diversification helps out. "There's no period that's really slow for us. For example, we have a lot of retail business [such as department stores], so even Christmas time evens out."

Quantity Questions

With the other variables in front of you, it's time to calculate quantity. Do you fill your machines to the brim or leave some air between product and rim? Obviously, the answer hinges on your research on each location and how often you'll service each machine.

Operators with more expensive inventory may start with less than full machines and increase the number of products based on how quickly they sell out. Conversely, when selling less expensive inventory, the trend is to fill each machine to the brim. "Generally, I fill my machines completely," reports Janice M., who dedicates her Saturdays to filling machines. "That generally gives me about a two- to three-week time span before I have to come back and fill them up again."

The thinking here is simply that if you do not sell a less expensive item, you are not losing much money and may, in fact, be coming out ahead in the long run because of volume. However, a higher-priced item is costing you more if it does not sell.

Regardless of the type and quantity you choose, remember to figure your first refill into your startup costs. "The first time you refill a machine, you must have more inventory," comments Pat W., an operator in Preston, Washington. "If you've got, say, $1,000 in prepaid phone cards, shipping fees, and taxes for a machine, the first time you go in to collect money, you need to have purchased that many cards to fill the machine at the same time you take the money out. So you actually have a startup

Stat Fact

A 2012 report from *Automatic Merchandiser* released a forecast from The NPD Group, a leading market research company that stated "Kids meals have been the focus of legislative and health advocacy activities over the past few years and that focus is expected to continue throughout 2012." Analyst, Bonnie Riggs suggests that in order for operators to tap into this growth trend, they will need to "understand the influences that affect consumer behavior and drive traffic in the next 12 months."

cost of not $1,000 but $2,000 because you have to fill that machine back up before you have the money out of the machine to buy more cards." To help you understand in more detail how to budget for your first machine fills, we've provided a sample startup inventory expense sheet on page 153.

Priced to Sell

Before we move on to discussing where to purchase your inventory, a few words about pricing are in order. Virtually every other retail business is your competitor. Therefore, unlike businesses that offer a service, such as consulting, your pricing process requires less guesswork.

While consumers expect to pay for the convenience a vending machine offers, their generosity only goes so far. One way to determine going rates is to survey your competitors' vendors. In established vending specialties, such as snacks and sodas, industry figures show your goods will cost 50 percent of the sales price. In other words, if a candy bar costs you 35 cents, a consumer will pay about 70 cents.

Erik A. Borger talks about being the lone ranger in a geographic area just starting its awareness of a trend that is spreading like wildfire in other areas of the country. "The problem with healthy vending is that it is still hard to turn a good profit," he says. "Most operators seem to be generating 70 to 90 cents on the dollar whereas a 'healthy' operator will produce only half that if they're lucky. You have to pay more for healthy products and sell them for around the same price as the traditional companies to really compete."

Indeed, wholesale pricing for healthy vending snacks seems to be more challenging through traditional venues, but there are alternatives. Sites such as www.vitacost.com and www.luckyvitamin.com offer sales and extreme discounts on natural products.

"Pricing is hard especially here in the Midwest where health is by no means in," says Borger. Until the Midwest catches up to those resonating more in tune with current national trends, Borger has his 50 cents on the dollar soda sales, which do very well, peace of mind from working for a goal he believes in, and his health.

Bargain Basement

While it's tempting to set your prices lower than the average to attract new clients, successful operators stress running the numbers or you'll run in the red. "I've been at the cash-and-carries with the guys that are just one-person operations running out of their van, and they're crying in their milk," Becky P. observes. "And I say to them, 'What are you charging? What are you paying for that product?' I can't tell you how many of them could not tell me what their unit cost was."

"Then I pull out a piece of scratch paper," she continues. "I say, 'Look, you're charging 50 cents for a candy bar and it's costing you 32 cents. It's costing you 8.25 percent sales tax and 10 percent commission. What do you have left? You need to charge 60 cents, and you need to educate your customer on why you need to charge 60 cents.' "

Paying Your Client's Commission

Many operators take location commission into consideration when establishing price. "If we don't pay commission, then it's one price; otherwise it's another," comments B.J. S.

Which begs the question, why commission at all? The answer: Your competitors may offer commissions, which means clients will expect it. Although clients don't depend on commissions to balance the books, they do use them to fund incidentals such as holiday parties, birthday or other cards, flowers, productivity rewards such as dinner certificates, etc.

It's a Planogram!

Operators with a wide variety of items in each machine, particularly food vendors, are turning to a formal way of determining what and how much to buy.

Called "planogramming," the basic idea is making a simple line drawing (like a tic-tac-toe grid, only bigger) of each of your vendors. Then, inside each cell of the grid, note where you intend to place products in a given machine.

Creating a planogram, or map, for each vendor gives you a visual representation of what your customers will see and allows you to make adjustments before you spend hours filling machines to the brim. In addition, planogramming assists you with matching location survey data to machine columns, helps you identify product trends, allows you to purchase inventory more cost-efficiently, etc.

Planogramming is part of the big-picture process of optimizing sales. Sales optimization is known in the industry as category management.

To set up a planogram, you need to start by identifying the categories and allocating space in each category. Then comes the big question . . . what products will you list in each category? Remember, you want enough variety so that you have more possibilities of making money. Just as investors diversify in the stock market (in case one stock tanks, they have others to count on), you typically want to diversify as well. You may choose to diversify in one broad category, such as those listed above. This might mean selling a variety of beverages. For other vending operators it means selling items from various broad categories. This is a judgment call. Fewer categories make planogramming easier and allow you to maximize your time on your route(s). However, more categories can produce more income if managed properly. You'll be able to decide based on how well you attend to detail and manage numbers.

Generally speaking, there are three basic types of products, from a sales perspective. You have your core products, or standards, that customers come to expect in a category group. These are steady selling products in all of your machines. Then there are cyclical products that you rotate because they sell, but not at the same pace as your core products. This is where you can have variety and introduce some new offerings. Finally, there are special products that are geared for a specific machine or for several machines because they are in demand at that location.

We'll delve into planogramming and category management in more detail when we discuss product merchandising in Chapter 13. For now, it's enough for you to know that maximizing sales goes beyond simply purchasing the right inventory.

Sourcing Resources

As you're getting up to speed on inventory issues, it's important to know where to buy your consumables. Just like any other retail business, your supplier options range from manufacturers to wholesale warehouse clubs and fall into the following basic categories:

- *Manufacturers.* Producers of goods, manufacturers often sell directly to operators in nonfood vending specialties such as pantyhose. In food vending circles, you're more likely to purchase from any of the other supply sources until you become large enough to warehouse products yourself. However, manufacturers' sales representatives may call on you to tell you about their products, purchasing incentives, and/or consumer promotions.

- *Brokers.* Another term for brokers is "independent sales representatives." Brokers represent manufacturers that are too small to—or choose not to—maintain their own internal sales forces. They may work for a number of different manufacturers but generally don't represent manufacturers of competing products such as Snickers and Nestlé's Crunch candy bars. Like manufacturers' representatives, brokers inform you about product offerings, offer purchasing incentives, and clue you in to special consumer promotions. However, brokers neither produce goods nor warehouse them. If you're a large vending operation, you'll receive products you buy from your broker through the manufacturer or a local distributor. If you're a small operation, you'll pick the products up from the distributor yourself.

- *Distributors.* Warehousers and sellers of goods, distributors rarely maintain sales forces that call on operators. Instead, distributors either deliver goods sold to you by manufacturers and brokers or allow you to purchase from them directly, passing on purchasing incentives and alerting you to consumer promotions. Many distributors also offer cash-and-carry services, as described below.

- *Cash-and-carries.* This is the industry term for warehouse clubs such as Sam's Club and Costco. The main difference between a distributor and a warehouse club is minimum quantity. Distributors generally require purchasing by the case while warehouse clubs permit purchasing as little as one bag of chips if you so desire. Because they allow single-item purchases, the cost of goods at warehouse clubs tends to fall between distributor and retail. While cash-and-carry once applied only to warehouse clubs, distributors are now establishing cash-and-carry services to compete with warehouse clubs for smaller accounts.

- *Commissary.* Commissaries prepare and sell sandwiches, salads, and other fresh refrigerated foods. In the past, when a vending operation grew very large, an in-house commissary was established. Today many large operators still support in-house commissaries, but the trend is toward outsourcing to reduce the myriad of costs associated with fresh food handling and preparation.

> **Beware!**
> An incomplete understanding of your specialty's commission structure can spell disaster. During startup, Wayne D. lost one-third of his business after reducing the commission on an account. "I didn't have a complete understanding of how the beverage business worked," says the Burnsville, Minnesota, full-line operator. "The bottler came in and took the account away from me."

To locate suppliers in your specialty area, consult the annual buyer's guides produced by *Automatic Merchandiser* and *Vending Times* magazines. Associations such as NAMA also offer listings of suppliers who are members, allowing you to cross-reference your findings and evaluate industry reputation.

The Broker Connection

At first glance, it may seem a startup's best bet for purchasing inventory is a distributor. Certainly, distributors offer an array of advantages, but astute vending operators know that brokers perform a vital industry role. According to Jim Patterson of Patterson Co. Inc. in Kenilworth, Illinois, brokers evaluate the available manufacturers and products before selecting the ones they represent. "Brokers can give you supporting reasons why a particular brand is better or who it appeals to, such as a consumer who wants more quantity than quality," he says. In addition, a good broker knows consumer purchasing trends and can advise you when to reduce your salty snacks in favor of more pastries. "Because we handle multiple brands, we recognize trends," Patterson says. "We see things moving back and forth within categories and between categories."

A broker also provides marketing and merchandising support. "We provide static clings to put on your machines that promote a consumer contest, particular brand, or concept such as value meal," asserts Patterson, a member of the National Vending Brokers Association. "For example, some campaigns promote the concept of purchasing a sandwich and a beverage as a way to compete with the fast-food chains."

Distributor Distinction

While a distributor will inform you of consumer promotions and purchasing programs, such as rebates, you will have to do the legwork yourself. On the other hand, distributors don't have a vested interest in particular products. Instead, their motivation is helping you boost sales, regardless of the brand or manufacturer.

"Most distributors have a monthly price book containing every product they carry," says John Ochi of Five Star Distributors. "It's a catalog, ordering guide, and inventory-monitoring tool all in one. We try to make purchasing as efficient and brainless as possible."

As a startup operator, you should expect precise information and advice from distributors on the types and quantities to stock in your machines, Ochi says. This takes the guesswork out of initial inventory purchases and jump-starts your sales by ensuring you offer what's most desirable to consumers in a given area at a given time.

A superior distributor also provides ongoing support. "First and foremost, you should expect a good distributor to be a conduit of information," Ochi notes. Distributors know local purchasing trends, monitor industry issues, and answer just about any question you might have.

In addition, quality distributors even track operator purchases and report statistical information to manufacturers, according to Ochi. "Then, the manufacturers have data that they can translate into purchasing programs specific to regional consumer preferences."

> ## Dollar Stretcher
>
> To minimize inventory costs, consider joining a purchasing cooperative. By soliciting suppliers as a group, each member of the cooperative benefits from volume pricing that's otherwise available only to very large operations.

Finally, expect your distributor to extend credit. "Assuming you have an open credit background, you should expect to get credit," Ochi says. "If your history's not good, you'll have to earn credit."

Take a peek at the "Application for Credit" on page 151 to find out what kind of information suppliers want before they'll give you credit. For an example of a distributor's monthly price book, turn to page 149.

Take a peek at the "Application for Credit" on page 151 to find out what kind of information suppliers want before they'll give you credit. For an example of a distributor's monthly price book, turn to page 149.

Smart Tip
Tip...

You want to make sure you don't just look for the best rates. Make sure you're dealing with reliable people who have been in the industry for a long time.

Credit Where Credit Is Due

This brings us to a more general discussion of credit in the vending industry. As in the case of food distributors, some suppliers will extend you credit based on your history, and some will require you to build a positive payment history with them.

Once you receive credit, expect to be granted what's typically referred to as either "30 days net" or "net 30," for short. "With one of my hosiery suppliers, I can pay half down, and they finance the rest for 30 days," reports Janice M. "I have one company where I just order my stuff, they ship it to me, and I pay it in 30 days. Sometimes I'm a few days late, and sometimes I'm a few days early, so it works both ways."

Ratios Are Key

OK, so you hated figuring out ratios back in high school math class. Well, you're going to be doing a lot of it now—in fact, you and your trusty calculator are going to be very ratio programmed in this business.

You will need to continuously keep track of the ratio between your expenditures and your sales, and account for each of the line items that contribute to both. If you don't keep track of the expense-to-sales ratio, you won't be able to stay ahead in the key "profits" category and you will have a hard time growing your business. Ratios you need to keep tabs on include:

- The growth margin percentage between cost and pricing of goods.
- Operating expense percentage, which focuses on controlling your expenses.
- Inventory turnover, which reflects how well you manage your inventory.

Distributor's Monthly Price Book

Item	Product Description	Mfg	Pack		Promo	Case/Unit 125-UP	Case/Unit 1-124
FLORIDA NATURAL							
630400	FN ORANGE JUICE 100%	14901	24	11.5 OZ		18.14 / .756	18.61 / .776
630440	FN FRUIT SPLASH DRINK	14904	24	11.5 OZ		15.21 / .634	15.61 / .650
GATORADE							
630832	GATORADE LEMON LIME	00901	24	11.6 OZ		10.08 / .420	10.53 / .439
630833	GATORADE FRUIT PUNCH	30903	24	11.6 OZ		10.08 / .420	10.53 / .439
630834	GATORADE ORANGE	00902	24	11.6 OZ		10.08 / .420	10.53 / .439
630840	GATORADE LEMON LIME BOTTLE	32866	24	20 OZ		15.90 / .663	16.61 / .692
630841	GATORADE ORANGE BOTTLE	32867	24	20 OZ		15.90 / .663	16.61 / .692
630842	GATORADE FRUIT PUNCH BOTTLE	32866	24	20 OZ		15.90 / .663	16.61 / .692
630843	GATORADE COOL BLUE BOTTLE	32481	24	20 OZ		15.90 / .663	16.61 / .692
GATORADE POWDER							
630854	GATORADE LEMON LIME POWDER	03967	14	51 OZ		77.25 / 5.518	79.24 / 5.660
630856	GATORADE ORANGE POWDER	03968	14	51 OZ		77.25 / 5.518	79.24 / 5.660
630858	GATORADE FRUIT PUNCH POWDER	33690	14	51 OZ		77.25 / 5.518	79.24 / 5.660
GEHL'S							
084101	GEHL MIXED BERRY SMOOTHIE	50016	12	11 OZ		16.85 / 1.404	17.54 / 1.462
084103	GEHL STRAWBERRY SMOOTHIE	50017	12	11 OZ		16.85 / 1.404	17.54 / 1.462
084105	GEHL PEACH SMOOTHIE S	50018	12	11 OZ	SPO	16.85 / 1.404	17.54 / 1.462
LIVING ESS./5 HOUR ENERGY							
632994	BERRY 5 HOUR ENERGY CASE		108	2 OZ		172.48 / 1.597	178.53 / 1.653
632995	BERRY 5 HOUR ENERGY CARTONS	58812	12	2 OZ		19.67 / 1.639	20.36 / 1.696
ROOSTER BOOSTER							
015100	SUPER ROOSTER BOOSTER 16 oz	25603	24	16 OZ		20.87 / .870	21.61 / .900
SWEET LEAF TEA							
661101	SWEET TEA ORIGINAL 15.5 oz	07010	24	15.5 OZ	1.00	13.38 / .558	13.88 / .578
661103	SWEET TEA RASPBERRY 15.5 oz	07013	24	15.5 OZ	1.00	13.38 / .558	13.88 / .578
661105	SWEET TEA LEMON 15.5 oz	07014	24	15.5 OZ	1.00	13.38 / .558	13.88 / .578
661107	SWEET TEA CITRUS GREEN 15.5 oz	07015	24	15.5 OZ	1.00	13.38 / .558	13.88 / .578
WELCHS							
635000	ORANGE JUICE 100%	379-00	24	11.5 OZ		17.40 / .725	17.86 / .744
635010	GRAPE JUICE 100%	380-00	24	11.5 OZ		17.40 / .725	17.86 / .744
635020	APPLE JUICE 100%	382-00	24	11.5 OZ		17.40 / .725	17.86 / .744
635100	FRUIT PUNCH DRINK	309-00	24	11.5 OZ		12.84 / .535	13.17 / .549
635103	ORANGE PINEAPPLE DRINK	378-00	24	11.5 OZ		12.84 / .535	13.17 / .549
635104	APPLE CRANBERRY DRINK	456-30	24	11.5 OZ		15.05 / .627	15.44 / .643
635112	STRAWBERRY KIWI DRINK	311-00	24	11.5 OZ		12.84 / .535	13.17 / .549
635150	ORANGE JUICE	281-00	48	5.5 OZ		21.11 / .440	21.66 / .451
635151	APPLE JUICE	283-00	48	5.5 OZ		21.11 / .440	21.66 / .451
635152	GRAPE JUICE	205-00	48	5.5 OZ		21.11 / .440	21.66 / .451
635160	CRANBERRY JUICE COCKTAIL	288-00	48	5.5 OZ		21.11 / .440	21.66 / .451
635170	GRAPE JUICE 100% PLASTIC	354-00	24	10 OZ		17.68 / .737	18.14 / .756
635171	APPLE JUICE 100% (PLASTIC)	316-00	24	10 OZ		17.68 / .737	18.14 / .756
635172	ORANGE JUICE 100% (PLASTIC)	344-00	24	10 OZ		17.68 / .737	18.14 / .756
635175	CRANBERRY JC CKTL (PLASTIC)	394-00	24	10 OZ		16.53 / .689	16.98 / .707
635180	ORG PINEAPPLE DRINK (PLASTIC)	317-00	24	10 OZ		12.24 / .510	12.56 / .523
635181	FRUIT PUNCH DRINK (PLASTIC)	490-00	24	10 OZ		12.24 / .510	12.56 / .523
635183	APPLE CRANBERRY DRINK (PLS)	456-10	24	10 OZ		12.24 / .510	12.56 / .523
635285	ORANGE JUICE 100% P BOTTLE	404-12	12	15.2 OZ		11.54 / .961	11.84 / .986

▲

- Sales per employee, once you have people handling specific routes. This allows you to know how much each employee is contributing to the bottom line versus how much you are paying.

Your Network for Success

Regardless of your inventory source, building good supplier-vendor relationships is key to your success. "If you don't [establish good relationships], chances are you're going to be an island unto yourself," warns Five Star Distributors' Ochi. "You're going to make a lot of mistakes, and it's less likely you'll succeed."

"Your relationship with your suppliers and your banker is just as important as with your customers," echoes full-line operator Becky P. "It's so important to have relationships with everybody because they will back you up. For instance, when it's 105 degrees outside and you are out of cups for your cold beverage machines, [you want to count on] your distributor to drive clear across town to bring you cups. Your distributor wants you to succeed. Because when you succeed, then they succeed, too." Keep the lines of communication open between you and your distributors and your business will thrive.

Application for Credit

A-1 Vending Machines

000 Fairway Ave.
Vernon Hills, IL 60000
Phone: (000) 555-9900 Fax: (000) 555-9910

STANDARD CREDIT TERMS

Company name: _____

Contact: _____

Billing address: _____

City: _____ State: _____ Zip: _____

Shipping address: _____

City: _____ State: _____ Zip: _____

Phone: _____ Fax: _____

Email: _____

Type of business: _____ In business since: _____

Form of business: ❏ Corporation   ❏ LLC
        ❏ Partnership   ❏ Sole proprietor

Is a purchase order required?: _____

Name of individual with authorization: _____

If it is to be a blanket PO, please list the number and expiration date.

Number: _____ Expiration date: _____

To whose attention should invoices be sent? _____

Is your work taxable? _____ If not, please attach signed certificate and list your tax exempt or reseller's number: _____

Application for Credit, continued

If you wish to pay by credit card, please provide information below:

VISA card number: _____ Expiration date: _____

MasterCard number: _____ Expiration date: _____

AmEx card number: _____ Expiration date: _____

Bank references (please list name and address of local banks):

_____

_____

_____

_____

Trade references (please list name, address, phone number, and account number of three references. Do not list credit cards.):

_____

_____

_____

_____

Our terms are net 30 days. Accounts not paid in this time frame will be charged a 1.5 percent interest rate per month and future orders will be on a C.O.D. basis until the account is current. Should collection or legal action be required to collect past dues, fees for such action will be added to your account.

Print name: _____ Title: _____

Signed by: _____ Date: _____

Quality Snacks Startup Inventory Expenses

To help you budget, here is a sample inventory list and product cost for Quality Snacks, the fictional snack vending operation we introduced in Chapter 6. Quality owns 15 snack vendors, which, for ease of illustration, are considered to be all of the same configuration and offer the same products.

Inventory Type	Approximate Unit Cost	Unit Count Per Vendor	Approximate Cost Per Vendor	Cost for 15 Vendors*
ROW #1—LARGE SINGLE-SERVING SALTY SNACKS				
Snyders Olde Tyme Pretzels	0.267	8	$2.14	$32.10
Fritos Corn Chips	0.292	8	2.34	35.10
Cheetos	0.292	8	2.34	35.10
Doritos Nacho Tortilla Chips	0.292	8	2.34	35.10
Cheese & Bacon Tato Skins	0.267	8	2.14	32.10
ROW #2—SALTY SNACKS				
Sunshine Cheez—Regular Flavor	0.180	10	1.80	27.00
Jays Oke Doke Cheese Popcorn	0.160	10	1.60	24.00
Jays Regular Potato Chips	0.160	10	1.60	24.00
Jays Open Pit BBQ Potato Chips	0.160	10	1.60	24.00
Snyders Mini Pretzels	0.163	10	1.63	24.45
ROW #3—COOKIES/CRACKERS/SNACKS				
Ritz Bits Cheese Crackers	0.283	10	2.83	42.45
Austin Zoo Animal Cracker Cookies	0.180	10	1.80	27.00
Knott's Berry Farm Raspberry Cookies	0.222	10	2.22	33.30
Kellogg's Rice Krispies Treats	0.350	10	3.50	52.50
Famous Amos Chocolate Chip Cookies	0.250	10	2.50	37.50
ROW #4—CANDY/SNACK BARS				
Snickers	0.344	18	6.19	92.85
Starburst	0.344	18	6.19	92.85
Reese's Peanut Butter Cups	0.344	18	6.19	92.85
Planter's Peanuts	0.208	18	3.74	56.10
Butterfinger	0.344	18	6.19	92.85
Kit Kat	0.344	18	6.19	92.85
Oreo Cookies	0.233	18	4.19	62.85
Twix	0.344	18	6.19	92.85
Twizzlers	0.344	18	6.19	92.85
NutRageous	0.344	18	6.19	92.85

Quality Snacks Startup Inventory Expenses, continued

Inventory Type	Approximate Unit Cost	Unit Count Per Vendor	Approximate Cost Per Vendor	Cost for 15 Vendors*
ROW #5—CANDY/SNACK BARS				
M&M's Peanut	0.344	18	$6.19	$92.85
PayDay	0.344	18	6.19	92.85
Milky Way	0.344	18	6.19	92.85
Baby Ruth	0.344	18	6.19	92.85
ReeseSticks	0.344	18	6.19	92.85
3 Musketeers	0.344	18	6.19	92.85
Tootsie Roll Twin Pack	0.306	18	5.51	82.65
Hershey Almond	0.344	24	8.26	123.90
Nestlé Crunch	0.344	24	8.26	123.90
ROW #6—PASTRIES				
Kellogg's Pop Tarts Sugar Cinnamon	0.361	12	4.33	64.95
Kellogg's Pop Tarts Frosted Strawberry	0.361	12	4.33	64.95
Cloverhill Big Texas Cinnamon Roll	0.391	12	4.69	70.35
Plantation Olde New England Brownie	0.323	12	3.88	58.20
Cloverhill Baking Jumbo Chocolate Donut	0.392	12	4.70	70.50
ROW #7—GUM & MINTS				
Wrigley's Doublemint Gum	0.175	20	3.50	52.50
Wrigley's Juicy Fruit Gum	0.175	20	3.50	52.50
Carefree Bubble Gum	0.200	20	4.00	60.00
Life Savers Five Flavor	0.240	20	4.80	72.00
Life Savers Pep-O-Mint	0.240	20	4.80	72.00
Cost of Beginning Inventory				**$2,872.95**
Cost of First Refill (each vendor one-half full)**				**$1,436.48**
Total Startup Inventory Cost				**$4,309.43**

Minimum purchase is one case.

**Suggested servicing is at half-full to avoid empties. See Chapter 13 for more information.

Source: Five Star Distributors Inc.

10

Hired Hands

If you're planning to launch into vending solo, you're in good company. Industry estimates say that as many as one-third of all vending businesses are one-person bands. However, few businesses, regardless of their industry, go it alone over their entire life span.

Teamwork or Sole Achiever?

There are benefits and drawbacks to both working with a team and operating on your own. If you work alone, you have no one but yourself to blame if things don't work out, but when they do, you get to keep all the profits and don't need to put work into a partner relationship, which some business owners find taxing. On the other hand, many partnered entrepreneurs say they wish they would have linked up with a partner sooner and could have achieved expansion quicker had they done so. If you want to work on growth areas of the business but don't have anyone to hand off the day-to-day duties to, then you're stuck unless you hire someone.

It's nice to be free, though, having complete control over all the decisions and not having to talk things out or worry about how to split the business if you and a partner have to part ways.

Whichever path is the one for you, it's best to be choosy about anyone you do decide to employ or team up with, addressing all legal formalities and using educated communication skills.

A Family Affair

Many vending entrepreneurs follow the time-honored tradition of involving their families in the day-to-day operation of their businesses. In fact, many start out as husband-wife combos. Involving family members not only supplies the business with low-overhead labor but also helps the family unit hang together through the inevitable three to five years of long hours any entrepreneurial effort requires.

"I wouldn't consider this a partnership even though my husband, Jared, and I own the business, which we bought from my parents three years ago," says Jennifer Berdoll Wammack. "It's a family business. Brandon, my brother, helps my father, Hal, in the orchard and Brandi, my sister-in-law, manages the retail store. We are very, very lucky. We all work well with each other and get along on both a business and personal level," Berdoll Wammack happily reports of life at the pecan farm, gift shop, and vending endeavor.

"Although it's not essential, it's a great help to have your family involved," points out full-line operator Wayne D. "Especially if your objective is to build up to being a full-time business—if it's part of you, it's part of them."

Like many all-in-the-family outfits, Wayne's wife and son have assisted with filling machines, answering trouble calls, and keeping the books. Involving his family even allowed him to act on a growth opportunity only a year after starting the business. "We bought a small route that was a spin-off of a larger vending company's routes," he explains. "My son was in high school at that time, and he serviced the route two or three evenings a week."

The Professional Family

Organizational psychologist and leadership specialist Dr. David G. Javitch wrote "10 Tips for Working with Family Members" for *Entrepreneur* magazine online. Some of his ideas include:

❍ Acknowledge and discuss a professional relationship that's not working.

❍ Agree to be more professional and less personal.

❍ Clarify specific goals to work toward the company's mission with, together.

❍ Clarify the work processes that will be used to achieve goals.

❍ Build trust by opening communication on sticky subjects.

❍ Make sure you're competent or engage in training to make it so.

❍ Demonstrate respect for everyone equally.

Read the rest of the article at www.entrepreneur.com.

While Wayne's situation is typical, you don't need a traditional family unit or older children to pull it off. A single mother of three children, Baltimore operator Janice M. takes her children along for her Saturday filling routine.

The key to family success is having everyone focus on the goal of the business. For young children, it's important that they learn the business in kid-friendly terms. They should share in some of the responsibilities and some of the rewards. A toy or gift for all of their hard work shows them that you can work and receive a payoff or a reward. Make it fun for the family and you can have a strong team for years to come. Make it an unpleasant chore and the kids will leave as soon as they are able. It's important to remember that family and hired employees are separate entities—you can act as if you're treating them the same way, but in the long run, you cannot, since your family members are an integral part of your life whether they do a good or a poor job.

Acquaintance Assistants

Hiring people with which you have a nonprofessional relationship means making it clear that you are separating business and the personal relationship.

▲

Green Drivers Have All the Fun!

A recent article by Joan Rattner Heilman in *AARP* magazine listed nationwide benefits to driving a green vehicle:

- ○ Utah gives a $605 income tax credit for new purchase of a "clean fuel" vehicle.

- ○ Oregon gives income tax credit of up to $1,500 for electric vehicle purchases.

- ○ Albuquerque, New Mexico; New Haven, Connecticut; and Salt Lake City, Utah, offer free meter parking.

- ○ Florida, Colorado, Virginia, Utah, and some highways in New Jersey and New York allow single drivers of green vehicles displaying their state license plates to use the carpool lanes.

Some hotels also offer free or discounted parking to guests with hybrid vehicles.

"Listen, if I get angry about something work related, it doesn't mean anything personal," is one way to start such a relationship. Also, don't get into the habit of taking advantage of people you know because they are willing to help. Treat people fairly.

Because her pantyhose machines must be mounted on clients' walls, Janice M. uses a temp agency to ensure experienced individuals mount her machines. The charge for these workers runs about $16 per hour. "Although it generally takes only two hours, I usually have to pay a minimum of four hours," she says. "But I don't mind paying for four hours because the quality of the workmanship is better."

Before hiring anyone, make sure you have a clear idea of exactly what you need them to do. It's a waste of money to have people standing around no matter what you are paying per hour. Write down what each person should be doing and explain it clearly—also ask for questions so that there is no misunderstanding. You'd be surprised at how many businesses—vending and otherwise—hire people who then end up doing nothing for a while because the employer isn't prepared to have them start immediately.

Retraining Programs: A Good Source

One approach to acquiring qualified help is seeking out government retraining programs. In addition to tax incentives for hiring so-called "disadvantaged workers," Janice M. discovered this avenue offers monetary and retention rewards.

"Through the welfare-to-work program, they pay me to train people, and they pay the people a wage during training," she says. "In return, I have to hire the people I train, with health benefits, and they have to work for me for a year. Since I have to train people anyway, I might as well get paid. Also, it guarantees me a worker for a year, which is great."

The pantyhose vendor also looks at the program as an investment in marketing. "Most of these people have never had a job before, so it's good to have [working for me] on their resumes. And it's good for me to be on their resumes."

Ready for a Route Driver

For most vending operators, the first true employee is a route driver. Although the term implies someone who simply transports items from one place to another, a vending route driver does everything short of accounting, marketing, and major repairs. Route drivers assist with purchasing at cash-and-carries, load their own inventory, decide on product rotation at locations, fill machines, conduct preventive maintenance, and handle routine trouble calls.

At what point you'll need regular assistance varies. For food operators, the most likely scenarios are growing into, or purchasing, an operation with several hundred thousand in gross sales. "At around $300,000 gross, annually, you'll need a route driver or maybe a half-time route driver," according to Donald Blotner of DCB Consulting in Eagan, Minnesota.

Full-line operator Becky P. concurs. "We had no employees our first five years, and we were growing the whole time. But

Stat Fact

In addition to the 76.2 percent of consumers who want healthier food options when they shop, according to Deloitte's 2011 Consumer Food and Product Insight Survey, 49.3 percent of the respondents want packaging that displays a row of standardized "nutrition keys" on the front (in addition to the standard ingredients listed on the back), as it would be helpful for purchasing decisions. Some companies are currently doing this on a voluntary basis. According to the survey, 51.1 percent of shoppers read ingredients on unfamiliar food items. While this study targeted "shoppers," one might apply the same logic to vending. Operators, you would do well to choose products with nutrition keys.

there gets to be a point when there's just no way. You get to a certain volume, and you require support.

"Today, our theory is, to support a truck it has to do $5,000 to $6,000 per week in gross sales," she continues. "So when a truck gets to $7,000 or $8,000 a week, then it's time to start thinking about getting another truck and more employees," says Becky, who takes the unusual approach of employing two people for every truck.

"We run two to a vehicle for safety, morale, and service," explains the Los Angeles–area operator. "In one hour, they can do two hours' worth of servicing at a single location. While one driver is filling a machine, the other one cleans and repairs malfunctioning equipment."

The Right Stuff

To find employees, successful operators use the standard tactics of placing newspaper ads. "We choose not to recruit or hire from other vending companies," says Wayne D. "We feel they bring too many bad habits—they don't want to do things our way; they want to do things their way."

While many operators voice similar opinions, not everyone agrees. "We put up fliers at the cash-and-carries," notes Becky P. "Guys who come to us from other companies tell us other people train for one to two weeks. We have intensive training for 90 days. We will not turn them loose for 90 days. We tell them upfront we're going to break all their old habits, that this is a philosophy that you've never heard before. But it works for us, and this is the way you're going to do it."

Places to seek employees include local bulletin boards, community newspapers, putting up posters (where permitted to do so), through word-of-mouth (offer a small finding fee if someone stays employed for six months), and on community online job boards.

Wherever you look for employees, remember they're on the front lines. No longer will you be interacting with clients and customers at the locations you pass off. Instead, your workers will be representing you and your company. This means you're placing your business reputation (your most valuable asset) into their hands.

You need to specify the attributes you are looking for in any job ads you might place in local papers or on websites. This includes:

- Good communications skills
- Good aptitude for numbers
- Ability to multitask
- Attention to detail

You need to then look at resumes carefully, get references, and contact those references.

When you interview potential candidates, you need to determine what they bring to the table in terms of honesty, integrity, and the understanding that this is more than just carrying boxes or placing products in the right slots. While software can help with planograms and product decision making at your end, you need employees who are alert and aware of the sales on their routes. They need to have a sales savvy and be outgoing, or at least understand the importance of establishing a good rapport with customers.

You want to explain to all prospective employees what the industry requires from an employee and see if they "get it." Establishing a working chemistry will be important; you need to determine whether or not you believe you can do so with the individual.

Interviewing

Your interview questions should be prepared in advance and should focus on aspects of the job that they will be doing. Present broad situations (since they won't know the specifics of the business yet) and see how they might handle such situations. Determine what prior experiences they have had that they can use while handling a route. Someone who has customer service experience or has maintained an inventory for a retailer may have some of the skills. You may not find people who possess everything you'd like in the "ideal" candidate, but you need to have a good feeling about the individual and that he or she has a solid foundation from which you can build. Don't hold candidates up to some unrealistic image or you'll be interviewing forever.

Also, remember, as mentioned earlier, to do background checks. It is surprising how many employers do not check up on the backgrounds of the people they hire and later wonder why the person did not work out. There are several background checking businesses on the internet, such as www.easybackgrounds.com and www.employerschoiceonline.com, that can assist you in checking up on employees that you are seriously considering hiring. Also, ask references (who are always ready and willing to say positive things) what is the one thing they would change about the person or find some other polite way of asking if there is any downside to hiring this person.

Hint: Remember, when interviewing someone, by law, you are not supposed to ask personal questions. Stick to business. You may inquire if someone is over 18 and

Smart Tip

You don't have to reinvent the wheel when establishing hiring guidelines, training procedures, and employee policies. Industry associations such as the National Automatic Merchandising Association, (312) 346-0370, www.vending.org, offer industry-specific publications and training tools to help new employers succeed.

if they can legally work in the United States (citizen or have working papers). Beyond that be very careful—discrimination lawsuits are popular in our litigious society.

Training

Whether you hire old hands or fresh faces, the bulk of employee education is typically done in the field. "All of our training is hands-on," states B.J. S. "A supervisor rides along with them for a couple of weeks. After that, they let them go for a couple of days and then send someone along with them again to see how they're doing."

While informal training is the historical norm, vending, like many industries, is beginning to realize the competitive advantages of more formal instruction. Specific product manufacturers, such as Nabisco and others, now offer training programs and materials to help operators and their employees improve their product merchandising.

Recently, articles devoted to the value of training abounded in industry publications such as *Automatic Merchandiser* and *Vending Times* magazines. NAMA's forward-looking Hudson Report also emphasizes increasing the amount and sophistication of training to remain competitive. "The business environment surrounding the vending and food-services industry will be faster-paced, more complex, and more challenging in every respect than in the past," the Hudson Report says. "The key to competitive advantage in any field is to have a superior team of managers and employees. Invest in your organization's human capital—educate and train your people."

Paying a Fair Wage

However you locate and train employees, compensation will be the first thing on their minds. If you're wondering what's fair, NAMA's "Wage Rates and Benefits Survey" can be your guide. Updated regularly, the manual breaks down wages and benefits by job function and by region, making quick work of knowing what your competitors are offering. The Bureau of Labor Statistics is another place to learn the average wages across the country for vending professionals.

Successful operators advise going beyond your local average. "We compensate above industry standards because we want a quality person," Wayne D. emphasizes. "That's been one of the problems with the industry as a whole—it's been noted as low-pay."

To get quality work, Janice M. recommends paying even occasional employees a reasonable rate. "There's a high school student I pay minimum wage. I pay my adult worker $10 an hour to compensate her for her knowledge and experience."

Most operators also pay route drivers commissions as part of their regular compensation packages. "We pay above industry standard, and all our route drivers are on commission," says B.J. S.

Reading the trade papers will help you keep up with wage hikes and competitive salaries so that you will not fall behind and risk losing your help. You also need to stay abreast of the labor laws. The United States Department of Labor (see Appendix for details) can be the source for labor-related questions.

Bonuses and Bennies

Bonuses are another popular way to both compensate and encourage. "We show employees how to make more money through proper servicing, maintaining equipment, etc.," says Wayne D. "Then we pay cash bonuses based on various factors such as limited stale quantities and proper ratio of products."

What's less common in vending are typical corporate-world benefits. "When we first started hiring employees, we had no benefits except vacation—no medical and no sick pay," Becky P. admits. "We gave one week [of vacation] for a year of service, two weeks for two years, and on up. As we grew, we added three days of sick pay. Recently, we were able to add medical insurance—we pay the employees' premiums, and they pay their dependents' premiums. I'll be perfectly honest: It's a big nut for us to cut, but with 4 percent unemployment (in 2007), we had to. We couldn't get anyone of consequence without giving medical."

But this doesn't mean Becky left her employees without a safety net. "We have a wonderful urgent care center. When we did not have medical, our employees went there if they had sore throats or the flu, and we always paid it. They also have a pharmacy there, and I bought their prescriptions—the whole nine yards. I just had

---

Better Doesn't Mean Faster

When motivating route drivers, you need to remember that doing a better job does not mean doing the job more quickly. While you'd like route drivers to stick to a schedule and cover a reasonable amount of territory, you do not want them to increase daily production at the risk of:

- ❍ Driving too quickly and possibly increasing your liability by not being safe on the road.
- ❍ Disregarding machine sanitation and cleaning protocols.
- ❍ Ignoring basic mechanical maintenance procedures.
- ❍ Not testing machines after filling them.
- ❍ Not listening to and talking to customers who may have suggestions or complaints.

▲

it set up with the doctor that he could send me the bill. In the long run, it was so infrequent, it cost a lot less than what medical insurance would have cost us."

All of these are important aspects of the job. Therefore, by motivating route drivers to improve productivity, you do not want to do so at the risk of any of the above-mentioned areas, as featured in *Vending Times*.

Know Your Employee Requirements

When hiring employees you are required to have an EIN, Employer Identification Number, and pay regular payroll taxes, Social Security (FICA), and workers' compensation. State requirements will vary, so you need to know what is required within your state.

You also need to be aware of and adhere to the Fair Labor Standards Act, which can be found on the Department of Labor website (www.dol.gov). Accordingly, you must maintain the following statistics for each employee (in some manner, whether that is on computer or on paper):

- Employee's full name, as used for Social Security purposes, and on the same record, the employee's identifying symbol or number if such is used in place of name on any time, work, or payroll records
- Address, including zip code
- Birth date, if younger than 19;
- Sex and occupation
- Time and day of week when employee's workweek begins; hours worked each day and total hours worked each work week
- Basis on which employee's wages are paid
- Regular hourly pay rate
- Total daily or weekly straight-time earnings
- Total overtime earnings for the work week
- All additions to or deductions from the employee's wages
- Total wages paid each pay period
- Date of payment and the pay period covered by the payment

Source: United States Department of Labor

Government fines or audits, from places like the IRS, are not the way you want to spend your money. Make sure you are on the up-and-up when hiring and paying your regular employees. The few dollars you may save by having someone "off the books" can come back to cost you big time later on.

Evaluating Performance

Regardless of what type of perks they offer, successful operators recommend basing them on concrete documentation. A written employee policy manual is a must for laying out expectations, as are proper accounting practices for tracking monetary rewards.

Because writing a policy manual probably isn't your forte, you can obtain NAMA's complete employee guide, "Employee Policy Manual." If not, look for another employee manual for a similar business—even a retail business—and use it as a template for your own guide. Essentially, the key is to spell out all of your rules and regulations, letting employees know what is and is not permitted—and the consequences of not playing by the rules. Discuss how activities including theft, drug, or alcohol use (or possession), harassment, physical violence, or any criminal actions will be handled. Spell out what are considered grounds for dismissal. Also, provide the ways and means

---

To the Hard Worker Go the Spoils

With margins so tight and benefits minimal, most vending operators turn to creative ways to reward a job well done. Dinners at fancy establishments, tickets to sporting events, and company picnics complete with drawings and prizes are common choices.

In addition to such standard offerings, Becky P. subsidizes new employees' Thanksgiving dinners and purchases them outright for longtime staffers. "At Easter time, they get a $25 gift certificate to the market and I always send lilies home for their wives or—if they're young guys—for their moms.

"We try to do things centered around the family because it makes them a hero," she continues. "It's important for an employee to have the backing of his family. That way, the wife helps push him out of bed in the morning. Or when he has to work on Saturdays, the family supports him and makes arrangements to do things when he comes home.

"It gives you a better employee," Becky says. "His attitude is different toward the company. For what you get in return for what you're giving—it's tenfold."

Since you are typically watching your budget closely, other inexpensive perks can be gift cards, an extra day off, or, if you are accruing points through your corporate credit card, you can pass along some of the perks you may be receiving.

in which employees will be evaluated and what is expected from them, should they seek advancement or more responsibility. Finally, list all parameters and structures, such as time schedules, hours of duty, number of sick and vacation days, and so on.

Finally, have an attorney look over your manual to make sure you are not saying or doing anything to violate anyone's civil rights.

As an adjunct to your employee manual, you can evaluate route people using a form similar to NAMA's "Self-Inspection Checklist for Machines and Location" (see page 168).

Safeguarding Your Route Drivers

It's no secret that there have been robberies along routes and that safety is a paramount concern of most vending business owners. While there is no foolproof system for guarding your assets, you can provide drivers with safes, alarms, cell phones, and common sense advice, such as knowing where to park—in well-lit, busier areas during daytime hours, and limiting the amount of cash on the individual at any given time. Route drivers should also vary their route schedule to avoid showing up in the same place at the same time every day.

You need to train route drivers to be very aware of their surroundings and the potential for robbery, and even a physical attack. Self-defense training is also a possibility.

You can also help by not making it obvious that the vehicle is that of a vending company and by installing the necessary alarms.

Oh, My Aching Back

In any labor-intensive industry, injuries will happen. In bygone days, wounded workers were discarded like old rags and thus, workers' compensation insurance was born.

While most operators admit to carrying insurance for themselves, mention workers' comp and the teeth-gnashing begins. But as industry associations and publications note, employers share the blame for high workers' comp premiums.

For years, vending industry premiums soared in part because employers failed to teach and enforce basic safety practices, according to *Automatic Merchandiser*. More recently, overall safety has improved because operators began to realize the impact of "experience modification" discounts. In addition, employers are learning the value of including employees in the process of making and enforcing safety policies. After all, reductions in comp claims mean more profits and, in turn, more profit-sharing.

Workers' comp premiums are based on annual payroll and vary by state. Figure about $825 per year for a single employee who makes $12 per hour. To bring this amount down, use NAMA's publication "Developing a Work Place Safety Program" as a basis for mapping out your own safety practices. As part of your program, consider including NAMA's video "Be a Buddy to Your Back."

Inspiring Efficiency

Motivating employees is one of the most difficult management tasks for nearly every employer. Loyalty—on the part of both employer and employee—once was the glue that bound bosses and workers. But the downsizing trend of the 1990s broke that bond, causing today's workers to be wary of long-term promises.

For employers, this means taking out the carrot and deep-sixing the stick. "We try to get our work environment to be a 'family' atmosphere," says B.J. S., whose employee morale was low and turnover high when he purchased the company. "Everybody knows why I'm here, why I'm doing the job the way I am, and what the goals are for the company. And they know there's room to move up and make more money."

Originally from Sweden, B.J.'s approach is born out of his European experience. "Where I grew up, the government's the safety net. But here, this [company] is the safety net. If an employee gets in trouble or needs some money, I will support them. They know they will get rewarded for their work and the company is here to protect them. For example, I have lent employees money up to $5,000, and the payment plan depends on the individual," B.J. continues. "If someone gets hurt or has problems at home, I give them a week off with pay to straighten things out."

His reward for what others might see as a pricey system? "I haven't had any workers' comp claims since I bought the company," says B.J., the five-year owner of a decades-old operation. "And retention is better. You expect 25 percent turnover, but there was nearly 100 percent turnover when I bought the company."

Toughing Out Turnover

As B.J.'s comments point out, no matter how exceptional your work environment is, turnover is a fact of life. Vending wages simply can't compete with companies in hyper-growth industries like technology, and the work is demanding.

"Turnover is a big issue in today's market," Wayne D. notes. "You've always got that core of people who are going to be at work every day," he assures. "Then there are some positions that will turn over more often—like the guy who's only been with you six months to two years."

Although every employer hits staffing slick spots, successful operators recount tale after tale of how their employees become not only valuable workers but also partners and friends.

Now that you're a hiring pro, let's explore the subject of where to locate your machines.

▲

Self-Inspection Checklist
for Machines and Location

Company name: _____

Location name: _____

Address: _____

Date of inspection: _____ Route person & no.: _____

Instructions: Self-inspections of locations assure your clients they are being pro-vided with the best possible service. This checklist provides you an opportunity to show your route persons their strengths and weaknesses. It will also help you in reviewing the condition of your location and machines by pointing out a variety of items that need routine attention.

CONDITION OF LOCATION	OK	NOT OK	REMARKS
General Conditions			
Floors, platforms cleanable?	❑	❑	_____
Floors, platforms clean?	❑	❑	_____
Insects, rodents under control?	❑	❑	_____
Light adequate for servicing?	❑	❑	_____
Light adequate for customer use?	❑	❑	_____
Service Utensils & Equipment			
Cups, bowls inverted?	❑	❑	_____
Spoons wrapped or in dispenser?	❑	❑	_____
Microwave ovens clean?	❑	❑	_____
Condiments (if offered)			
Clean dispensers or packeted?	❑	❑	_____
Protected from flies, dirt?	❑	❑	_____
Trash Containers			
Adequate containers present?	❑	❑	_____
Lids, covers self-closing?	❑	❑	_____
Emptied and cleaned routinely?	❑	❑	_____
Water Supply			
Approved source, safe quality?	❑	❑	_____
Connections, fittings properly installed?	❑	❑	_____

Self-Inspection Checklist
for Machines and Location, continued

CONDITION OF VEHICLE	OK	NOT OK	REMARKS
Truck compartment clean?	❏	❏	_____
Products protected?	❏	❏	_____
Perishable foods stored below 45°F?	❏	❏	_____
CO_2 tanks blocked?	❏	❏	_____
Vehicle saftey check conducted?	❏	❏	_____

EMPLOYEE CLEANLINESS

	OK	NOT OK	REMARKS
General appearance?	❏	❏	_____
Uniform clean?	❏	❏	_____
Hands clean?	❏	❏	_____
No smoking during service?	❏	❏	_____
Hands washed when necessary before servicing?	❏	❏	_____

Types of machines:

Suggested Code:

1._____   A   OK

2._____   X   Not Satisfactory

3._____   C   Corrected at Inspection

4._____   N   Does Not Apply

CONDITION OF MACHINES	MACHINE					REMARKS
	1	2	3	4	5	
Cabinet Outside						
Front, sides, top clean?	❏	❏	❏	❏	❏	_____
Delivery door, good repair?	❏	❏	❏	❏	❏	_____
Utility, bolt holes closed?	❏	❏	❏	❏	❏	_____
Vent openings screened?	❏	❏	❏	❏	❏	_____
Cabinet Inside						
Splash, spillage removed?	❏	❏	❏	❏	❏	_____
Waste pail emptied, cleaned?	❏	❏	❏	❏	❏	_____
No insects, rodents present?	❏	❏	❏	❏	❏	_____
No product left in machine?	❏	❏	❏	❏	❏	_____
Filters, cartridges, screens cleaned or exchanged routinely?	❏	❏	❏	❏	❏	_____

Self-Inspection Checklist
for Machines and Location, continued

Product Containers & Piping

	1	2	3	4	5	
Product surfaces in good repair and cleanable?	❑	❑	❑	❑	❑	_____
Canisters, reservoirs, tanks, troughs, bowls, chutes, tubes, brewers, valves, pipes, etc., clean?	❑	❑	❑	❑	❑	_____
Vend stage routinely cleaned?	❑	❑	❑	❑	❑	_____

Routine Cleaning

Sanitation kit present?	❑	❑	❑	❑	❑	_____
Sanitation kit used?	❑	❑	❑	❑	❑	_____
Product contact surfaces routinely cleaned?	❑	❑	❑	❑	❑	_____
Fixed pipes, tubes, brewers properly & routinely cleaned?	❑	❑	❑	❑	❑	_____

Temperature Controls

Cold foods kept below 45°F?	❑	❑	❑	❑	❑	_____
Thermometer in cold food compartment?	❑	❑	❑	❑	❑	_____
Cut-off control operable?	❑	❑	❑	❑	❑	_____
Temperature of hot water checked periodically?	❑	❑	❑	❑	❑	_____
Ice production checked?	❑	❑	❑	❑	❑	_____

COMMODITY FILLING

Commodities correctly handled?	❑	❑	❑	❑	❑	_____
Cups properly handled, stored?	❑	❑	❑	❑	❑	_____
Food contact surfaces not touched in reloading or exchange?	❑	❑	❑	❑	❑	_____
No commodities left in machines?	❑	❑	❑	❑	❑	_____

Signature of route person at time of review: _____

Date reviewed with route person: _____

Supervisor conducting inspection & interview: _____

Location name: _____

Source: National Automatic Merchandising Association

Location, Location, Location

Location, location, location. It's a mantra all successful operators keep in mind when trying to determine where to set up business—or in this case, components of their overall business, the vending machines.

As we've said before, vendors are simply miniature retail stores. Given two machines of equal quality, offering the same products and serviced with the same care, the difference between one that's unprofitable and one that's profitable is location.

Learn the Art of Locating or Hire a Locator

Since proper location is key to your vending sales success, you need to either learn the art of locating, and do a lot of research and legwork to master it, or you need to hire a professional locator.

The operators interviewed for this book were torn about hiring locators, many of them expressing disappointment in the gap between what was promised and what was actually delivered. If you decide to hire a locator you can expect them to work on a 50 percent deposit to start looking for locations. Once the location is found, they bring you, the client, to the site for approval. If you decide to purchase the location you pay the locator at that time. Locators usually provide a 90-day warranty that says if you lose the location through no fault of your own, they will replace it.

Before handing over any money, or being impressed by promises and glittery locations, ask for a complete resume of successes the locator has had with other operators. Ask for references. Call each resume reference and make sure it pans out. Ask the operator if he or she was impressed or left desiring of the service. Network the contacts at *Vending Times* for reputable locating services.

Looks Can Deceive

Traditionally, companies with fewer than 50 employees haven't been profitable for operators. "Most of the people who come into our facility think they've found a niche market in small locations," notes machine distributor Vince Gumma of Chicago's American Vending Sales. "If there isn't a machine in that location today, then there's probably a reason."

Ferreting out that reason can sometimes be a challenge, but talking to the office or building manager is a good place to start. Most likely, the problem has been cookie-cutter vending. If so, collect enough demographic, wage, and related information to determine whether the location offers profitability if you customize.

Reputable locators are becoming more common, and some startups have grown into handsome enterprises with the assistance they've received but more often than not the feedback we got was negative due to the persistence of unprofessional posers taking advantage of people who have not done their research. When we asked Erik A. Borger what he thought, as you may have guessed, he advised, "Never, ever do it. It is a horrendous experience. At least for me it was."

You might want to have a professional locator help you get started, but once your business is off the ground, you may prefer to go it alone and keep more of the profits for yourself.

The trick is to find locations where:

- There is significant traffic
- There are no competing machines (or similar products)
- The demographic market for your products is likely to buy
- There are no competing retailers
- There are good places available to put your machines

Additionally, you want places where business is growing and not where downsizing will limit your customer base or renovations will end all foot traffic.

The problem you will run into is that many places that allow—or want—vending machines already have them. After all, this is a very competitive business. Places that don't have vending machines may:

- Not permit them
- Not want them
- Not be very good locations

Of course, you may be lucky and find places that just have not yet been approached by vending operators. Perhaps an operator thought they were too small for a full-sized Dixie Narco machine, which holds 501 products. However, they might be just right for a smaller machine, such as the espresso and cappuccino machines mentioned previously, or perhaps for another creative concept.

Some of the keys to success are to present a product that is not found in the existing machines; find another location in the same facility—such as a building on a college campus that doesn't have machines; present a better machine and a better commission deal; and/or find a location that is just being built and get in on the ground floor, so to speak.

In addition to finding locations, you will have the ongoing job of evaluating them and determining whether or not they are still profitable. A great location may turn into a poor one for a variety of reasons. For example, a row of machines that have

When the Going Gets Tough, the Tough Use Profit Protection

Operators are a crafty bunch and have devised strategies for handling higher costs. The 2011 "State of the Vending Industry Report" illustrates how operators got tough in 2010. With fewer operators in the business and the competition fierce since the start of the recession, operators focused on delivering a more dedicated work force to their companies, along with a list of profit protection techniques that helped their profits improve, despite trying times. NAMA lists the top methods operators used to handle higher costs in 2010 as:

Raised prices	18.2%
Absorbed the extra cost	15.2%
Reduced service frequency	11.3%
Rearranged routes	10.6%
Eliminated unprofitable accounts	9.0%
Lowered commissions	6.8%
Postponed parts/equipment buys	5.7%
Rearranged job responsibilities	4.9%
Reduced company travel	4.6%
Reduced equipment in accounts	4.4%
Adjusted compensation benefits	3.7%
Reduced product variety	3.0%
Postponed equipment repairs	1.7%
Switched to more cost-efficient trucks	0.8%

always done well for you in a food court might suddenly stop doing as well if the store next to those machines suddenly goes out of business—no one is leaving the food court through that exit anymore because there is only an empty store. A machine in a parking garage may no longer be profitable if a garage with better lighting and lower rates opens down the street. There are many reasons why a location can go bad.

In the food court, you may want to move the machines to the other end of the facility, closer to a busier location, with the permission of the food court owner. It is these kinds of moves and strategies that keep you always in the right place for sales volume. In the garage scenario, you may want to check in with the owners of the new facility or stay put for a while, but not load machines fully until you see if business picks up again.

Conversely, there are reasons why a bad site may suddenly become much more promising. Since many of the longtime vendors may have written a site off, you may be able to seek out business at a location that has suddenly taken an upswing because of new tenants or a change in management.

John Ochi of Five Star Distributors puts it best: "You should be careful not to get volume just to get volume. A lot of operators just grab an available location and don't worry about it. Those are the people who call us up and say, 'We're going to be late making payment.'"

This isn't to say some locations are inherently bad and others good, but that a variety of factors affect whether a particular location is right for you.

Beyond Counting Heads

The size of the population at a given location once was the measuring stick for most vending specialties. With food operations, any location with more than 100 employees generally assured sufficient sales to warrant placing machines. When marketing Telecards, for example, interstate truck stops were the prime target. However, as more operators enter any given specialty, fewer large locations remain untapped.

Today, successful operators concentrate on the quality of the population at a given location. "For example, banks have a lot of employees but they [usually] don't buy from machines," full-line operator Wayne D. explains.

As a rule of thumb, the food industry now concurs on the benchmark of 50 employees as a minimum. "There are plenty of 50-person accounts that can be profitable," assures Vince Gumma of American Vending Sales.

Does this mean completely ruling out smaller or less active locations? Not necessarily. As we've mentioned before, vending is a relationship-oriented business largely dependent on referrals as a source of new clients. Serving an underperforming location that's keen for vendors can pay off in the long run. A small cafeteria may support a specific vending machine if it's the only game in town. For example, if no local establishment sells ice cream and you put an ice cream machine in a community center with plenty of kids, teens, and young adults, you might see very positive results.

Since your clients are also in business and understand solvency concerns, Wayne D. suggests asking them to bring underachievers up to breakeven. "If there are 20 people at the location, you tell them, 'It has to do X number of dollars, or you'll have

▲

to subsidize it.' We don't tell people they can't have a machine; we tell them it has to pay for itself, or they'll have to help pay for it."

Space in Between

Although vending operators rarely state finances in terms of hourly rates, they do stress travel time as the number-one consideration when placing vendors. "I highly recommend that people who are starting out don't travel outside a limited geographical area," says Wayne D. "Too many people get involved with saying, 'It's just my time, and my time isn't worth anything.' Sure your time is worth something!"

Not only does the amount of time you spend traveling define the number of machines you can service under ideal conditions, but you must also factor in trouble calls. "If you're 20 miles away, and you have to run back to fix a coin or dollar bill jam, that's an expensive proposition," says Wayne.

Operators and experts recommend securing a sizable account and building around it. "The hub-and-spoke theory works," says Five Star Distributors' Ochi. "If you get an anchor account, you should build the spokes around it." This means that you should seek a number of clients in one general area so that you can collect from, and restock, several machines without having to make long trips in between, especially with the spiraling price of gas.

Who's in the Neighborhood?

Next, consider what you're up against. In food vending, this means fast-food restaurants and convenience stores. "If people in an office building can walk out and buy something in two minutes, I'll sell less," says Wayne D. "If there are 30 people on the day shift, 20 on second shift, and 25 on third shift, the third shift will buy more than the other two combined because the convenience stores aren't accessible."

Another factor is the type and amount of break time. Are employees allowed to leave the premises? Do they have an hour or a half-hour? If breaks are generous, further investigation may be in order. If breaks are limited and there isn't enough time for a "sit down" lunch, or if students (for example) cannot leave the building, then you have a more "captive" audience. Prisons, hospitals, summer sleep-away camps, and assisted living facilities are all profitable "captive" audience opportunities.

Surveying the population may turn up a need for "quick eats" options. In a recent nationwide survey by the National Restaurant Association, nearly 40 percent of adult workers reported they did not take a real lunch break, notes the National Automatic Merchandising Association's Hudson Report. Additionally, pressed to put in longer hours, many office employees are eating lunch at their desks, meaning a well-packed sandwich and a selection of favorite beverages may be very good options.

The Future of Candy and Snack Sales

CHART 14E: **TOP 20 CANDY/SNACK/CONFECTIONS IN DOLLAR SALES, 4-YEAR REVIEW**

#	PRODUCT	2007	2008	2009	1-YEAR CHANGE	2010	1-YEAR CHANGE
1	Masterfoods USA 2-oz. Snickers Original	73¢	76¢	83¢	9.21%	88¢	6%
2	Masterfoods USA 1.74-oz. M&M's Peanut	73	77	84	9.09	89	5
3	Masterfoods USA 2-oz. Twix Bar	73	78	85	8.97	89	4.7
4	Frito-Lay 1.5-oz. Ruffles Cheddar & Sour Cream	71	81	85	4.94	88	3.5
5	Frito-Lay 1.75-oz. Doritos Nacho Cheesier Big Grab	79	80	83	3.75	86	3.6
6	Frito-Lay 1.5-oz. Lay's Chips	77	79	81	2.53	84	3.7
7	Frito-Lay 1.125-oz. Cheetos Crunchy	59	64	87	35.93	75	-13.7
8	Masterfoods USA 2.13-oz. Three Musketeers Original	71	77	84	9.09	88	4.7
9	Kellogg/Keebler 3.6-oz. Poptarts Frosted Strawberry	84	88	91	3.41	95	3.2
10	Kellogg/Keebler 1.7-oz. Rice Krispies Treat	77	78	84	7.69	89	5.95
11	Kellogg/Keebler 2-oz. Famous Amos Chocolate Chip Cookies	71	79	87	10.12	91	4.5
12	Kellogg/Keebler 1.5-oz. Cheez-It Original	57	61	69	13.11	73	5.7
13	Frito-Lay 2.125-oz. Cheetos Crunchy	80	80	82	2.5	83	1.2
14	Masterfoods USA 2.17-oz. Wrigley Skittles	76	79	87	10.12	91	4.5
15	Masterfoods USA 1.69-oz. M&M's Milk Chocolate	72	76	84	10.53	88	4.7
16	Nestle 2.1-oz. Butterfinger	73	75	84	12	89	5.9
17	Inventure Foods 1.75-oz. TGI Friday's Cheddar & Bacon Potato Snacks	75	76	84	10.52	88	4.76
18	Kellogg/Keebler 2-oz. Cheez-It Original	NA	81	87	7.4	88	1.1
19	Frito-Lay 2.25-oz. Fritos Chili Cheese	77	79	82	3.8	84	2.4
20	Frito-Lay 2.75-oz. Grandma's Peanut Butter Cookie	68	68	72	5.88	78	8.33

Editor's Note: Percentage gains have been affected by rounding.

Source: Elliot Maras and *Automatic Merchandiser* magazine

For nonfood vending, other competitive pressures warrant consideration. Baltimore pantyhose vending pioneer Janice M. says her machines compete with virtually every other purchasing option. "My market is mostly last-minute customers but not always.

▲

If I sell a good product at a good price, I get repeat customers who, instead of going to a store and buying ten pairs of hose and keeping them in their desk, might just say, 'I'll get them from the machine.' "

Purchasing Patterns

Demographics also play a starring role in locating your vendors. The demographics of prospective locations speak volumes about whether or not your offerings are a good match. Gender, ethnicity, work classification, and transience are leading indicators of not only what your customers will buy but also whether they'll purchase it from a machine. "White-collar workers are more likely to go somewhere else than blue-collar," B.J. S. asserts. "It's an attitude about machine food." Additionally, it may be part of the job. Blue-collar employees are less likely to be having a "client lunch" than a white-collar employee.

Of course, there is also the opposite argument that with the right snack options, white-collar employees, who may be earning higher salaries, will be quick to spend on snack foods throughout their work day. The latest in "high-tech" machines does make it easier to fit vending into technology companies, typically run by a younger demographic group (in their 20s). This is because this type of service goes along with their mindset—buying things quickly through technology. Hence the success of the iPod vending machines in Macy's . . . a young audience that has grown up with technology, buying something through the push of a button or two, just as they do over the internet.

Visibility and Signage Count

For some vending specialties, another profitability factor is visibility. Vending machines need to be in good locations so that people can spot them as they walk into a specified area or along a corridor. If possible, you may want to put them near ATM machines, where people have available cash. Obviously, you want well-traveled locations, but you also need to make sure that access isn't blocked. The signage on the machine needs to be well lit for the best visibility, and part of your job is to make sure the vending machines maintain proper lighting and remain in good locations. Remember, a good location

> ### Smart Tip
> No matter what you vend, always seek out ways to maximize your servicing time. "I do one location this week and one another week and two another week," says Baltimore operator Janice M. "That way I'm not stressing myself out trying to run around to six or seven different locations in one day."

can change based on numerous factors including construction being done in or around the location. Rethink the location regularly.

If you are limited to inadequate locations for any reason, you may be best seeking a new location entirely.

On the Right Route

When fuel was cheap, cities were compact, traffic was light, and the vending industry was growing, operators didn't worry much about how they organized their routes. Today, however, the cost of travel has risen and competition has driven prices and margins down. Now the name of the game is reducing dead time. "We've done time studies," Wayne D. asserts. "We know it takes just as long for a guy to fill a machine with $50 of product as $100. The significant cost is the time getting there and opening the machine."

To bring these costs under control, the buzz is proper route structuring. Simply put, your route structure is how all your locations fit together on the map and how often (and in what order) you service them. To be effective, you must determine the most efficient service schedule at the machine level.

The Index Card Challenge

Try this exercise to create the most efficient route:

1. Create an index card for each location.

2. On the front write your stat facts: how much of each product is purchased weekly, where the location is, and what its challenges are.

3. Next to each challenge write how much time you allot for it.

4. On the back write in abbreviated form what the weekly maintenance issues on the vendor are and how much time they require.

5. On the front of the card in the upper right hand corner write the total time that location takes and a rating of how difficult it is from one to five.

6. Now arrange the cards in a straight line across the table, imagining the drawbacks and benefits of the best combinations. Once you find the perfect sequence, write it down!

"If I go to a snack machine every week for $60, the maximum I'm going to make is $3,000 annually," says Wayne D. But if that same machine is serviced every two weeks, you'll still make $60 per week (in half the time) and you'll have time to service a similar machine at another location, effectively doubling your sales volume. "If I go there 26 times a year [instead of 52], I'll have 26 fewer times I count bags, and 26 fewer entries in the computer," says Wayne D. "It takes only a little more time to fill 250 items than it does 80 items. It's the time getting there—driving to the location, loading product onto a dolly, and walking into the building. If an operator doesn't learn this in the beginning, he'll stumble around and never be able to properly train those he hires."

While it's logical to conclude that it would be even more cost-effective to service machines once every three weeks, the cost of lost sales due to empty columns outweighs savings from fewer rounds of service. Generally, industry experts and trade publications suggest planning to service a machine when it is between 50 and 60 percent of capacity. As you may have guessed, proper route structuring doesn't necessarily mean you'll skip a location entirely, rather that you design your route so that the vendors require less tending. If you pay attention to the specific needs of each location, your route plan will function like a nicely choreographed dance with hardly a motion wasted.

For Erik A. Borger, creating the most efficient route plan possible is essential because picking up wholesale goods from suppliers already incurs a lot of driving. It's a good thing he's got a Prius to save money on gas. "I deal with too many suppliers, but with healthy vending you have to. No one is going to be a one-stop shop; it can certainly be a long day of driving at times," Borger laments. Although fine-tuning route structures is an ongoing process, the importance of considering how a prospective new location fits into your current route structure can't be overstated. Of course, you can't know the exact rate or volume of sales until you actually begin servicing that location. What's important is estimating as closely as possible to determine if it's worth pursuing at all.

"It's time, time, time—in pennies, nickels, and dimes," Wayne D. stresses. "A location has to be right for your business."

Ochi adds, "If you aren't efficient with your route structure, you won't survive."

Steering Clear of Crime

As we discussed in Chapter 8, wear and tear on your machines affects your bottom line. A workhorse candy and snack machine

> **Bright Idea**
>
> If the industry organization for your specialty doesn't offer a sample contract, the makers of the popular small-business accounting software QuickBooks offer a solution. The Quicken Family Lawyer contains a basic business contract template and will walk you through the process of creating a document that's legal in your state. Nolo (www.nolo.com) also offers free guidance for drawing up contracts.

Telemetry

One of the best aspects of modern computer technology is that machines can now let you know when they are empty or which columns are empty, helping you to plan your route accordingly. As mentioned earlier, they can also alert you as to when the machine may be on the verge of failing.

Remote monitoring is picking up acceptance in an industry that has, on occasion, been resistant to change (not the coins).

"NASA calls it telemetry so we call it telemetry," says Tim Sanford, editor-in-chief of *Vending Times.* "The old way of thinking was you made stops on Tuesdays and Thursdays and that was your schedule. If you suggested that perhaps they could make stops on Tuesday and Friday sometimes if you didn't really have to load the machine on a Thursday, the operator would say 'that's not the business we're in,' basically not wanting to make a change. Then people came along 15 years ago and said there will be ways for the machines to communicate with you. Today, however, because the cost of driving a truck is so great now, you find more people looking to decrease the number of trips they have to make without losing control of the account or selling out," explains Sanford.

"Vending operators always have 'overserviced' their machines, effectively scheduling a service stop on a schedule designed to preclude anything from 'selling out' before the driver arrives," says Sanford. "And every stop costs money. Various strategies have been devised to extend the time between services, such as 'double facing' the most popular items. In recent years, vending management software has been developed for forecasting the sales of each machine, and this now is being supplemented by 'remote monitoring' (telemetry). This is a long story, but the punch line is that machines in the field can report their inventory levels, item by item, on a frequent basis. Forecasting and remote monitoring can enable the operator to schedule service only when the machine needs it. That results in fewer stops, and thus more sales between stops, larger collections per stop, and lower annual cost. These things are not yet in widespread use, but many bellwether operations are reporting good results with them, and they are sure to gain greater and greater traction over time."

Even with telemetry, Sanford also notes that many route drivers begin to instinctively know when a machine is going to sell out by looking at their data

▲

Telemetry, continued

(via software or handwritten notes). For example, if a machine is reloaded every Monday and is 75 percent depleted by Wednesday afternoon for the last 40 weeks in a row, then you know you'll want to go back every Thursday. You'll get into a rhythm. Telemetry—or communication from the machine—is helpful in places that are difficult to gauge, because the patterns are not as consistent, because you're trying new products, and for varying the sizes of the machines. It can help you strategize without having to drive to each location as often.

can rack up sales for 20 years if it's maintained correctly and doesn't fall prey to abuse by customers or passersby.

For this reason, successful operators advise entrepreneurs to leave public locations to large operations that can better absorb the costs of insuring, repairing, and replacing easy targets.

Along with the crime against the machines, you need to consider your own personal safety (also mentioned earlier). One tactic is to join your local vending association to tap into warnings about crime sprees. "We have a hotline," says John Ochi, referring to the Illinois chapter of the National Automatic Merchandising Association. "Every time someone gets hit, the information gets distributed and at least you're forewarned. The best thing you can do is join NAMA. Even your biggest competitors will help you along because it doesn't do any of us any good in this industry when crimes happen."

What's My Cut?

Utter the word "commission" in vending circles and you'll elicit a cascade of four-letter expletives. Be that as it may, vending operators have offered clients commissions as an incentive for decades, which means clients today just plain expect to take a cut.

No matter what you're vending, commissions take as much as a 25 percent bite out of gross sales. As we discussed in Chapter 9, the average commission varies by vending specialty and geographical region as well as the size and type of client. Therefore, when you are evaluating a location, be certain to discuss your prospect's expectations upfront. Otherwise, your location may pocket your profits and leave you running in the red.

Contract Essentials

Among the essentials of a good contract, you will need to include for how long the contract is valid and how (and by whom) it can be terminated. You also want exclusivity, thus preventing competitors from also setting up vendors in the same locations. There may be other types of vending machines permitted and this too needs to be spelled out. There should also be a confidentiality clause in the contract to keep matters private.

Get It in Writing

Those who look out for operators' best interests urge newbies to consider only locations willing to sign contracts. A good contract is much more than just protection from breaches of faith, such as allowing a competitor to place their machines at the same location. Instead, think of contracts as multipurpose documents. Contracts spell out who is responsible for providing power so your bill acceptor works. They state commission amounts and dates when you will pay them. They lay out responsibility for damage to your equipment. They require your client to give you written notice of termination in advance, rather than suddenly telling you to remove your machines as you walk in for a regular servicing. If the machine is unplugged or blocked by construction, or moved, the results of such actions are also spelled out in the contract. In short, contracts protect your bottom line by stating your right to remove a machine if the location is unprofitable. You should discuss with local vending associations and other operators what a standard client contract should include and have an attorney look over the contract.

For an example of a detailed vending-specific contract, see NAMA's "A Guide to Location Contracts or Service Agreements" on page 184. A shorter format can also be found on page 188, "Agreement for Sale/Lease of Goods." You might also visit Vendline at www.vendline.com and click under Route Manager (in the contracts category) for a sample that you can use as a template.

Keep in mind that there will be specific details that some locations will want to put in place—such as a school may not want high-sugar items or they may not have the vending machine open until after classes. Make sure to discuss any such as a school that may not want high-sugar items or to have the vending machine open until after classes.

▲

A Guide to Location Contracts or Service Agreements

Compensation, Accounting, Licenses, Cost Changes

Operator agrees to pay Location the following sums subject to other provisions of this agreement:

_____% of gross receipts or

_____% of gross receipts of (Product)

(list each Product)

The term "gross receipts" shall not include any applicable sales or use taxes.

Operator will report on the basis of 13 four-week accounting periods, and will submit within 20 days after the close of each such period to Location a report of gross receipts through the machines together with a check for the sum due Location under this agreement. Operator shall maintain an accurate record of all merchandise, inventories, and receipts in connection with performance under this agreement. Location is authorized to inspect such records at all reasonable times during business hours.

Operator agrees to obtain and display, if required, all applicable federal, state, and local licenses.

It is understood that compensation paid to Location under this agreement is based on federal, state, and local taxes and license fees and on the cost of merchandise sold through the machine existing at the date of this agreement. In the event of an increase in taxes, license fees, or the cost of merchandise sold through the machines under this agreement, which are not reflected in an increase in the retail selling price, then the compensation to Location provided for in this agreement shall be reduced to reflect such increases.

Maintenance and Sanitation

Operator shall operate and maintain all vending machines and other equipment in a clean, sanitary condition in accordance with recognized standards for such machines in accordance with all applicable laws and regulations. Location will keep the areas in which the vending machines are located in all service areas in a clean and sanitary condition and shall dispose of all refuse that results from the operation of the vending service and will replace expendable items as needed.

Personnel

Operator's personnel will at all times be dressed in clean, neat uniforms and will observe all regulations in effect on Premises. Operator shall not employ at the Premises any employee not acceptable to Location. Operator's employees shall have health examinations as frequently and as thoroughly as required by law and good practice. Location agrees to furnish Operator's personnel with any identification

A Guide to Location Contracts or Service Agreements, continued

passes required for entrance to and exit from the Premises. Location shall not impose any regulations on Operator's personnel not imposed on Location's personnel. The parties hereto agree that they will not hire employees of the other within six months of the date of termination of their employment with the other without the written permission of the other party.

Indemnity

Operator will indemnify and hold Location, its employees, guests, and visitors harmless for any loss, damage, injury, or liability occurring because of the negligent performance by Operator's employees, contractors, or agents under this agreement. Location will pay Operator all losses from theft of money and merchandise and from vandalism or other intentional damage of Operator's vending machines and other equipment. In no case, however, shall Location's liability for such losses exceed the lower of 1) the repair or replacement cost of machines and equipment damaged plus the value of money and merchandise lost or 2) $_____ per occurrence.

Insurance

Operator will procure and maintain the following insurance:

(a) Workers' Compensation as prescribed by the laws of the State of Missouri.

(b) Comprehensive bodily injury, property damage, liability, and casualty loss, with limits of $_____ for injury or death of one person and $_____ for injury or death of two or more persons in any one accident; and $_____ property damage in any one accident.

(c) Product liability as shall protect Operator and Location, their employees, agents, and independent contractors in minimum limits of $_____.

Location shall promptly notify Operator in writing of any claims against either Location or Operator, and in the event of a suit being filed, shall promptly forward to Operator all papers in connection therewith. Location shall not incur any expense or make any settlement of any such claims or suit without Operator's consent.

Alterations

Location agrees to notify Operator of any alteration that will affect any of the areas where services are performed under this agreement before such alterations are made. Operator agrees to make no alterations in the Premises unless authorized in writing by Location. Location agrees to cooperate in making any alterations that may become necessary for proper performance of the service under this agreement.

▲

A Guide to Location Contracts
or Service Agreements, continued

Term, Renewal, Business Interruption: Cancellation and Breach

This agreement shall become effective _____ and remain in force for a period of three years and for any additional period due to business interruption. Unless canceled by written notice at least _____ days prior to the termination date, this agreement is deemed to be automatically renewed for additional periods of one year thereafter upon the same terms as set out herein.

If, because of riots, war, public emergency or calamity, fire, earthquake, or other Acts of God, government restrictions, labor disturbances, or strikes, operations at Premises are interrupted or stopped, performance of this agreement, with the exception of money due, shall be suspended and excused for so long as such interruption or stoppage continues. This agreement shall be extended for a period of time equal to the time of the interruption or stoppage.

Either party to this agreement may terminate this agreement by giving _____ days notice in writing to the other party of its intention to cancel this agreement. This agreement may also be terminated by Operator by reason of unprofitability by giving _____ day's written notice to Location.

In the event any provisions of this agreement are violated by either party, the other party shall serve written notice upon the breaching party setting forth the violation and demanding compliance with the agreement. Unless within _____ day's after serving such notice, such violations cease and corrections are made, the aggrieved party may terminate this agreement immediately by written notice to the offending party.

Termination

Upon termination of this agreement, Operator shall vacate the Premises and shall return the Premises together with all furniture owned by Location to the same condition as when originally made available to Operator, normal wear and tear, fire, and other casualty loss excepted. If Operator fails to remove its property and effects within a reasonable time after termination, Location shall have the right to remove and store Operator's property and effects at the expense of Operator.

Damages

It is understood and agreed that Operator has incurred, in anticipation of sales to be made over the term of this agreement, expenses in purchasing and installing machines and other equipment, hiring or rescheduling employees, purchasing inventory, and other expenses. It is understood and agreed that these expenses form part of the consideration for this agreement. In the event this agreement is canceled, or terminated by breach by the Location prior to its termination date, Operator shall be entitled, as a

A Guide to Location Contracts or Service Agreements, continued

measure of the expenses incurred and earnings lost as agreed by the parties hereto for such period, to recover 1) any unamortized expenses for machines and other equipment installed under this agreement plus 2) _____% of the average monthly gross receipts or sales made through the machines during the months prior to such cancellation or breach to the date this agreement would have terminated had there been no cancellation or breach.

Miscellaneous

It is understood and agreed that this contract establishes an independent contractor relationship between the parties. Notices to Location required herein shall be addressed to the Ace Computer Company, 123 Main Street, St. Louis, Missouri. Notices to Operator required herein shall be addressed to the ABC Vending Company, 456 Main Street, St. Louis, Missouri.

This agreement shall be construed under the laws of the State of Missouri.

This agreement is entered into by Operator on the expressed representation that Location owns the business at the Premises or has the authority to enter into this agreement.

This agreement constitutes the entire agreement between the parties and all previous communications between the parties with respect to this agreement are canceled and superseded.

Witness our hands this _____ day of _____, 20xx.

_____

Operator   Location

_____

By   By

_____

Address   Address

_____

City, State   City, State

Source: National Automatic Merchandising Association

Agreement for Sale/Lease of Goods

Memo Form

Agreement made _____ , through_____ , between
month/day/year month/day/year

_____ and _____
Name of Buyer Name of Seller
herein referred to as buyer, of herein referred to as seller, of

Address_____ Address _____

City_____ City _____

County_____ County _____

State _____ State_____

This memo confirms the sale/purchase or lease on: _____
month/day/year

Quantity   List items being purchased/leased:

_____   _____

_____   _____

_____   _____

for_____ Dollars ($_____)

Is this a deposit?   ❏ Yes ❏ No

Deposit will be returned upon removal of all vending equipment in good condition from location and if purchased deposit will be applied toward purchase.

Dated _____ month/day/year

Signature of Buyer Signature of Seller

_____   _____

Source: McLean Machines & Co. Inc.

Likewise, you may need to have certain provisions, such as access to refill the machine when it is an optimal time on your route. A location that cannot let you into the facility until x time of day may put a serious crimp into your route planning. Security measures are tighter than ever and some locations will have policies that stipulate when you can and cannot enter the premises. Ultimately, you will need to work out an agreement that is best for both parties, which may mean some negotiating and making compromises—as long as they do not affect your ability to make money from that vendor.

Putting It All Together

Judging prospective locations can be tricky. Use the measures we've discussed here in tandem with the market research you conducted as part of Chapter 4. In addition, survey a prospect's employees, consult local demographic information, and review sales data generated by a previous vendor.

Develop an evaluation worksheet such as the "Location Evaluation" form on page 190 to help you with qualitative and quantitative analysis. When the information is all in, take a step back to see how each location fits into your business as a whole.

Remember, the more thoroughly you evaluate upfront, the more likely you are to sort the gems from the gravel. In the end, you'll be a more successful entrepreneur.

Location Evaluation

These are important questions for you to ask each location owner or manager. This enables you to evaluate if it would be profitable for you to pursue this account.

Company name: _____

Contact _____

Address _____

Phone _____

Location _____

Employees _____ Shifts _____

Hours open _____ Weekends _____

% Male _____ % Female _____

Average age: _____

Eat/drink at location? _____

Leave building? _____

How long lunch? _____

Breaks? _____ How long? _____

Nearby fast food? _____

Cafeteria? _____

Food trucks? _____

Reasons for change _____

_____

Referred by? _____

Equipment the customer requests _____

_____

Commission requested? _____

Willing to sign agreement or contract? _____

Notes: _____

_____

Evaluation by _____ Date _____

Source: The Vending Connection

Blow
Your Horn

Most businesses have only one target
audience—either the mass market they sell to anonymously or a
small group of buyers they serve one-on-one. As you already know,
vending entrepreneurs sell to both.

Because of your unique dual-clientele situation,
blowing your own horn means marketing to the first group

▲

and merchandising to the second group. As the industry magazine *Automatic Merchandiser* explains it, marketing is determining whom you're selling your product to and how you're going to do it. Merchandising is determining the exact brand, color, flavor, size, type, and quantity someone wants to buy and then presenting it to them in a manner that encourages them to do so.

Since you must market your vendors effectively before you can merchandise the products they sell, in this chapter we'll talk about marketing. Then, we'll discuss merchandising in the following chapter.

Before we move on, it's important to note that your marketing strategies should be relationship-based. Some of our sage operators suggest that cold-calling or contacting prospects directly by telephone or in person results in the most sales.

Others, such as Randall Sutherland, get a high sales return from a small mailing investment. If it's done right, your mailer won't wind up in a pile of junk mail. Says Sutherland, "I spend about $200 on a great business mailing list, and add another $150 for beautiful, colorful postcards and postage combined, and it usually results in about four sites converted to sales."

Build on the Basics

Before you pick up the phone to make inquiries or slip on your dress shoes to pound the pavement, invest in the marketing essentials. For any successful entrepreneur, the most basic marketing tools are also the most valuable, and in vending, this means business cards, online business listings in as many places as possible (which we'll get into in detail in Chapter 14), Yellow Pages ads, and vehicle signage.

- *Business cards.* Whether you whip them up on your computer, use a print shop, or rely on an online printing service, business cards are the currency of the marketing trade. Handing a prospect a business card (or mailing them one to follow up a phone conversation) shows you are a serious businessperson. Without a card, you're just a wannabe—someone who's not serious.

- *Yellow Pages ads.* As a serious businessperson, you'll already have a business telephone line, which means you are automatically eligible for a Yellow Pages listing. Due to the operators out there who don't take cues from their customers to upgrade technologically or cater to specific appetites, there are always locations in need of a vendor with great customer service, so make sure you're listed in as many directories, offline and on, as possible.

- *Vehicle signage.* The more time commuters spend in their cars, the more valuable your vehicle's exterior becomes. Let's face it—you want the

Postcard Pointers

○ Do some research. Prove to your future customers that having a vending machine in their space will result in higher employee productivity, less time spent on lunch commuting, and whatever else applies to the type of site you're targeting. Use the front of the postcard to display statistics and facts along with high-quality photos of your most current trend, cohesive products, and sparkling, well-kept machines. Use facts from the many articles and reports at www.vendingmarketwatch.com and www.vending-times.com.

○ Use some of those research skills to ferret out conventions, networking events, and convergences of office managers, such as office supply-related events. Contact the big chain corporate offices of Office Depot, OfficeMax, Staples, and Best Buy and search online to see national convention listings for this industry. Network like crazy and keep these contacts organized and ready to use for mailings, follow-up calls, and sales visits. All these activities give your mailing cards extra power whether you use them as a calling, business, or mailing card.

○ Appeal to current health concerns by promoting the products that according to the "State of the Vending Industry Report" consistently do well and reflect consumers' growing education on nutrition. A "Did you know?" section relating energy levels to various aspects of nutrition found in your products (based on factual, traceable sources) placed in a callout box on your card separates facts from promotion and makes the card easy to read.

○ Check out the print and design deals to be had at www.modernpostcard. com, www.123print.com, and www.vistaprint.com. Easy, do-it-yourself templates and design services are featured at each of these companies.

○ This would be the perfect opportunity to incorporate the scratch-and-sniff aspect of marketing, too.

beleaguered procurement officer who's unhappy with his current vending operator to spot your vehicle and write down your telephone number. The downside of this is that by advertising on your vehicle that you are in the vending business, you are also attracting the attention of would-be thieves.

▲

Therefore, you might have a sign that can be shielded or removed when necessary—or, if you have more than one vehicle, you might opt for the less obvious target when going to certain areas on your route. The other option is to have excellent safety devices in the vehicle, travel by daylight, and park in busy areas. Magnetic signs are the perfect solution at $49 and under. See www.wholesalemagneticsigns.com.

All set? Good. Now it's time to ponder your next moves.

Whom Do You Know?

Your initial efforts should target those you know. Not only is this tactic more likely to net you paying accounts, but you'll also hone your presentation skills on individuals most likely to cut you some slack.

As equipment distributor Vince Gumma puts it, "Usually, when new operators come in to [purchase equipment from] us, they have something already lined up—a friend or relative at a factory or office building—and they've got some kind of verbal commitment." In fact, waiting until you've made your first sale makes good business sense. After all, you won't know the right machines to purchase until you've evaluated the location.

Janice M. turned to her own congregation. "My first client was my church. They were willing to give me a shot, and I was so happy. I still have that same account."

Wayne D. tapped into contacts he was making as a sales representative for R.J. Reynolds. "Once we established the business, there was a lot of word-of-mouth—people began to refer us to other people," he says. The experience of these operators clearly supports the importance of drawing on your existing relationships.

Targeting Prospects

After you have pitched your services to those you know, you are ready for total strangers. Use your market research from Chapter 4 to generate prospects.

Bright Idea

Small towns near famous national parks with camping features usually have little cafes that campers feast in on their way in or out of the untamed wilderness. A vending machine with forgotten essentials such as natural mosquito repellent, sunblock, hand wipes, toothbrushes, biodegradable soap, water tablets, water bottles, portable rain ponchos, mini flashlights, magnesium fire starters, matches, first-aid kits, compact travel pillows, chemical hand warmers, and folding utility knives would be a welcome sight for absent-minded travelers.

"I basically go after large buildings with a lot of women who circulate throughout the building," says pantyhose operator Janice M. of her prospecting tactics. "Every week, the *Baltimore Business Journal* compiles lists such as 'the biggest warehouses,' 'the biggest female-owned workplaces,' or 'the biggest churches.' They break the lists down into categories so you can see the number of female employees, total employees, where they're located, and what they do. That generally tells me a little bit about the company and helps me make a decision."

Make a list of the companies in each office building or location you plan to target. Research each company by combining the methods you learned in Chapter 4 and calling the receptionist at each place for a general query about their respective worker demographic. This will help you decide the types of businesses to target, considering the product you offer.

> ⚠ **Beware!**
> The September 2011 issue of *AARP* magazine featured a specific fraud alert for the benefit of senior citizens warning that like everyone else facing financial insecurity, aging con men (and women) also need to keep working longer, and they make up part of this sleazy crowd. The aged are preying on the gullible and have beneficial features that make it easier for them to do so. They try to find common ground, promoting themselves as Christians, or war veterans, and use long lists of bogus references including prominent figures in the community. They also count on people respecting their elders and use the "reciprocity rule," taking their prey out for expensive dinners, knowing the pressure will be on to invest in their schemes.

Making the Calls

Armed with as much advance information about your prospects as you can dig up, now it's time to start cold calling. The positive aspect of cold calling by telephone is that you can knock out numerous calls in one sitting. The negatives, however, are that you may not get the person in charge (who may be different from the one on your list) and you may be just one of many solicitations the person is receiving in the course of business, meaning they are quick to say "not interested." There is such a glut of telemarketers and cold callers out there today that the modern-day business owner is very likely to be very skeptical.

Therefore, you will also want to mix in some in-person cold calls, especially if you see potential for several clients in one area—such as a new shopping mall or office complex.

The first thing you want to find out, in either manner of cold-calling, is who the contact person is regarding vending decisions. "It may be the owner of the company; it may be the secretary; it may be the facilities manager. It may be an apartment manager or an office manager. It depends on where you're going," Wayne D. asserts.

"If possible, survey the location. Do they have old equipment there? What can you offer that the current operator doesn't offer?" continues the full-line operator from the Twin Cities. "Then, just walk in, drop your business card off, and say, 'If you're dissatisfied with your current vendor, give me a call. I'd like to make a proposal to you. If you are satisfied, maybe I can satisfy you better.'"

Randall Sutherland, also a victim of being overcharged for machines, told us the now-defunct business that he purchased them from did have one thing going for it: They set him up with a great list of business leads, which he was able to use productively for his business reply mailings. Part of their program was to coach him on how to talk to prospects and present his ideas once he got on site. "Cold calling is tough, but their marketing expertise was great and I was given contact sheets full of target market prospects. And since I didn't know anything else at the time, that was the way I got myself ahead," Sutherland remembers. "It really helps if you're very upbeat about your company once you get in the door for a follow-up or even just coming in off the street, dressed in crisp khakis, a polo shirt with your company logo, and of course fully armed with colorful brochures and business cards."

For a sample calling script, see page 198.

Rhino Hide

As the scenarios presented by our operators suggest, cold callers quickly develop thick skins. Successful salespeople also take rejection in stride since they get a very small percentage of sales from the amount of calls they make. The key is to hone your selling skills and make enough cold calls so that you get a reasonable number of placements from which to build a business.

The modern business owner is also armed with a great backup tool for doing business and closing deals . . . the internet. Many businesspeople today have become more familiar with using the internet and less comfortable with person-to-person encounters. Most businesspeople today also need to take some time to evaluate anything that requires making a commitment, so the internet is an ideal backup tool. It allows your prospective client to evaluate your offer at his or her own convenience. By making the initial contact and letting the individual know that he or she can find out more on your website, or from an email, you can then let them take it from there.

Set up a time for a follow-up call to see if he or she has looked at the site or at your email. You might also ask if you can email more information, again, allowing the person to read it at his or her own pace without the pressure of making a decision.

A website can be a strong backup tool and help you close deals. In a very "guarded" business environment, this is the option that more and more salespeople

Website Optimization

Today, if someone is looking for vending machines for his or her business, they will do as everyone does when searching for a product or service and search the internet. From their search, lists of vending companies will come up and they will typically look through the first few pages and make a decision of which one, or which ones, to contact. The problem, however, is that you may come up on page number 92, meaning they may never see your website. Therefore, in an effort to come up more quickly in their search, you need to do what is called website optimization, whereby you try to get your site to come up higher on the listings.

There are numerous ways to go about this, and there are web optimization specialists who can help you raise your web page to where it is among those that business owners find when searching. Seeking a local expert is one option, and buying a book on the subject, such as Khoa Bui's *Increasing Your Website Traffic*, is another.

In Chapter 4 we experimented with key word searches to find out who is searching for what right now. Since 80 percent of searches are two words or more, you need to think of two- or three-word key phrases that people would use that would bring them to your page. Know your market, your products, and your area of service. For example, most people won't just type in "vending," but "vending machines" or "vending machines Boston." Remember to be specific and include key phrases.

Also, for each unique service that you feature, you should have a separate page. So, if you sell coffee, have a separate page for coffee; that way, if someone is searching for coffee vending machines, your page will be more likely to come up—perhaps not your entire site, but the page labelled xyxvending/coffee (company name/product). Also, have the keyword high on the page, since some search engines only look at the first few lines. Also make sure your website is in basic HTML format and that other file extensions besides HTML are not used, since they are not always picked up by search engines.

There are many tricks to optimization, which is why entire books are written on designing websites and long articles can be found in the archives of *Vending Times* and other trade (as well as computer and web-related) publications.

Keep it in mind, because moving up on search engines can result in a great deal of business.

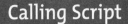

Calling Script

Hi. I just want a few moments of your time. [This has become an important phrase in our very guarded, fast-paced culture.]

Did you know that vending machines are a $25-billion per year business?

[If you anticipate offering a commission:] You can cash in on a piece of that business.

The public is buying from vending machines on a growing basis.

We at ABC Vending can supply you with the latest in high-tech vending machines and give you a cut of the sales.

It's a great way to make a profit. We offer x, y, and z [products] among other possibilities, all of which allow for your staff to get what they want quickly and conveniently and return to work, rather than having to take breaks to go to the nearby convenience store. You can even have [name of your most enticing product]!

We also service and tend to the machines on a regular basis to make sure they stay fully stocked and in working order.

Would it be possible to set up an appointment to show you some of our products and the latest in machines that we offer?

[If the respondent is wavering]

You could also look at our website at www.abcvending.com and we could talk next week.

[or]

I could email you with some specific information about our products.

This is a great opportunity to cash in on the growing high-tech vending industry.

---

are taking, and in this case, you are also a salesperson. Of course, this is not to say you cannot make deals the old-fashioned way—through the telephone and in-person meetings. However, it adds a major timesaver and selling tool to your arsenal.

Whatever the script is that you use, or however you plan your in-person script, you want to sell without being the "annoying in-your-face" salesperson. That means listening to the feedback that you are getting—if the person is interested and asking questions, keep talking about the products and the opportunities for them. Remember, most people want to know what's in it for them in the first minute or they will tune you out. You can no longer use the old four-minute script, which no one will listen to in a fast-paced world.

If the person is politely trying to get rid of you, use your website as a place they should "check out" just in case they change their minds. Most businesspeople will punch up a website just to see what's there, even out of curiosity.

A good salesperson today knows when to move forward and when to step back and let the website or emails take over. You need to be persistent, but in a beneficial way—therefore, if you call back in four months, give them a new benefit such as telling them about the new machines you now have or the new products you sell.

Sales Statistics

It is estimated, as is the case with direct mail, that you will receive a 2 to 4 percent sales rate, meaning if you call 100 places, about 3 will result in sales.

Over the five years since he purchased the business from his father-in-law, B.J. S. collected statistics on his sales calls. "I keep track of every sales call on my computer—what I did, what I talked about. You get somebody interested every 40 phone calls, so that's the success rate—1 in 40. You have to have some type of sense of humor," he continues. "Part of sales is being persistent and never giving up. Some of these guys know I'm going to call them every four months. You have to be stubborn as hell and not take 'no' for an answer."

Stat Fact

The highest priced cold drinks reported in the 2011 State of the Vending Industry Report were energy drinks, selling at $2 and up. While they did not sell in high volume, they conditioned customers to accept higher prices for other products, according to operators. It was also noted that energy drinks carried a high level of brand loyalty. Customers who pre-ferred one brand were not likely to buy an alternative.

Promoting a Concept

For those pioneering new vending frontiers, changing a "no" to a "yes" can hinge on your ability to show your prospects a benefit they might not immediately see. "With pantyhose vending, presenting the concept as an employee benefit is crucial," says Janice M. "When I'm calling and the response is, 'He's not in. What are you calling for?' I say, 'My name is Janice and I offer a new service for your female employees. We sell pantyhose vending machines.' And especially if it's a female assistant, they usually go, 'Oh, pantyhose? Oh yeah, that's great!' Generally they say,

▲

'I'll take your name and number and I will have him call you. Or if you want you can send some information in and I will make sure he looks at it.' "

Postcall To-Dos

When you hit one of those one-in-40 responses, B.J. S. recommends being ready to go into high gear. "Obviously, when someone says, 'Send me information,' you have to have something nice to send them," he says. "Instead of just sending them a flier, you have to make up a nice proposal that's multicolored." Even if you have a website, with plenty to look at, having something ready that you can send over quickly, as in a sales kit or sales presentation, is a good way of making the process more personal.

Incorporate as much information as possible about how your prospect will benefit from your service and supply a list of trade references—clients, your banker, suppliers, a relative who's a business owner, or anyone with whom you have established a solid relationship.

"Include everything except specific machine information because you haven't seen their break room yet, and you don't really know their needs," advises B.J. But do furnish a listing of machines you carry (or plan to purchase) along with some narrative drawn from marketing materials supplied by the equipment manufacturer. "In that section, you say you want to meet with them to see their break room and see how you can fit the machines to their needs." Write a short cover letter (see the sample on page 201) and place it on top of the proposal.

Janice M. expands on this advice. "I include a general introduction, pros and cons of having a pantyhose vending machine, why we think it works, and articles that have been written about me as well as customers and their comments," she says. What she intentionally doesn't mention in her proposals is the availability of commissions. "Some clients want commissions and others don't. I try to figure out the person I'm meeting with and go from there." This allows you to determine whether or not to work commissions into the conversation based on the response you receive.

If you're answering an RFP (request for proposal), the process of assembling a proposal is essentially the same. However, with an RFP you must speak to each requested point, even if you normally withhold such information until you meet. Failing to address a point in an RFP is a red

---

Bright Idea

Respect receptionists, secretaries, and security guards, for they are the gatekeepers of organizations. A tiny sample basket with mini-sized treats can go a long way in helping you get past the front lobby.

Cover Letter

March 5, 20xx

Mr. Gordon Bleu
1111 Market Street
Baltimore, MD

Dear Mr. Bleu,

Enclosed please find some information on A-1 Vending Machines, a pantyhose vending service. Let us show you how to profit from space you already own and impress your female employees at the same time.

My name is Jill Smith. I will call you when I am in your area to see if we can meet and discuss which opportunities will work for you.

Thank you in advance for your time. I look forward to talking with you soon.

Sincerely,

Jill Smith

Jill Smith

Enclosures

Source: McLean Machines & Co. Inc.

flag to a prospect—you might as well be stating you're unconcerned with meeting their needs.

Asking for the Sale

Once you've sent a proposal, don't sit on your hands waiting for your phone to ring. The name of the game is follow-up. Prospects expect you to call. To ensure your follow-ups are timely, construct a simple system for recording your prospecting activities. A sample of such a form, "Contact Sheet for New Clients," is below.

Sealing the Deal

Although one of the attractions of operating a vending business is casual attire, successful entrepreneurs emphasize preparing for your sit-downs by dressing for success. You need to maintain a very positive attitude and focus on the needs of

Contact Sheet for New Clients

Date	Name and Type of Company	Contact Person	Phone	Result

the client—if the client has you in his or her establishment and has looked over the material or your website or both, and has determined that he or she wants to do business with you, it is at that point you should stop selling yourself and your business. Too many salespeople never stop hyping their products or their services, even once the sale is nearly completed. The key, at that point, is closing the deal. This means talking about a contract and a date on which to bring over the machine and to set it up. Move to the aspects of sealing the final deal.

Each business deal is a process and it needs to have a beginning, middle, and end. Sure, the deal can result in future deals as well, but each specific deal should end with a signed contract.

> **Tip...**
>
> **Smart Tip**
> Make sure to acknowledge holidays in a nonreligious, yet grateful fashion. People are so busy between the end of October and early January that they barely have time to eat lunch. Randall Sutherland suggests having a surprise pizza delivery for the employee break room with a card attached that thanks customers for their business and wishes them happy holidays.

Reputation Sells

As we've mentioned before, successful vending entrepreneurs guard their reputations with their lives. Even early on, veterans say a good reputation is all that matters.

"When you're starting out, your clients are going to be your best source of new business," stresses 20-year veteran Wayne D. "If you've satisfied them, they're going to recommend you because there are enough poor vending companies out there that there are always bids available. Even today, we get 60 percent of our business through referrals."

B.J. S. emphatically agrees. "The biggest selling point in vending is word-of-mouth," he says. "Having a good reputation is key. A lot of our business is people who have had a different vending company, and then they come to us."

The Art of Being Wired

Slowly but surely, the vending industry has joined the internet age. The Vending Connection Yellow Pages lists vending machine service operators online in a state-by-state directory. In some regions of the country nearly every operator listed has a website, while in a few states only a few are utilizing the far-reaching power of the internet.

Here's where savvy entrepreneurs can gain a competitive advantage. While you may have little interest in surfing the web, your prospects are almost certainly wired.

Smart Tip

To let your website help you build your customer base, you can add some popular items that readers will forward to a friend. An e-card (electronic greeting card) for example or maybe a nonoffensive joke, bit of great trivia, or (if you are market-ing to one particular group such as hospitals or schools or shop-ping centers) some fun facts that one person will see and want to send to a friend can immediately promote you from one potential client to two potential clients. In fact, you can offer some incentive if the friend signs up as a client. This type of marketing, called viral marketing, is a great way to spread the word about your company without having to do a thing—except have a link that allows them to easily forward that bit of information to a friend.

Many of them will already be accustomed to using email as their primary form of communication.

There are numerous web providers and places to contact when looking to build a website—even the Vending Connection Yellow Pages lists nearly a dozen website designers or marketers. Visiting a site like www.web.com can help you build a simple site very easily. Also, asking other business owners (not only in the vending industry) whom they hired to build their websites can provide you with leads.

Your Website

Building a website today is not a particularly difficult proposition, and can serve as a place where potential customers can go to see what you have to offer. In addition, if someone sees your company name on your vehicle, hears about you from a satisfied customer, or sees your business card, it gives them a place to see your vending machines and your products. You do not need to make any deals through your website, but having an online presence can support your sales efforts enormously.

A couple of pages highlighting (with quality color photos) exactly what you are selling can speak volumes. A page about your background as a dependable, reliable company can be a selling point in your favor. A page of quotes from satisfied customers can always be added as your business grows. In addition, you can provide information on the costs and the services you provide (including emergency services). An email address (on a "contact us" page) and perhaps some fun facts, a survey, or even something humorous (to keep them coming back) can round out an inexpensive website, which you can use for promotion and marketing.

Some tips that you should keep in mind when building a website, or having one built for you, include:

- Look at other sites and decide which you like the best and would want to model yours after.

Tips from a Web Master

Consider these tips from website branding and marketing guru Khoa Bui:

1. *Find out who your target customer is.*
   Congratulations on taking the first step in building your first website. Now let's get to work! First you need to know everything about your customer such as age, occupation, and interests. Be as specific and narrow as possible. You'll be using this information later when writing your website copy to optimize it for clarity and recognition so that the search engines prefer and promote it. Optimizing involves editing your site's HTML (the code responsible for how you experience a website) so that search engines quickly find it relevant to the key word searches your audience uses to find what they want. If your site is optimized correctly the search engines can more easily promote you as a match to the searchers. Having an optimized site will gain favor with the search engines and help you generate sales.

2. *Register a powerful domain name.*
   Once you've isolated who your target customer is, it's now time to register your domain name (your web address or website name). Here are some tips to help you create a domain name that gets found on the search engines: Make sure your domain name includes a major keyword that your customer is searching for. Don't just include your business name; remember you want people to find you. If you still want your business name as a website, just register another domain name for it. You can later link the two sites together to refer to one another, should some customers search online for you with your company name. Include your area location as part of your domain name so people looking for your services in your area will find you.

3. *Purchase a good host for your website.*
   Make sure your hosting provider is fast and secure. People don't want to wait too long for your website to load. It's also important to have 24-hour tech support so your site is never down or malfunctioning. Finally, make sure your hosting provider is a reputable one and isn't prone to hacker attacks and crashing servers.

Tips from a Web Master, continued

4. *Get your marketing materials together and launch your website!*
   List testimonials, awards received, featured media sources, quotes, books, and anything else your business has taken part in. This will help you convert your traffic to sales. Once you've gathered all your marketing materials, it's now time to build your website. Image is everything online; therefore invest in a professional website design company to build it for you. Never cut corners with your business.

5. *Optimize to increase your website traffic and watch your sales explode!*
   You can start generating sales for your website by increasing its website traffic. Here are just a few ways to help do that:

   - Write articles and submit them to ezine directories.

   - Set up a new blog site and write keyword-rich blog posts to attract free traffic.

   - Create advertising campaigns.

   - Use Facebook and Twitter.

   - Communicate with newsletters to feature your site.

   - Search engine optimize your website.

   - Keep learning and applying new traffic-generation techniques to increase your sales and sell more than ever before!

For in-depth instruction on making the web work for you, we highly recommend Khoa's Bui's book *Increase Your Website Traffic* (www.khoa-bui.com).

- Avoid "bells and whistles" (i.e., technical gadgets that can slow your site down, like fancy videos).
- Select colors that are easy on the eyes.
- Don't pack so much onto a page that it is impossible to figure out what is going on (remember, sometimes less is more—your quality merchandise will stand out if you don't put a multitude of stuff on one page).
- Make it very easy to navigate—if someone clicks to see a photo of your candy selection and gets something else, they will most likely not bother with your site, so make it simple.

Before you put a website up, check to see that everything that is supposed to appear actually works. Also proofread it, since many sites have misspelled words and horrendous sentence structure. Make it look professional since it reflects your business.

Introducing Yourself

After you ink a contract at a new location, take a final marketing step. Broadcast your new service to the crew on location.

> **Smart Tip** Tip...
>
> Whenever you make a sales pitch, provide opportunities for your prospect to talk. Ask questions, listen attentively, and take notes. This shows your client you're interested in what he or she wants, not just what you want. At the same time, the data you collect will help you determine what will be profitable and what won't.

"We place signage on our machines saying a new vending company is here," Wayne D. says. "In a factory setting, we place signs around the building. In an office building, we pass out fliers. On all of them, we say, 'Call our office and tell us what you want.'"

Grabbing the Spotlight

If you're serving a specific community or population in a unique way—as is full-line operator Becky P., with her unique approach to nonnative speakers (more about this in Chapter 15)—or if you're pioneering a new specialty, such as Janice M.'s pantyhose vending concept, the media will want to hear.

"Initially I talked to a reporter from the *Baltimore Business Journal*," explains Janice. "I ran into him at a small-business seminar, and after I started my business, I went through my business cards and gave him a call.

"He wrote a story about me, and I got a new customer from his column," she continues. "Later on, I got a call from Channel 13, our ABC-TV affiliate, which saw the story in the *Baltimore Business Journal*. Then, the *Baltimore Sun* got it from Channel 13. After that, our NBC-TV affiliate did a story, and then the NBC radio affiliate did one. Then the CBS-TV affiliate called and, finally, *Black Enterprise* magazine."

From there, word-of-mouth took off, and Janice's marketing efforts soared. Enthuses the entrepreneur, "Since then, I've done local cable access talk shows, local radio station talk shows, and interviews for the local and national black press."

Introducing yourself to your potential customers serves the same purpose as any other marketing effort: encouraging customers to buy. Blowing your own horn is especially critical in circumstances where a previous operator may not have delivered as high a level of service as you do. While you have obviously convinced the boss you're the best, the only way employees will know is if you tell them.

The key to a press release is grabbing the attention of the reader and providing the who, what, when, where, how, and why of the story in a couple of paragraphs, followed by a general paragraph (sometimes called a boilerplate, since it can typically be used again and again) about your business.

For example, you might see something like the fictitious press release on page 210 for a new marketing concept, starting on top of the page (upper left-hand corner) "For Immediate Release," with the date on the right and the headline centered.

PR can come about by generating press releases about newsworthy information in your business. This does not mean self-indulgent news about you and the inner workings of the company, but about that which you are doing for the benefit of customers, clients, or the community. To let newspaper, magazine, and other editors know what innovative concept you have just introduced or what fundraising endeavor you are taking part in, or what local sports team you are sponsoring, you will write a short, one-page press release.

Good Vibrations

Public relations is a misunderstood and underutilized marketing tool. Although many people define PR as an article in the newspaper, in truth it's much more.

What doesn't work? In vending circles, special events such as grand openings, celebrity appearances, and holiday gatherings are rarely used because they require attractive commercial office space, which startup operators usually lack. It's also generally ineffective to seek media attention. The media's job is covering the "new" or the "novel," and most vending operations are neither. (Caveat: If you're starting an operation in a smaller city, your local newspaper might want to know.) This isn't to say that being the first to sell pantyhose, iPods, or Chinese Food through a vending machine won't make the local press if you are truly doing something unique. Likewise, the new machines with LCD screens warranted an article because they were the first of their kind.

There are ways of grabbing attention in the media with new products or items, with unique ways of selling items, or perhaps with an interesting location. Perhaps you are the first to put a vending machine in city hall or on a major cruise liner or on Mount Rushmore.

Another opportunity for PR is cause-related marketing. As the name implies, cause-related marketing is allying yourself with a worthy cause. To be effective, you must choose causes of interest to your prospects. For example, if your market is health-care clinics, supplying snacks or sodas to a fundraising event for a cancer center will generate some noteworthy attention. After the event, distribute a news release to doctors and clinic administrators telling precisely how your donation benefited the fundraiser.

Be sure to include a rundown of your charitable efforts in your sales proposals, as well. And remember to write off the cost of the inventory on your taxes.

Another vital strategy is one-on-one networking. "To get to know people in the community, get involved in the Optimists, Rotary, VFW, American Legion, Shriners, or other groups or associations," advocates Wayne D.

Joining your local chamber of commerce and shaking hands at monthly after-hours events also helps. Participating in appropriate professional association activities, such as trade shows for corporate procurement directors, is also wise.

Press Release

For Immediate Release November 29, 20xx

XYZ Vending Introduces the Doggie Vending Machine

No, they are not for the pet to use, but the new vending machines provide a line of pet products for the pet owner on the go. Dog food, doggie clean-up bags, doggie bones, squeaky toys, and other favorites for your pooch are now readily available in a handy vending machine. Perfect for anyone traveling with their pup or even out for a walk without an essential item for their four-legged partner, the vending machines are both secure and have the latest in weatherproofing for outdoor locations.

Complete with 20 selections, the Doggie Vending machines have already been spotted in areas near dog-runs, at pet salons, veterinarians' offices, and along popular walking locations. XYZ Vending refills them on a weekly or biweekly basis as necessary and can stock them with a wide selection of canine choices, including leashes and rainwear.

XYZ, founded in 1982, is based in Plumsburgh, Vermont, and serves the entire New England area with vending products that also include... etc., etc.

After completing the basic paragraph on the business, you make sure to include all contact information at the bottom, including address, phone and fax numbers, email addresses, and website.

The point is to provide the news that is of interest to the reader in a concise manner since most editors, publishers, news reporters, and journalists are inundated with press releases and have little time to read each and every one. You can also email press releases if you have the contact info of the editors most likely to be interested in the type of story you are offering. While this example is on the sillier side, the more exciting, unique, and/or innovative your news, the better chance you have of showing up in the media.

Finally, remember to proofread your press releases before sending them to media outlets, most of which can be found through local directories (at libraries or online), or for very local coverage, check the newspaper addresses in the local business listings.

Getting Them to Buy

Whether you're reading this book cover to cover or consulting it step by step, the first thing to know about merchandising is that it's the most important ingredient to your vending operation's success. You can place the nicest machines in the most lucrative locations, but if people don't buy what you're selling, you'll quickly be a has-been.

▲

Fortunately, when it comes to merchandising, you're not going where no one has been before. The tools and advice you'll need are readily available. Best of all, the concepts are easy to learn and apply.

Because food vendors, from snacks and soda to frozen desserts, offer more selections than other specialty machines, we're going to use edibles to explain merchandising basics. However, the techniques you employ to maximize sales in a 20-column snack machine also apply to a 4-column Telecard unit, except it's all less complicated with a 4-column device.

Merchandising 101

Merchandising is determining the exact brand, color, flavor, size, type, and quantity of products your customers want to buy and then presenting them to consumers in a manner that encourages them to do so.

"If we have a facility that has all truck drivers and blue-collar workers, we would not merchandise the same items as in a heavily female area," says full-line operator Wayne D. "In a predominantly female location, we'd offer more low-fat items and diet sodas." In addition to the right products for your customers, proper merchandising means stocking the right amount of items. "If chips are the biggest item, then I need to put more rows of chips in the machine," Wayne D. says. "If a location needs more Cheetos, we'll give you three rows of Cheetos. You may see two or three empty columns, but that's because people are buying more Cheetos."

Of course, product presentation plays a major role in merchandising. "If you put sandwiches in a machine on a Monday, and you don't show up to service the machine until Friday, no one's going to touch that machine after Tuesday," explains full-line operator Becky P.

Just as grocery stores offer specials on certain items to introduce new offerings or encourage increased buying, the same goes for vended items. Using an interactive system such as scratch-off cards to showcase new products makes it more exciting for your clients. You can order them at Scratch Off (www.scratchoff.com) and choose whatever snack item you want to give away. The winner gets the treat, but everyone else's scratch-off reveals promotions of your newest products.

Merchandising is also a matter of making items within the machine stand out. We are a culture highly sensitive to, and influenced by, appearance. A good photo on the machine is worth a thousand words, and may bring you a thousand dollars in sales very quickly. Manufacturing companies are testing out various designs and other means of signage and video broadcasting. The goal is to make the items as tempting as possible at the point of purchase. The LCD monitors now being included in some of the state-of-the art machines can be programmed so that they show either a photo of, or words about, the product . . . or alternate between both, plus provide pricing. Touch-screen information is also being tested and employed for high-end vending machines.

Razzle Dazzle Visual

Both Randall Sutherland and Erik A. Borger concur that because children are attracted to machines, the appearance of the vendor and even a child's ability to watch the operator load everything up can work to your advantage. "My biggest audience is kids; they like the pictures on a lot of my healthy products," says Borger. "I make sure the light bulb isn't burnt out so they can see everything. Kids are kids and they love anything that will take money and spit products out. If I had a dollar for every child who screamed out a 'Whoa!' when seeing me stock my machines, I would be a rich man."

Since it is presumed that a high percentage of people make their selection at the point of purchase, it is right there at eye level that you want to have the product photos or signage. It is also at the machine itself where you obviously want to have the most popular products most prominently displayed. Depending on the machine, this can be done in various ways. Whether it's a superball or a cup of coffee, the consumer wants to see an actual product or product photo that entices them to put money in the machine.

"It would be really cool if machines matched the environments that they are in, more so than they do," says Randall Sutherland. "There are so many things you can do to a machine that make it a really attractive option for the customer. It can be seen as a piece of art, not just this box that dispenses food with brand names all over it. You've got a place like an ad design firm, really hip and cool, and then there's this big ugly machine with Coke branding on it. It doesn't quite fit in."

Sutherland elaborates: "Just imagine if you had your machine outside a surf shop

Route Cards/Delivery Receipts

Route cards or delivery receipts, such as the samples below, are vital to tracking inventory and merchandising effectively.

RTE	SERV #	SERV TYPE		CHANGER AMT	EMPLOYEE							MACH #	MACH DESC		MACH #
3	16	COLLECT		33.00								1879	SNACK LFT		1879
DATE		**WEEK**	**DAY**	**LOCATION**											**RTE/SERV. #**
11/18/99		1	THU												3/16
PRODUCT		G&M	CHIP	CNDY	COOK	SNKS	DEBY	BAG	G&M						**WEEK** 1
PRICE		0.50	0.60	0.65	0.75	0.75	0.60	1.00	0.75						**DAY** THU
PAR		60	99	534	15	15	30	45	20						11/18
FILLS															(CHECK ONE)
															REFUND
DAMAGED															CHARGE
REMOVED															C.O.D.
INVENTORY															
METER 1 READING				**METER 2 READING**				**TESTS**	**REFUNDS**			**CASH COLLECTED**	**AMOUNT**		
CONTACT						**SERV TIME**	**BEG**	**END**	**SLUGS**	**CASH COMM**					
COMPANY NAME MIDWEST VENDING, INC.				**DELIVERY RECEIPT**					**REC. BY:**				**NAME**		

The format of a route card is operation-specific. Many operations begin with one type of route card and adjust it to help merchandise products more effectively. The sample above tracks products by category and sale price.

RTE	SERV #	SERV TYPE	CHANGER AMT	EMPLOYEE				MACH #	MACH DESC	MACH #
DATE		**WEEK** **DAY**	**LOCATION**							**RTE/SERV. #**
PRODUCT										**WEEK**
PRICE										**DAY**
PAR										
FILLS										(CHECK ONE)
										REFUND
DAMAGED										CHARGE
REMOVED										C.O.D.
INVENTORY										
METER 1 READING			**METER 2 READING**				**TESTS**	**REFUNDS**	**CASH COLLECTED**	**AMOUNT**
CONTACT					**SERV TIME**	**BEG**	**END**	**SLUGS**	**CASH COMM**	
COMPANY NAME			**DELIVERY RECEIPT**				**REC. BY:**			**NAME**

Use the blank route card above to assist you with developing appropriate forms of your own.

Source: Midwest Vending Inc.

Machine Collection Form

Although route cards (or delivery receipts) are common in food vending, other specialties use different systems. Instead of a card, this one-page form is used to track inventory and sales for pantyhose vending.

Performed by: _____ Date: _____

Location: _____

	Slot 1 Machine 1	Slot 2 Machine 1	Slot 1 Machine 2	Slot 2 Machine 2
Color/size style				
Previous number in machine				
Number added				
New number in machine				
Money collected				
Short/over/even				
Notes				
Total				

Source: McLean Machines & Co. Inc.

and the graphics were beautiful scenes of surfers riding the waves. Imagine matching any vendor to its environment in an attractive way and you've got yourself another selling point. I recommend going into motorcycle detailing shops and talking to the artists who work there. You can get them to work on a variety of your accounts with extreme creativity and elaborate workmanship."

Also, a lot of companies will give you promotional materials that go with their products, so you can catch the eye of potential customers. There are plenty of things you can do today to enhance the look of a machine.

Stocking by the Numbers

Not surprisingly, the goal of proper merchandising is selling the maximum amount of products while limiting out-of-stock columns. An empty column isn't selling anything, and if it remains empty too long, it essentially sends the message "Don't trust this machine; seek what you want elsewhere."

To know what to stock the very first time, rely on statistics compiled by your suppliers or information you've gathered as part of your market research. To illustrate, let's use the "Quality Snacks Startup Inventory Expenses" form in Chapter 9, which shows a sample starting inventory for a 654-unit snack machine as proposed by Chicago's Five Star Distributors. Regional statistics gathered by Five Star show 54.1 percent of purchases will be candy/snack bars, 15.3 percent will be gum and mints, 9.2 percent pastries, 7.65 percent cookies/crackers/snacks, 7.65 percent salty snacks, and 6.1 percent large single-serving salty snacks.

Therefore, if you were an operator in the Chicago area with a 654-unit snack vendor, the first time you filled the machine you'd need 354 units of candy/snack bars,

---

High-Tech Monitoring Companies

As mentioned earlier, more vending companies are going more high tech. ProTel, a company in Lakeland, Florida, was among the first companies to equip vending operators with a remote monitoring system which includes a monitor located at the machine and management software at your base office. Together the combined devices allow operators to monitor their machines from afar. Jennifer Berdoll Wammack relies heavily on the USA Technology system that tracks and relays detailed sales information every 24 hours to her email account.

100 units of gum and mints, 60 units of pastries, 50 units of cookies/crackers/snacks, 50 units of salty snacks, and 40 units of large single-serving salty snacks.

As you will recall from Chapter 11, it is recommended that a machine be serviced (filled) when 50 percent of its products have sold. Why fill a machine when it's half-empty? Industry statistics show that servicing a machine when 50 percent of its products are gone minimizes the number of empty spirals and, therefore, lost sales.

In addition to minimizing empties, servicing at 50 percent (rather than 60, 70, or 80 percent) maximizes your income/expense ratio. "We strive to make at least $100 per 500-unit snack machine at every servicing," notes Wayne D. "If you merchandise correctly, you should be able to make $100 every time you open a machine."

Another way to understand these concepts is by thinking of them in terms of your local grocery store. "If a grocery store carries Charmin toilet tissue, employees load shelves using a space-to-sales ratio," Wayne says. "They know through their data what they need on the shelves every day and every week. A vending company is the same. If an operator doesn't do space-to-sales ratios, then he's continuously filling that machine."

Although operators and experts recommend relying on your distributor's statistics to start, you should develop your own data for each vendor as quickly as possible. Keep track of sales each time you open a machine using route cards (also called delivery receipts) or machine collection forms, such as the samples shown on pages 214 and 215.

If you have joined the computer age, as recommended in Chapter 7, transfer information from the route cards to your computer. If not, use a ledger book to track information by hand.

Managing Your Stash

As you may have already guessed from reviewing the "Quality Snacks Startup Inventory Expenses" form in Chapter 9, within each product category you'll be stocking a variety of different items. The reason for stocking different items within each category is simple: Customers want variety.

While figuring out the right merchandising strategies on an item-by-item basis is still somewhat a matter of trial and error, a fact-based system called category management has begun to catch on in the vending industry. According to *Vending Times*, category management is already familiar to mass-market retailers and uses a research-based approach to stocking machines in a manner that makes the most money from the space available. See the "Category Shelf and Location Assignment" form on page 218.

As noted by *Vending Times*, research by Nabisco Inc. says when selecting items within each category, consider each of them as belonging to one of three groups:

1. *Core.* Items that will be in every one of your machines every day; these should occupy about 20 percent of available slots.

2. *Cycle.* Items that will appear in every machine every day within specific time frames or menu cycles; these include leading consumer brands in each category and products that present different taste profiles, as well as branded new products. These should occupy about 60 percent of machine-selling space.

3. *Choice.* "Wildcard" items placed in machines to serve requests at a given location; to improve "turns" (in other words, sales), Nabisco recommends limiting the "choice" items to three products or brands.

Again, relying on your suppliers for guidance the first time you fill your vendors, and carefully tracking sales at each location, allows you to fine-tune menus to appeal to the greatest number of customers. See the "Example of Core, Cycle, and Choice Product for 45-Select Machine" on page 219.

As we discussed before, there are good reasons to pay attention to the awareness your distributor has of your local audience, but your copious attention to addressing customer cravings, recording what requests result in sales (remember Randall Sutherland's tattletale of the women requesting diet products for viewing only), and analyzing all your data from a pulled-back perspective biannually will give the most accurate guidance on what you should stock.

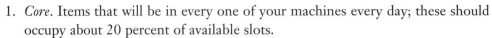

Category Shelf and Location Assignment

LSS Salty Snacks		LSS Salty Snacks		LSS Salty Snacks		LSS Salty Snacks		LSS Salty Snacks		Salty Snacks	13
Salty Snack		Salty Snack		Salty Snack		Salty Snack		Salty Snack		Crackers	3
Bagged Cracker		Bagged Cookie		Salty Snack		Salty Snack		Microwave Popcorn		Cookies	4
Choc. Candy	Choc. Candy	Choc. Candy	Choc. Candy	Choc. Candy	Choc. Candy	Choc. Candy	Choc. Candy	Choc. Candy	Choc. Candy	Chocolate Candy	10
										Nonchocolate Candy	2
Non Choc. Candy	Non Choc. Candy	Nuts	Cracker Sandwich	Cracker Sandwich	Granola Bar	Break-fast Bar	Pastry	Sleeve Cookies	Sleeve Cookies	Nuts	1
										Granola/ Breakfast Bars	2
Pastry		Pastry		Pastry		Pastry		Large Cookie		Pastry	5
										Gum	3
Gum		Gum		Gum		Hard Roll Candy		Hard Roll Candy		Hard Roll Candy	2
										Total	45

Example of Core, Cycle, and Choice Product for 45-Select Machine

Fritos		Cheetos Snacks		Doritos Snacks		LSS Salty Snacks		LSS Salty Snacks	
Salty Snacks		Salty Snacks		Salty Snacks		Salty Snacks		Salty Snacks	
Bagged Crackers		Bagged Cookies		Salty Snacks		Salty Snacks Premium		Microwave Popcorn	
Reese's PBC	Snickers	M&M Peanuts	Choc. Candy	Choc. Candy	Choc. Candy	Choc. Candy	Choc. Candy	Choc. Candy	Choc. Candy
Non Choc. Candy	Non Choc. Candy	Nuts	Cracker Sand-wich	Cracker Sand-wich	Granola Bar	Break-fast Bar	Pastry	Oreo	Sleeve Cookies
Pastry		Pastry		Pastry		Pastry		Large Cookies	
Gum		Gum		Gum		Hard Roll Candy		Hard Roll Candy	

Core=9 spirals (20% of machine)

Cycle=28 spirals (62% of machine)

Choice=8 spirals (18% of machine)

Empty Avoidance

In the real world, nothing is as simple as fact-based merchandising plans. For instance, just because a machine holds 60 units of pastries doesn't mean you will sell enough pastries every two weeks at every location to keep them from going beyond their freshness dates. To compensate, use one of the oldest tricks in the book: Fill only a portion of the slower-moving column with pastries and the balance of the column with something else. Putting something that is popular behind the slower selling item will make sure that the column stays full and that the few items that need to sell in a short amount of time will stay fresh.

Fun Fact

When President Obama signed the Federal Health Care Reform Act in March 2010, along with it came a mandatory calorie disclosure at the point of sale for vending operators with 20 or more machines. As you know from much of the material we've covered, most people now want to see nutritional information, preferably on the front of the package. But don't fret if you've got less than 20 machines. You can volunteer to become subject to new federal menu labeling requirements. View details on signing up here: www.fda.gov/Food/LabelingNutrition/ucm217762.htm.

▲

Pulling Product

Sometimes no matter what merchandising alternatives you try, sales just aren't cutting it. In such cases, you may be faced with tough choices. You may elect to set a minimum, whereby the location guarantees a minimum amount of sales. If the customer doesn't meet the minimum, you need to evaluate the reasons. Perhaps some

> ### Bright Idea
> For assistance with your first planogram, turn to a product sales representative for a major vending player, such as Nabisco Inc. Sales reps are familiar with planogramming and can quickly get you up and running.

selections should be changed. Perhaps the location of the machine should be moved within the same facility to a busier area. You need to discuss the possibilities. Of course if a McDonald's just opened next door, you may have the answer to your problem. This may mean stocking the machine with something that McDonald's doesn't sell, or bringing in a new machine.

"If you dialogue with your clients, an explanation will usually become clear," says B.J. "You need to be more price competitive, or you need to put a different selection in. Whatever it is, you try to work it out first, and then, if there's no hope, you're just going to have to pull [your vendors]. By that time, you should have made the client aware of your decision," he continues. "It's pretty tough. That's part of where being a good salesman comes in. As long as you're upfront with the client, you're most likely to develop some type of relationship. You always hate to lose clients, but sometimes it's unavoidable."

Of course, it's highly advisable that if you foresee pulling a machine, you ramp up your placement efforts and have a place in mind to move the machine. A machine sitting in your garage is definitely not going to make you any money.

Planning It Out

With so many variables to consider, perhaps you're wondering if there's any sort of road map that can help you reach your proper merchandising goals. Enter the ink-on-paper tool known as a planogram. There are also software programs that can help you with planograms and save you time. RouteSail® Millenia from Validata® (www.validata.com) is one of the software programs that can make planogramming (plus route mapping and other aspects of your business) much easier once you get used to it.

As stated earlier, a planogram is a graphic display of your merchandising plan. In other words, you draw a rectangle that represents a machine, divide it up into columns according to your machine's layout, and write the names of individual items in the slots. More specifically, you place items in slots using the core, cycle, and choice columns as discussed earlier. Many operators even take it a step further by planogramming for machines based in different demographic areas.

"We have a different planogram for schools than for office buildings," comments Wayne D. "In a 20-column machine, for example, there will be 12 that are mandatory, 2 that are brand of the week, and 6 that are at the route person's discretion. Based on our sales statistics, we know what our 10 or 12 top selling items are. Those 10 or 12 will be basically the same in every location."

Does this mean you need a different planogram for each machine? Not necessarily. Depending on your vending specialty, and the areas you serve, you can determine if they are similar enough to use the same planogram. Some vending operators have a basic plan with a few tweaks here and there for certain locations.

Changing the Plan

Operators and experts suggest reviewing all your sales figures regularly and adjusting your planograms accordingly. How often you do this depends on your operation, but monthly reviews are most common.

"Variety is the life blood of vending," emphasizes broker Jim Patterson of Patterson Co. "If the customer can memorize the machine before he goes there, the operator's in trouble because he can make a decision from his desk.

"Vending originally grew from forced coffee breaks," he continues. "But it's changing to become more customer demand–oriented, so operators need to be more sensitive to consumers' demands and wants. Even among the products that need to be there, you have to move them around. If a customer sees the same product in the same slot, they may think that it never sells and it's still there when, in fact, it's always there because it moves so well."

Like Wayne D., Patterson evokes the grocery store model. "Just like a grocery

Stat Fact

The 2011 "State of the Coffee Industry Report" by Elliot Maras of Vending Market Watch reveals that though economic conditions continue to impact office coffee service (OCS) along with most industries, it has suffered less since the start of the recession than the rest of the vending industry. Additional findings from the study include:

- In 2011, coffee consumption increased in all age groups in the study (ages 18 through 39).
- A significant portion of total coffee consumption is the gourmet variety, indicating that consumers want to maintain coffee quality even in an uncertain economy.
- 60 percent of all coffee drinking employees consider free coffee an employee benefit.

store resets the store periodically, you need to reset the machine and move products from column to column."

By moving items around, you maintain the same sales of popular favorites, but you also force the buyer who is always looking at the same column, or has the number of his or her favorite item memorized, to look at some of the other products. This may cause them to try something new.

Adding Excitement

In addition to the basics we've discussed, merchandising includes promoting products or concepts. For example, placing clear-plastic promotional stickers, known as "static clings," on your vendors highlights certain items. Supplied by your sales rep or your product broker, static clings can publicize a consumer contest, a single product, a particular brand, or a concept such as the ubiquitous fast-food "value meal"—buying a sandwich, side item, and a beverage.

Also available from suppliers are posters you may ask clients to display in various areas. Such posters promote individual items, the idea of purchasing from a vending machine, or the suggestion to buy a product from your machines to take home.

When it comes to contests, you can come up with your own or work with your suppliers. In vending, a contest is generally a random stickering of products in a category or column you wish to promote; the customer who buys the winning item earns a prize. Stickers can be as simple as small labels you purchase at any office supply store.

"We'll provide X winning stickers and X number of prizes, such as T-shirts," says Peterson. "Then we either give you the prizes or list a toll-free number on the sticker that the consumer calls to redeem the prize themselves."

To set up a contest yourself, affix a vending token or coupon to packages. While you won't make any cash on items purchased with the tokens, you'll encourage more usage of your machines and generate immeasurable goodwill. If you go the sticker route, you don't have to give away the farm. "We sticker items and the lucky sticker wins something like a two-liter bottle of pop," Wayne D. says.

Especially when you're new to a location, working with suppliers on co-sponsoring promotions helps draw customers who might not otherwise use your machines. "We work with our suppliers to offer a two-for-one special on a certain type of candy bar," asserts Wayne. "We put up signage so it is promotional for our supplier, too."

Whatever methods you use to add excitement, just do it. (For some ideas, see page 223.) "It's important you don't just put product into your machine," asserts John Ochi of Five Star Distributors. "Spotlight it to bring it to your customers' attention."

Special Promotions

The purpose. . . to build a better business relationship with the clients and to move more product! Place a note on the front of the machine for special promotions or promotional-priced items. Keep holidays and the day of the week in mind for special location promotions.

Fantastic February

All candy is on sale

ONLY **50¢**

Stock Up!   Stock Up!

MMM. . . *Muffin Monday*

The Vending Company
will be bringing muffins for everyone on:
Monday, May 1st

"Thank you for your business"

Doughnuts

will be supplied **Wednesday**

the 4th of July. . .

Courtesy of *The Vending Company.*
Thank you for your business!

PIZZA PARTY FRIDAY!

Pizza will be served
Friday, October 7th
courtesy of
The Vending Company

"It is just our way of saying THANKS!"

Win Gift Certificates

for three movie rentals
or **$10** at Denny's
or 2 tickets for the hockey game.
**Check your purchase for a
winner's sticker!**

Redeem your prize by calling
The Vending Company at 555-1234.

Win a pair of
Movie Tickets

If your purchase
has the winning
sticker, take it to
the receptionist,
and pick up your
prize!

Just a special
"Thank you" from
The Vending Company

TERRIFIC TUESDAY!

Ten cents for coffee

Thank you for your business, from
The Vending Company

Source: The Vending Connection

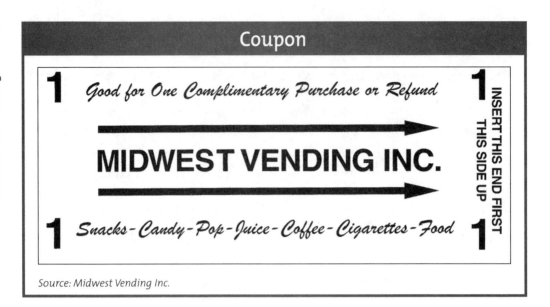

Coupon

1 *Good for One Complimentary Purchase or Refund* **1**

MIDWEST VENDING INC.

INSERT THIS END FIRST
THIS SIDE UP

1 *Snacks - Candy - Pop - Juice - Coffee - Cigarettes - Food* **1**

Source: Midwest Vending Inc.

Free Vend Allure

Another way to encourage customer loyalty is by placing your machines on "free vend" under given circumstances. Just as the name implies, a machine set to free vend dispenses product without requiring customers to insert any money.

Because free vend can quickly put you in the red, you'll want to work with your clients to limit the number of free-vend customers. For example, your clients can use free vend during an after-hours meeting as a way to encourage and reward attendance. When the cost of a free vend is significant, a reduction in a location's commission is a common method used to offset the loss.

Couponing Arrives

The advent of the bill acceptor has provided operators with a valuable promotional opportunity that was impossible before. Because newer bill acceptors are actually small computers that read the metallic content of paper currency, they can be set to read a coupon that has an operation-specific metallic signature.

In the past, vending operators passed out coin-shaped tokens to promote usage of their machines. However, tokens are generic, which means the customer can use them in any machine. This is especially problematic when more than one operation services a location, such as when you handle snacks and a bottler supplies sodas.

Although coupons cost more than tokens because bill acceptor companies charge operators for software that's needed to program a machine, according to industry magazine *Automatic Merchandiser*, the use of coupons has increased some operators' overall sales as much as 25 percent.

"We may give a client ten coupons a week or ten a quarter," says Wayne D. "The coupons allow customers to take one item, regardless of cost. In some cases, we sell the coupons to clients at a reduced cost and they use them as employee rewards or incentives, such as for meeting productivity quotas or delivery deadlines. Before, when we used the free-vend system, people would take home extra items."

Coupons are also reducing refund costs significantly. As you'll learn in Chapter 15, a large part of good vending customer service is providing refunds for lost coins and bills. While the most common practice is to refund in cash, nothing guarantees the cash will be reinserted into your machines. "Coupons pretty much eliminated our refund problem," says Wayne.

14

Dream Team
Networking, Social Media, and Marketing

The powers of face-to-face networking, specific, targeted use of social media, and marketing combine to make a tool like no other. The results you'll get with minimal financial investment and lots of sweat equity can't be purchased.

▲

The Game Is Changing

Some of the key factors in growing your business are visibility, quality, consistency, and the ability to control the speed of your business's growth so that it runs just ahead of your customers' needs. Even if you attend to all these categories diligently, you've got to put a hefty commitment into networking to grow a solid reputation in your community.

Thrusting your business card into every new person's hand you meet, along with touting your wonderful vending services, isn't the way to gain ground with discerning possible clients. The old-fashioned way for people to choose service providers was simply to give their business to the few people in their immediate circle, or neighborhood, because they were the only option. Back in the days when there was only one grocer, cleaner, or baker in town, the choice was clear, and with that choice came the building of a solid relationship—or there was trouble. Additionally, the providers' products and services had better be good when every one of their customers was one of their neighbors, more or less.

Keep It Close to Home

Gary Vaynerchuk's book *The Thank You Economy* focuses on bringing the mom and pop warmth and quality back to today's business ethic with the modern tools found in various social media venues. His round-the-clock work ethic and understanding of how to satisfy customer desires in this unique era of online socializing have made him one of the leaders in creating and maintaining solid business relationships through social media. Check out his book, blog, web TV show, and businesses for inspiration (www.tv.winelibrary.com, www.garyvaynerchuk.com, www.obsessedtv.com, and www. vaynermedia.com).

Today, with so many choices and empty promises, not to mention the personal budgeting challenges most of us have faced in the last five years, confidence in service providers is mandatory. People now put their money where they find value mixed with sincere connections and follow-through, and often choose the most personal connections for business they can find. A basic idea is that it's good to know where someone lives if you entrust them with large amounts of money. That much hasn't changed. The difference now is the array of tools available to professionals for building personal relationships, which have the capacity to convert to business and retain old-fashioned standards.

Whether you choose to use one or all the methods we outline for you, be aware that the potency of your invested time will be most powerfully leveraged by applying quality, consistency, generosity, and sincerity to each of your connections. Now we'll review the methods and venues you can use to generate business.

The Magic Combination

Face-to-face networking, online networking through social media channels, and social media marketing through gifts make the magic combination that can connect you to more of your market and create a different kind of relationship with your clients than you can establish with traditional marketing and just showing up for the job (see "Networks Connections" on page 231 to see how these work together).

Each one of these facets works a part of the trio that is essential for the new kind of relationship entrepreneurs are having with their clients. Business and pleasure are mixed as gifts of special interest are shared through hobby sites and social groups and business is created.

Entrée, Side Dish, Dessert

Prioritizing which tools to put the most energy into is important, as is understanding which tool to use for each part of building business relationships. You don't want to spend hours and hours online creating wonderful, free tutorials for your audience if you haven't done any face-to-face networking to create a substantial persona behind the "virtual you."

Entrée

Think of actual, physical networking (the act of getting out of the house and showing up at events, ready to be an engaging, helpful, interested guest) as your entrée. Commit yourself to showing up at one event per week, dressed in your best impression outfit, and prepared to sincerely get to know people and learn about their goals. The purpose of going to these events is not to tell everyone how great your service is. It's to find out what the guests' needs are, what's going on in their lives, and how you can help them achieve their goals. Week after week, go back and build on those relationships, asking about the details of people's progress.

Wonderful, Addictive You

Most people want to be around someone who always cares how the other person's life is going, is in their corner, and helps them achieve their goals. In fact, they often feel indebted to that person and will go out of their way to return the generosity. You're setting yourself up to be someone other people want to be near because they feel good about themselves when they're around you. We're not trying to coach you to pretend to like people so you can get their business, rather, to get you to become part of what the best networking has to offer. This is simply how it works.

This is not going to work if you don't care about people or have a great work ethic. With all friendships that result in business, you've got to keep the same level of caring up and give that customer service all you've got. At that point everyone will know everyone else in your groups and quality service reputations will spread quickly (and negative ones twice as fast), which can be extra inspiration to throw in some TLC. If you're not a natural "people person" or particularly social, you'll start gaining an appreciation for the process as you practice, and may even start having fun.

Side Dish

In-person networking can be greatly complemented before or after events by using blogs and social connection sites such as Yelp, Meetup, and Facebook to:

- Brief members on news about the group
- Show off photos of the event
- Announce future engagements and speakers
- Re-engage group members on related topics for further online discussion
- Expose members of the group to elements of your business that would help them (if those elements relate to what people need or want)
- Post industry news links from other sites
- Review products, services, and places your audience uses

Go find your tribe (the group of like-minded thinkers out there you resonate with and for whom your products or service are geared) online (see Meetup information below on how), get to know them in person, build the relationships by creating valuable content for them to keep growing and connecting between events, use that content to attract an even wider social sphere, and turn all this into real-life connections. And so the cycle goes. But the key is giving. Read on to understand how and why.

Dessert

Think of the business you're given as dessert after eating your veggies and a nutritious main dish; it's something you can't sit down to dinner expecting, but you feel lucky if you get it. Just keep eating your dinner faithfully and consistently and you will gain a certain amount of dessert. We've provided a visual of how the cycle works on page 231.

Face-to-Face Networking

Good old-fashioned socializing can turn into business. But without direction or clear plans for how to convert social connections into business, you might as well stay home.

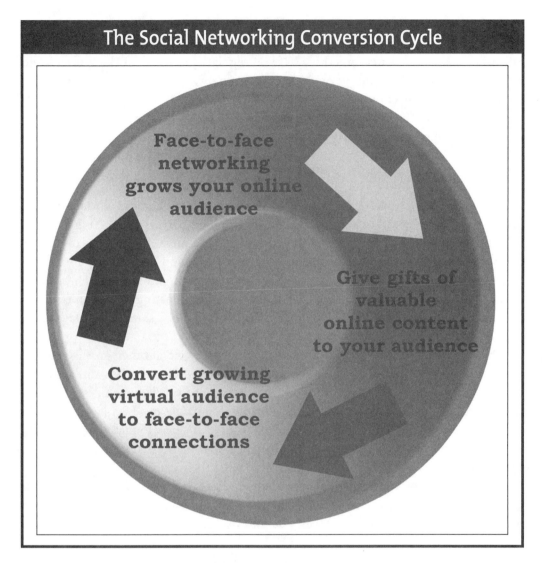

The Social Networking Conversion Cycle

Face-to-face networking grows your online audience

Give gifts of valuable online content to your audience

Convert growing virtual audience to face-to-face connections

In-person networking is still the strongest way to create business potential and is one of the reasons people choose their relatives and friends rather than strangers for projects—they've had a good long time to observe them and would rather give business to someone predictable. There is also a need for most people to invest their dollars locally, whether that means in family, friends, or their own community. The idea of "keeping it in the family" translates to solidly grown professional circles, networking communities, and trade organizations where people have had to go the distance over time to prove to one another that their work ethics are admirable.

People are either growing or nurturing their families (or networks) every day. Those networks for professionals are much like family and share similar functions.

For your network to have value, you need to care about what's going on in the lives of your "friends," express it, and become an asset to them (unlike that friend who only calls when he or she wants something). If you regularly go to networking events and offer your expertise, depending on which type of networks you join, you can expect to create solid connections that will eventually turn into business. When you give and are helpful and thoughtful, and people have experienced your reliable, consistent presence, you'll be thought of when it comes time to refer business.

Meetup

There are many trade organizations and clubs in which you can do face-to-face networking, but Meetup (www.meetup.com) is a unique virtual connecting site that transitions online socializing into actual gatherings. You can take advantage of the far-reaching demographic sorting of Meetup and meet any kind of audience your heart desires through the site. It is a social site, but many groups gather based on business or trade interests and business is likely occurring at those meetings. But don't go into using Meetup as a mass marketing campaign, because you'll be shunned, and it's rude, to boot.

The groups of people that gather and connect with one another on this site are special interest types who for the most part want to find one another and socialize. If you type in a special interest that you have and where you live, you'll see a list of established groups in your area that are already socializing and having a grand old time. If several groups are gathering on a similar topic, it's best to pick the group with the most members and the most active gatherings. If you join that group you can see a list of its past events, how many attended, and what their comments were afterward.

To make the most of Meetup for networking purposes, choose a few groups of your target audience and start going to their events, while following the words of wisdom from master networker Dr. Ivan Misner below.

Tips from the King of Networking

We asked Ivan Misner, founder and chairman of BNI, the world's largest business networking organization, to speak about how vending operators can use the face-to-face networking process to their best advantage. Last year alone, BNI generated 6.5 million referrals resulting in $2.8 billion worth of business for its members. Misner offers these tips for networking results.

Join several types of casual contact networks such as chambers of commerce, Rotary and Kiwanis clubs to diversify your demographic connections and avoid putting all your eggs in one basket. Misner likens only networking with one group to investing in the same kind of stock throughout your investment portfolio, which is not conducive to averaging growth. Misner explains, "In these types of organizations you'll have the opportunity for slow growth and high visibility. Even though Kiwanis clubs don't really conduct business (and in some you can get fined for trying to), you'll be rubbing shoulders with a lot of successful people while contributing public service and building your community presence."

"Later when you're established it's very beneficial to serve on the boards of nonprofits, but I wouldn't recommend that to anyone first starting out because they usually expect substantial financial contributions and your growth will be very slow," says Misner, who advises those building their businesses to join knowledge networks, professional associations specific to your audience (such as office manager and human resource professional organizations), and other nationally known professional groups. Misner also recommends sponsoring events or portions of events, which will get your business recognition, and adds, "When you're a sponsor, there is no hidden agenda and it's clear you're there to do business.

"BNI is one such professional organization," Misner points out, "with a sole purpose to generate business through referrals. We have strong contact networks that meet weekly, with opportunities to speak about one's business to the group at each meeting. A vending operator would be the one tradesperson of that type in his or her network and could generate business by appealing to subgroups within the networks they join. For example, one week the operator may talk about how their service would benefit school boards with a special school-focused program, and the next week the operator could highlight how large office corporations would benefit from the healthy choices their machines offer. About every three or four months each person gets to speak for a longer period (15 minutes) than at the weekly meetings (about five minutes), and that would be the time to really expand on what they do."

The 12 x 12 x 12 Rule

Misner teaches new networkers to use these three steps to ensure they're making the most of their first impressions.

1. *12 feet away*

    "How do you come across from 12 feet away at a networking event? You don't have to wear a three-piece suit, but you do have to dress the part for your profession. I remember a competent accountant who always came to events wearing a Hawaiian shirt and sandals, calling himself 'the casual accountant.' I remember thinking that I'd never refer this guy to a client because it's a reflection on me. It's sad, but first impressions count and if you're trying to do business with big corporations and dress inappropriate to your profession, that's networking suicide."

▲

2. *12 inches away*

Misner sees a lot of people whining about the difficult economy once they get into one-to-one conversations at events and points out that when someone talks about how bad business is during a recession it doesn't do any good because people don't care. Some of them have similar problems and others are just glad you're worse off than they are. Misner advises eventgoers to stop whining and be positive, adding, "Surveys consistently show that one of the leading characteristics of master networkers is a positive attitude."

3. *Your first 12 words*

To elicit interest and instigate probing curiosity Misner says the first 12 words that come out of your mouth after a face-to-face introduction should be attention getters and make people curious. Misner says the goal is to get the listener to ask "How do you do that?" If your unique selling proposition is reflected in an engaging statement such as Misner's: "BNI's mission is to help people work less, make more, and create referrals for life," people will want to find out more about your business than its superficial representation conveyed through small talk. Note that Misner's first words to a listener convey a message of giving.

Post Event Follow-Up

Misner encourages networkers to absolutely follow up after events, but to make sure to choose a method that they'll follow through on, stressing that a stack of blank notes intended to be written but weren't, or were delayed, doesn't do any good. He says although handwritten notes are the best choice for post event follow-up, he hates actually writing them and has found a way to make it easy. "I use an online service that has a scan of my handwriting (which is turned into a font) that enables me to just go online, type what I want the card to say, and then Send Out Cards (www.sendoutcards.com) creates this nicely written card and sends it for me," Misner says. "You can also just pick up the phone and tell the person you met what a pleasure it was and express interest in learning more about them. Remember that part about learning more about them, rather than just telling them more about you."

The VCP Process®

"The necessary, linear stages of growing a solid business relationship through networking are first visibility, then credibility, and finally profitability," says Misner. "You first must make yourself visible by showing up and letting people know what you do and who you are. Second, build your credibility by matching your message and intention with action, quality work, and professional ethics that are traceable. Third, you'll begin to profit as confidence is built on your growing reputation as a reliable, trustworthy, and predictable service provider."

Appropriate Gratitude and Acknowledgment

Misner believes in recognizing referrals, whether it's with a card, gift basket, or something more substantial for those people who have really given you a lot and coaches gift givers to think of author Dr. Tony Alessandra's platinum rule and treat the receiver the way they want to be treated, not the way you want to be treated. Misner says, "Give them something that is uniquely important to them, not just something that you think is nice. To know what that is you have to be observant and a good listener."

Combining Social Media with Face-to-Face Networking

"I remember this kid who drove an hour to interview me in Stockholm for a newspaper," says Misner. "He spent the first 20 minutes letting me know what an arcane, buggy whip system he thought face-to-face networking was. He thought online social networking was the best way to connect for business. I asked him why he just drove an hour to meet me, and he sheepishly replied that his boss said he had to interview me and a face-to-face interview is always better than using the phone or email. Point made.

"Online networks will never replace having actual conversations replete with eye contact and shaking hands, but it can be an essential, complementary tool. You can prime attendees online before meetings to get them interested in your topics, invite them to come hear you speak, inform them about what's going on in your organization, and let them know who will be guests or visitors to the event."

For more tips and a thorough study of this process, pick up a copy of Misner's *New York Times* bestselling *Networking Like a Pro* and visit www.bni.com.

Using Social Media for Growth

Think of the knowledge you currently have about vending, and related industries attracted to vending, as a gift to attract interest to your offerings. The old saying "You can catch more flies with honey" comes to mind. Deciding to only use social media networking to create business is a shortsighted perspective on the vast potential that the whole system can offer if you focus on two important goals: use the whole system (a sampling of the major sites and their free tools combined with in-person networking), and give, give, give. If you focus on exposing the target market and related audiences to your knowledge using all the tools available, you will build quite a reputation and will for the most part do it without fees.

Captive Audiences

Nielsen's 2011 "State of the Media: Social Media Report" tallied up facts that show just how important engaging consumers online really is.

○ Americans online spend 23 percent of their time on social networks and blogs.

○ Americans spend more time on Facebook than they do on any other website.

○ Tumblr nearly has tripled its audience since 2010, becoming an emerging player in social media.

○ 40 percent of social media users access the sites by mobile phones.

○ Men are the heaviest online video users, streaming more videos and watching them longer.

○ 70 percent of active online social networkers shop online.

○ Blogger, the second most accessed site, boasts users with the highest average income of $75,000.

Read the rest of the study at http://blog.nielsen.com/nielsenwire/social.

What Do You Know? What Can You Give?

Let's suppose for a minute that you're trying to capture accounts in office parks and would like to appeal to the office managers who make the vending decisions. We're going to give you a list of assignments that you can tackle each night when you come home from work, with minimal time requirements, to begin creating your social media presence. If your target market is something other than office parks, then change the topic accordingly.

Make a list of topics you have knowledge about that would help your target market of office managers or human resource personnel, for they will be the ones who get the idea to hire you after they see how wonderful you are. Some operators who offer knowledge through social media only target other operators, which is helpful to them and may get you referrals, but it doesn't capture the main audience you need to be visible to. Here is a sample list of topics:

- How "free" vending motivates employees
- Reward systems manage idle time
- Turn lunch and break rooms into media centers
- Seven tips for throwing a great company party
- Troublemaking employees lower morale; what to do
- Is your office haunted? Take the test and find out
- Egg hunts and matzo balls —keeping religion out of office décor
- Valentine's Day special report: Office romances, when to interfere

Humor and Originality Go a Long Way

How will you ensure that your business doesn't blend in with the woodwork? No one wants to hear boring ad copy or sales pitches. And they really won't hear or see something that is generic, floating in a sea of other generic ads. There's a reason why there are entire festivals dedicated to viewing the most outrageous commercials and ad campaigns. The clever, funny, shocking, or bizarre ad is remembered. We're not suggesting that you become an online shock jock just to get attention, but there are ways to make a point other than the barrage of beige ad communications that bore consumers to death or even insult them by being stupid and condescending.

Recently a new clothing store owner getting ready for a grand opening decided she needed to do something drastic to attract customers. She posted online announcements that the first 50 customers in the door on grand opening day would be outfitted from head to toe for free, with one catch: everyone waiting in line to get free clothes had to be in their underwear only, ready to try clothes on. No one wearing clothes or coats over their undergarments would be considered for the promotion. When a local news station got wind of the event (no doubt alerted by the store owner), cameras covered the shivering customers standing in line in their skivvies, all the way down the block. Talk about press! That one campaign got the store enough coverage to be talked about for months.

You don't have to go to such lengths or let go of as much inventory as that store owner did, but if you make your campaigns, alerts, events, and specials unusual, you'll get more attention for your efforts.

Why not try making funny ads based on the worst-case scenarios that occur when people don't have access to snacks and drinks? Do office workers go ballistic with one another when they don't get food? Do they steal one another's lunches from the company break room? Do they fall asleep under their desks? If your vending products are film, aspirin, tattoos, or toys in capsules, translate the idea accordingly. You don't have to be a great graphic designer to create a photo cartoon. Just take some photos of willing friends posing as actors in your ad charade and then insert hilarious thought and speech bubbles into the scene using a digital camera and the simple editing program your computer probably already has on it. When you're finished you can use the ad online and as a promotional postcard. If you don't have the equipment, hire a graphic design student from a local college to bring your idea to life for less than the going rate.

Have contests for your current customers, photograph the contest reactions and activity, and make a slideshow from the photos with funny captions (be careful not to offend anyone). Post the slideshow online and announce with signage on your vending machine where it can be viewed. Ask people to cross post your show and write to popular bloggers requesting the same.

What Now? Where to Illuminate Your Talents

The next step is to make a list of the ways you'll present these topics and the places where they will capture your desired crowd. These are the ways we suggest you get started, but the options are endless:

- *www.youtube.com*. Create a simple video tutorial with an inexpensive video camera or digital camera. The Kodak Easyshare runs about $100 and just as the name says, is easy to use and share with. Upload the video to YouTube. You'll be asked to create a channel, which you should name the same as your business if you want the same traffic directed toward it. Another option is to name it something such as "Corporate Office Management Tips Houston Texas [or wherever you are]."

- *www.wordpress.com and www.blogger.com*. Set up a blog on www.wordpress.com and/or www.blogger.com and write short, useful articles on your topic list. Post them every few days. Take photos that relate to the post and include them in your feature. The instructions on both sites include a help search box to use if you get stuck; if you can't find what you need there, these are such popular blog sites that a Google search will yield multiple answers to your questions.

  Make sure to enable readers to subscribe to your blog via email. That way they'll be alerted every time you post a new entry. Announce your new blog on Facebook and in all the venues where you hold a virtual presence, encouraging people to subscribe for free tutorials.

- *www.facebook.com*. Facebook is the most popular social information exchange site, with 61 percent of its users 35 and older, so it's a good bet for getting massive exposure. But it's easy to get lost in the shuffle if you don't post quality content. Create a fan page for your business and prominently display links to your other channels, blogs, and profiles. Collect "friends" on Facebook by doing key word industry searches and displaying a genuine curiosity about what people do and want.

Create polls on Facebook on scintillating topics related to your mission and watch the fun begin as users become interested in you. Try finding controversial, interesting, but not off-color news headlines about vending, nutrition, and office politics. Make sure your services and products are displayed during these interactions in an engaging, classy way that invites exploration.

Facebook has inexpensive, pay-per-click ads for varying rates that work well for specific, focused campaigns. Consider trying an inexpensive one to see if you get any hits.

Always Treat 'Em Right

If the key to attracting new accounts is a good reputation and giving people that which is valuable to them, then customer service is the key to building the reputation every successful vendor needs.

This trend is echoed in the business world at large. From the smallest startup to the halls of corporate conglomerates, the

▲

mantra for the millennium is customer service. Once thought of only as a department, it's now considered an essential element in every corporation's culture.

Service Never Sleeps

Jennifer Berdoll Wammack offers service 24 hours a day at her vendor, and seven days a week, from 9:00 A.M. to 7:00 P.M., in her gift shop. She gives out samples and educates people about pecans. Most people don't know that there are many varieties of pecans, just as there are many apple varieties. The key to quality customer service is listening and researching. You need to listen to what customers say, whether it is a complaint, a request for a product, or even praise for a job well done; you also need to research what your future customers need. Customer service is based on the 80-20 concept in business that says that 80 percent of your business will come from existing customers and 20 percent from new customers. You do not want to continue having to find new customers, which can always be more costly. By appeasing your existing customers, you are maintaining the base of your business—this is not only true in the vending industry, but in most businesses. Therefore, the $20 of freebies you give to compensate a dissatisfied customer is still cheaper than the $50 it will cost you to find a new customer.

From Start to Finish

For full-line operator Becky P., outstanding customer service means taking the initiative to greet customers and discuss their needs. "When I walk into the vending room, I always say, 'Good morning, good afternoon, how is everybody?' "

As she begins servicing her machines, Becky's always on the lookout for ways to reach out. "If someone walks up to a machine next to me and makes a purchase, I always thank them. I can't tell you how many times they'll turn around and say, 'For what?' or they think I'm being sarcastic. And I'll say, 'You thank your customers. You're my customer, so I'm thanking you.'

"They don't think of it that way," she continues. "They think of the vending machine as being cold. Right then and there, you've taken that cold, inanimate machine and given it a personality. They are going to think of your smiling face and you thanking them when they make their next purchase."

The same goes for when a customer interrupts her from servicing a machine. "If a customer comes up and asks, 'Can I get something out?' my response is always 'I'd be thrilled to serve you personally' and then I hand them the item they're interested in. And then, I always, always, always thank them."

Education Is the Most Powerful Tool of All

Stock your shelves for brief dips into wisdom. We know how busy new entrepreneurs tend to be. We're familiar with the morning rush: trying to get out the door to conquer the world, eating a fistful of something for breakfast while standing up and slurping coffee. But even five-minute indulgences can rub off on you and plant the myriad ideas of stellar service and shining habits to make you a better choice than your competitors. We suggest stocking your arsenal of trade "secrets" with the books below, written by today's top contenders whose success lies in appealing to what consumers want:

- *Raving Fans: A Revolutionary Approach to Customer Service* by Ken Blanchard, Sheldon Bowles and Harvey Mackay

- *Delivering Happiness: A Path to Profits, Passion, and Purpose* by Tony Hsieh

- *Customer Winback: How to Recapture Lost Customers—And Keep Them Loyal* by Jill Griffin and Michael W. Lowenstein

- *Exceptional Customer Service* by Lisa Ford, David McNair, William Perry, and Tony Hsieh

- *The Cult of the Customer* by Shep Hyken

- *The Thank You Economy* by Gary Vaynerchuk

- *"I Love You More Than My Dog": Five Decisions That Drive Extreme Customer Loyalty in Good Times and Bad* by Jeanne Bliss

- *2010 Culture Book* by Zappos

Leave these books all over the house for quick reads between activities. After a while you'll be surprised at how the new methods influence your daily activities.

Once she's finished servicing, Becky's exit mirrors her entrance. "When I get to the door of the room, I always turn around and say, 'Goodbye. Thanks, everybody. We really appreciate you.' And it's from the heart; it's not just something I say. I truly do thank them. I understand completely that a Snickers bar is a Snickers bar, and they can go to the 7-Eleven, the AM/PM, or the catering truck, but I want them to buy it from me."

Get It Now

In addition to overt friendliness, successful operators stress the importance of prompt action on customer requests. "If a customer asks for something that's not in the machine and you have it on the truck, even if you feel like your legs are ready to fall off, you immediately go and get that item and bring it back to the room," Becky says. "You have made that person feel important. We all love recognition, and it's remembered."

Wayne D.'s advice is the same. "Always be courteous and respond to requests for product in a timely manner. If our route driver doesn't have it on his truck, and he's not going to be there for a week, he calls the office to make sure he'll have the product the next week," says the full-line operator. "In most cases, you or your driver are there servicing a location for an hour or an hour and a half every week," continues Wayne. "You get to know people on a first-name basis, and fairly well."

> ## Smart Tip
> Goof Off is the recommended method for removing spray paint from vending machines. Goof Off is carried by Home Depot, Lowes, Meijer, Bed, Bath and Beyond, Ace Hardware, True Value, and Menards. Read more about Goof Off products at www.goofoff-stainremover.com.

This means that if you have drivers working routes for you, it is essential that they do not go out in a bad mood and take it out on your customers. You need to remind your staff that their actions are a reflection on your company and that they must take a deep breath and put aside their woes for the day, which might include traffic on the roads and personal problems. While in a location, they need to be cordial and helpful to anyone who approaches them.

Special Requests

Invariably someone's going to ask you to stock an item regularly for them. Whether or not you do so is a judgment call. Obviously, you won't get a watermelon into a vending machine, but if it is a logical request that fits your line, you can jot it down and try to include it if the cost is right.

"If two or three people end up buying an item every day, then we make a lot of money," comments Wayne D. "Generally, in a snack machine, there's enough room to add a special request. When they get those special requests, people who say they will purchase the product usually end up buying it."

However, at some point you're likely to be faced with a tough choice, regardless of purchasing frequency or profitability. "If the key executive at a location drinks Diet Dr. Pepper, then we put it in," acknowledges Wayne. "If the person is your

> ⚠️ **Beware!**
>
> Just because a customer requests and purchases a product doesn't mean you should overlook that item's profitability—or lack thereof. "It's important to stay on top of unit costs," full-line operator Becky P. stresses. "Otherwise, before you know it, you could be losing one or two cents on that product, and that adds up at the end of the year."

vending contact, you have no choice but to leave it in. Then, even if we change personnel, there's a note on the inside of the machine or on the route card stating the preference.

"If you're forced to stock a money-loser in order to profit overall, there's still a way to minimize the damage," explains Wayne. "Simply stock such products in a column that holds fewer items, or place them in a column that—for whatever reason—is slow no matter what you attempt to sell."

In some vending specialties, you'll have other alternatives to saying "no." For example, in pantyhose, successful entrepreneurs say you can offer to sell special products direct. "Sometimes [when I'm loading machines] customers tell me, 'The queen size pantyhose aren't big enough. Do you have any queen XXs?'" says Baltimore operator Janice M. When she can't stock a particular product she replies, "I have a catalog, and you can buy them directly from me.

"I like the fact that they realize they can just come up to me, and they can tell me what they think and what they want—what works for them and what doesn't work," she continues. "My mom and dad had a store and they always talked to a customer who had a complaint; they never said, 'I'm too busy.' I learned that from them."

I Want a Refund

Not surprisingly, another common customer request is for a refund. Most operators will be accommodating most of the time as a sign of goodwill and good customer relations. The only time when such requests become a problem is when they are coming more and more frequently from one location. This could indicate that the products are going bad (which may be the fault of a defect in the machine) or people are taking advantage of your kind nature. This may mean simply trying some new products in the machine. It may also mean that you take a loss on the machine for a little while until the "trend" dissipates. Last-case scenario is letting the client know the problem and working out a solution.

For the most part, you'll find giving some refunds ultimately means losing a dollar one day and gaining a steady customer because you've established credibility with the buyer.

But It Was Jammed

In addition to bad product, many refund requests stem from real or imagined coin and bill acceptor jams. In nonpublic locations catering to employees, such as offices and factories, most operators handle this situation with a refund slip system.

An envelope or similar container, such as a plastic bag, marked "blank refund slips" is mounted on the side of one of the vending machines. Another envelope, marked "completed refund slips" is mounted next to the blank slip envelope. The next time the machines are serviced, the completed slips are then collected. The appropriate amount of money owed a customer is placed in a regular business envelope, sealed, and the name of the person is written on the front. Refunds are then given to the location's contact person or a designated individual, such as a receptionist, to distribute.

Alternatively, a stash of coins and bills are provided to a certain individual, again the contact person or other designated person. In this case, the designated individual collects slips and hands out refunds immediately.

The second scenario is the preferred method. This is where one person is assigned to maintain a special pouch with some cash in it for such refund purposes—this can come from petty cash in an office situation. Then the person handling the money can take the slip and immediately pay the individual back.

Whatever system you employ, or the client requests, use the refund slips for more than just proper bookkeeping. This way you can have the individual write down the product they were trying to purchase so you can determine if the problem is inside the machine on a specific spiral.

Refund slips need not be elaborate or expensive. Necessary elements are space for the customer's name, refund amount, and reason for the refund. Including the name of your company on the slip visually reinforces your commitment to customer service and reassures the customer they're filling out the right form. You can even print them out on your computer. See the sample refund slip on page 247.

Stat Fact

The 2011 "State of the Vending Industry Report" showed operators using glass-front machines to successfully serve a diverse customer demand, and expose and sell their secondary, or less familiar, new product lines. "A successful cold beverage strategy in many vending locations was to have a closed-front machine for the high-volume sellers (such as soda) along with a glass-front machine for the secondary ones," reports Elliot Maras, editor of *Automatic Merchandiser* magazine.

Public Offerings

If your locations are open to the public, your refund system will more likely rely on telecommunications rather than pencil

Refund Slip

A Matter of Taste
Refund Slip

Print Name: _____

Date: _____   Item: _____

Location: _____   Amount: _____

Machine: _____   Reason: _____

This information is important so that we may improve our services. Thank you!

and paper. Prominently affixing your company name and telephone number or email address is key.

"I want people to be able to contact me for things like losing their money," says Janice M. Although she lists her business telephone number on her machines, her voice greeting encourages callers to contact her via pager.

An issue for refunding money from public vendors has always been lack of guaranteed reinsertions. Wayne D., who serves park and recreational facilities, discovered from the statistics he keeps that refund customers often were not plugging the money back into his machines.

With the advent of advanced electronic bill and coin acceptors, he's now solved the problem by giving free item coupons to those who call for their money back. "We really prefer coupons, because we know they're using the product."

If It's Broken, Fix It

Whether tied to a specific refund request or the result of watching your refund slips, you will be called on to repair your vendors. People want vending machines fixed quickly—and it's to your benefit to get out there and make quick fixes. You, therefore, need to make sure that your cell phone or pager is always charged and turned on, so that if you get a call concerning a broken machine you can make sure to work a repair trip into your schedule. You also need to have tools stashed in your vehicle at all times.

While your decision may vary with the circumstances, always provide clients and customers with your best estimate of when you'll be there.

"Our overall service turnarounds are logged on the computer," notes full-line operator B.J. S., whose operation includes two full-time service technicians. "We log from the time of the report to the time it was fixed. Our average is 47 minutes. And if somebody wants me to guarantee it, then I do, which is why we factor in travel time."

During off-hours, expect customers to insist on quick action. "If you're working a night shift and you go to a machine and it's not working, you want it fixed," says Becky P. "It's holidays, Saturdays, and Sundays. We may be in our pajamas, but we throw on our sweats and take care of the call."

Of course, you need to have some training in basic vending machine repairs, which you can usually get when purchasing the machines.

To reduce emergencies, successful operators and industry experts stress preventive maintenance, paying attention to refund slip trends, and tracking coin-to-bill ratios to spot fluctuations. For more on time- and money-saving tips, see Chapter 8.

Ask What They Want

Although we've spent a great deal of time discussing managing machine outages, handling product complaints, and giving refunds, an equally important customer service task is designing some pre-emptive strikes. Key to reducing griping on the back end is asking for customer input upfront.

"We survey locations to find out what they want," comments Wayne D. "If what's requested is off-the-wall, we can't do that. If it's within reason, we will. For instance, if two or three people request a specific name-brand soda, then we put it in the machine."

To get the most from her survey efforts, Janice M. includes both quality of service questions as well as product selection questions on index-card sized questionnaires she places inside her hosiery boxes. "It wasn't long after I started the business that I began including customer comment cards because it was the only way I could find out what people really wanted," she says. "At first, it was just a small card I printed myself—the same as the ones you use to print business cards on your computer."

As her business grew, she turned to a professional printer. "Now it is a two-sided card," notes Janice. "I have always put size, color, and style (such as Lycra or micro-fiber). But now it is a little more complicated because I have more things to offer."

Whether your business lends itself to a comment card or the more standard sheet-of-paper survey, follow Janice's lead by distributing a questionnaire that provides you with both service and product feedback. Using a dual-purpose form provides you with the maximum amount of information for a minimum amount of effort. For an example of a detailed form that you can adapt to fit your business's needs, see the "At-Location Survey of Customer Reactions" on page 250.

Use the Web to Collect Data

Another way to encourage feedback is to get on the internet and post a survey form on your website. If you don't have a site, at least post your email address on your vending machines and let people know that they can email you feedback on the vending machine or request a survey. Then, have a survey saved as a Word document (which is easiest for most recipients to open) and send it to who requests it. Some people will fill it out and others will delete it—nonetheless you can get some feedback.

> ### Bright Idea
> Scratch-and-sniff business cards and promotional postcards come in hundreds of scents, many of them for food. Be unique and people will remember you. Wouldn't you remember the person who handed you a mouth-watering card smelling of cappuccino, buttered popcorn, gingerbread, or apple pie? Here are some companies that provide this service: Highpoint Printing (www.highpointprinting.com), H&H Graphics Inc. (www.hhgrfx.com), and The Print Box Inc. (www.promobrands.com).

Of course, always remember that when soliciting feedback from the public, you will get a cross section of valid responses and junk. Don't ask people for identifying information—they will be less likely to fill out your survey. People today are very aware of identity theft and do not want to provide any potentially identifying information. To increase survey response, offer a reward or prize. Again, when you use email, they do not need to give you any identification information other than their email address. You can email a coupon or a download or something else that does not require you to physically send something to a street address.

Make Yourself Available

Whether it is in person, by phone, or via cyberspace, the customer service bottom line is being accessible. Savvy entrepreneurs know this goes beyond giving your main contact your business card. There is a tendency today for many business owners to be very hard to reach, guarded by administrative assistants and/or phone systems that require pushing numerous buttons and waiting a long time to get through. Since this is a very people-oriented business, you can't hide yourself away from your customers. Being available is a key to the business. Nonetheless, you have to plan your time carefully so that you can talk with customers as well as handle your many responsibilities.

At-Location Survey of Customer Reactions

XYZ Vending Company
Customer Questionnaire

We're doing a survey of what our customers think about vending machines and about the vending service at this location.

1. Have you used the vending machines here in the past two weeks? (Check one answer)

    ❑ Yes (Go on to question 2.)

    ❑ No: If no, why not? (Skip to question 3.)

2. (If Yes to question 1) In the past two weeks, how many times have you purchased the following products from a vending machine here? (Circle one code for each item below.)

Coffee or hot drink	0	1	2	3	4	5	6	7	8	9	10+
Soft drinks	0	1	2	3	4	5	6	7	8	9	10+
Juice	0	1	2	3	4	5	6	7	8	9	10+
Sandwich or salad	0	1	2	3	4	5	6	7	8	9	10+
Fruit, yogurt, etc.	0	1	2	3	4	5	6	7	8	9	10+
Candy, gum, or snacks	0	1	2	3	4	5	6	7	8	9	10+
Milk or ice cream	0	1	2	3	4	5	6	7	8	9	10+

3. I will read you some statements about the vending machines at this location. [Ask first whether the person agrees or disagrees. After telling you which, ask "agree strongly" or "agree somewhat"? "Disagree strongly" or "disagree somewhat"?]

About the Products	Agree		Disagree		
	Strongly	Somewhat	Somewhat	Strongly	No Answer
a. Most of the time I can find a sufficient variety of products in each machine.	4	3	2	1	0
b. I would rather buy brand-name products than a nonbrand item.	4	3	2	1	0
c. Products in our machines usually are fresh.	4	3	2	1	0
d. The quality of the products in our machines is as good as the same products in other retail outlets.	4	3	2	1	0
e. Prices in these machines are, for the most part, reasonable.	4	3	2	1	0

At-Location Survey of Customer Reactions, continued

About the Products	Agree Strongly	Agree Somewhat	Disagree Somewhat	Disagree Strongly	No Answer
f. The product I want is seldom sold out when I get to the machine.	4	3	2	1	0
g. I like the coffee from our machine.	4	3	2	1	0
h. I would prefer to have a larger selection of soft drinks.	4	3	2	1	0

About the Machines

	Agree Strongly	Agree Somewhat	Disagree Somewhat	Disagree Strongly	No Answer
i. The vending machines here are easy to operate.	4	3	2	1	0
j. If I don't have enough change, it's still pretty easy to use the machines.	4	3	2	1	0
k. The machines are usually neat and clean.	4	3	2	1	0
l. I wish there were more machines at this location.	4	3	2	1	0
m. The machines at this location are seldom out of order.	4	3	2	1	0

About the Service

	Agree Strongly	Agree Somewhat	Disagree Somewhat	Disagree Strongly	No Answer
n. The people who service our machines are usually friendly and courteous.	4	3	2	1	0
o. It's easy to get refunds when something is wrong.	4	3	2	1	0
p. During the past four weeks I've had no problems with the machines.	4	3	2	1	0
q. The machines at this location are serviced at least every two days.	4	3	2	1	0

About Company Identity

	Agree Strongly	Agree Somewhat	Disagree Somewhat	Disagree Strongly	No Answer
r. I have no idea who owns and operates the machines at this facility.	4	3	2	1	0
s. The company that services them seems to care about its customers.	4	3	2	1	0

At-Location Survey of Customer Reactions, continued

t. The name of the company that owns and services the machines here is:

_____

(write name as given)

❑ Don't know the name (check here)

4. Now I would like to ask your opinion about the products being offered. Tell me which products you'd like to see offered in the machines besides what's available now.

1. _____ 2. _____ 3. _____

4. _____ 5. _____ 6. _____

5. Which of the following products do you feel are reasonably priced? (Check all that apply.)

❑ Hot beverages ❑ Soft drinks ❑ Candy ❑ Snacks

❑ Sandwiches ❑ Salads ❑ Milk ❑ Juices ❑ Cigarettes

6. I'd like to ask you a few questions about yourself so we will be able to classify your answers according to the different groups of people we're talking to...

a. Sex: ❑ Male ❑ Female

b. Age: ❑ Under 18 ❑ 18–24 ❑ 25–34 ❑ 35–44 ❑ 45–55 ❑ Over 55

c. Occupation: _____

d. [If this is an employer area, or a school] How long have you worked here (or gone to school here)? _____ Years

How to Score and Total the Responses

The questionnaire statements are weighted: 4=agree strongly; 3=agree somewhat; 2=disagree somewhat; 1=disagree strongly; 0=don't know/no answer.

1. For each separate statement multiply each of the four numbers (1–4) times the number of responses each number received.

2. Add up the result of the four multiplications.

3. Divide the sum by the total number of questions answered on this segment (including the "0"-no answer responses.)

This will give you the score of responses on the scale from 1 to 4 (for example, 2.94 means "on average people tend to agree somewhat").

Source: National Automatic Merchandising Association

Get Personal

In closed, nonpublic locations, such as offices and manufacturing facilities, being personally involved in employee affairs is another way to encourage buying. "We get involved by bringing complimentary desserts and beverages to employee functions," says full-line operator Becky P. For an occasion such as the birth of an employee's baby, Becky says, "We bring them baby toys."

Once, after the death of an employee's family member, co-workers held a potluck lunch to help raise money for the funeral expenses. Becky brought in complimentary desserts and joined in on the fundraiser, including staying for the meal. "Our customers are very generous," she says. "If one doesn't have food to eat, they all pitch in to help."

It's that generous, energetic attitude of her customers that Becky's operation thrives on. "We feel vending is a benefit for employees. We also understand the morale of the lunchroom. If we can help make our customers' lunch break a more positive one, we do everything we can."

Beyond Training Sessions

It's one thing to train non-English-speaking employees in some key English phrase, but it is another to recognize that in some locations, you will also need to put labels on machines in other languages. It is very easy to have such labels printed up—either with your computer or at a printing business. You can then add them to your vending machines.

Old-Fashioned Service in a Modern World

Full-line operator Becky contends it's still possible in today's world to take care of the customer the old-fashioned way—with exceptional service—while still making a

Dollar Stretcher

If you need translators to help you communicate with ethnic populations, contact your local high school or community college and post an ad for student assistants. Students welcome opportunities to practice languages and gain valuable resume experience as well. Promise students a written recommendation and a real-world title such as translator or communications assistant.

profit. Once the language barrier is broken, the cultural diversity of her customers gives Becky additional opportunities to differentiate herself from her competition by providing a wide range of products and services.

Still, she admits, it takes some creative thinking. "Our clients have asked us not to get institutionalized with our company. They worry that if we do, they won't receive the personal service we give them now." But she's quick to add that she has no intention of sacrificing her customer-centered orientation. "We're still growing, learning, and having fun."

Monitoring Progress

Throughout this book, you've heard successful vending entrepreneurs emphasize the importance of a certain aspect of running a profitable company that many small-business owners love to hate: managing their finances.

Perhaps you're wondering why you need to crunch more numbers in the first place. After all, you already tackled the

▲

math in Chapter 6. The answer: That chapter covered what you need to begin. Once you're up and running, you'll want to periodically make sure your business is on a healthy track.

Respect Your Finances

Financial experts advise that respecting your money is key to succeeding financially. From keeping the bills in your wallet organized by denomination and facing the same way to knowing exactly what is going on in your bank account daily, staying aware is the key. Ignoring your money, not dealing with tracking dollars "right now," and failing to squirrel away padded amounts of acorns for winter will leave you looking like an empty-handed fool.

As someone with a bird's-eye view of vending operations notes, 15 to 20 percent of vending businesses that purchase from his company are bankrupt without even knowing it. "They don't watch the p's and q's of the economics. Just because you have cash flow doesn't mean you're in the black," says John Ochi of Vernon Hills, Illinois-based Five Star Distributors. How does he know? "When people apply for credit with us, we get a glimpse of their financial picture. Sometimes it just blows us away."

This doesn't mean your financial checkups have to be painful. Since you are armed with all the valuable tips in this book, your reports may demonstrate just what a savvy entrepreneur you are—maybe even more so than you expected. But if the numbers are below par, regular monitoring will give you plenty of time to make adjustments and save your business from failure.

It's All in the Tools

The primary accounting tool you'll use to track your progress is an income and expense statement, also referred to as a profit and loss statement (or P&L), which basically organizes your collections and disbursements for a specific period of time. Generally, businesses generate monthly income and expense reports as well as quarterly or annual summaries.

A monthly report gives you a snapshot of the current period but doesn't show you whether the strong months outweigh the weak ones overall. By adding up the months quarterly or annually, you'll see whether you are making the profits you desire or if some adjustments need to be made.

As Randall Sutherland points out, "When I sold Highlander Vending to become a consultant, what made my business sell was very concise record keeping. The thing that sells a route is a thorough spreadsheet that shows exactly the type of machine, location details, contact person, machine key numbers, profitability which is tracked,

Dollar Stretcher

Today's operators view computers as a savings, not an expense. Beyond saving advertising dollars by using social media, web, and blog marketing, Jim Patterson of Patterson Co. Inc. reminds us how computers can help in managing a business. "Previously, operators spent thousands of dollars on machines and trucks, but they wouldn't spend it on managing the business," he says. "Software helps you figure out how often you're at a particular location, manage your machine, organize your route structures, and so much more."

the number of stops you make per week, etc. That makes it easier for a potential buyer of your business (should you decide to change the type of vending you're doing or become a consultant) to envision how they'll succeed with your business. All of those comments I suggested making on each stop come in very handy, too, as the potential buyer can see the evolution of product offering decisions, how to deal with suggestions, and so on."

While some operators still do this work by hand, tracking your income and expenses is a good example of where computer software can be a real timesaver. Not only do popular personal finance programs such as QuickBooks add up the numbers for you, they also typically use a checkbook-style on-screen metaphor to make entering information as easy as writing it down in your checkbook register. You don't need to know anything about accounting or report generation; the software does it for you. The software will also calculate commissions you owe to a location automatically, giving you more time for your main income-producing activity: servicing your machines.

Keeping Track Monthly

By maintaining monthly profit and loss statements, you can see exactly where you stand and even notice cycles during the year, especially if you have products that sell more seasonally than others. For the most part, if you have a variety of machines, you should be able to establish a consistency from month to month that will paint a regular picture of how you are doing and what you can expect.

You can be very detailed or have some general categories when listing your expenses. The decision is yours, as long as you get an accurate picture of what is being spent in conjunction with what is coming in each month. See the "Income and Expense Statement Worksheet" on page 258.

On the Machine's Level

In addition to tracking the overall income and expenses for your business, use the same formats we've presented here to monitor each vending location. Otherwise, how

Income and Expense Statement Worksheet

Income	
Machine sales	
Other income	
Total Monthly Income	
Expenses	
Advertising/marketing	
Bank service charges	
Commissions	
CPA/accounting	
Depreciation	
Office equipment/furnishings	
Vehicles	
Vending machines	
Insurance	
Licenses and fees	
Office expenses	
Equipment/furnishings	
Office supplies	
Rent	
Repairs/maintenance	
Telephone	
Utilities	
Internet service	
Payroll	
Salaries/wages	
Benefits	
Payroll taxes	
Workers' compensation	
Product expenses	
Cost of goods sold	

Income and Expense Statement Worksheet, continued

Product loss	
Professional services (including contract)	
Sales/use taxes	
Subscriptions/dues	
Travel, meals, entertainment	
Vehicle expenses	
Vehicle purchases	
Lease payments	
Loan payments—principal	
Loan payments—interest	
Maintenance and repair	
Vending equipment expenses	
Machine purchases	
Lease payments	
Loan payments—principal	
Loan payments—interest	
Parts and repairs	
Storage	
Delivery/moving/freight	
Other miscellaneous expenses	
Total Monthly Expenses	
Net monthly profit (loss) before taxes	
Income tax (estimated)	
Net Monthly Profit (Loss) after Taxes	

will you know if a location is holding its own, going gangbusters, or falling on its face? "You need to look at every location as a profit center," explains veteran startup watcher Vince Gumma of American Vending Sales. "Keep a P&L on each of them and not overall." Vending-specific software programs, as mentioned earlier, can help you do this.

To track income and expense information by location, many of the line items will have to be pro-rated. To do this, just calculate the percentage of total gross sales each location represents. Use the location's percentage to allocate a portion of each general expense. Of course you will not pro-rate three key line items—income, product costs, and sales taxes—because they are specific to each location. Instead, assign the exact income and product costs generated by a location to that location. That way, you will know which locations are making a profit and which ones need fine-tuning.

For more on turning an underachiever around, see Chapter 13.

High-Tech or Low-Tech?

If you're purchasing an existing organization with a sizable number of machines, you may want to collect data with a laptop or notebook computer. You can punch in numbers and upon returning to the office, download the notes into the appropriate categories with your accounting software.

While it may take a little time to get comfortable with the latest software, the ability to enter data quickly and have it saved into a database is a timesaver. Being able to send email to otherwise hard-to-reach customers is also a benefit if you're on the road. In addition, you can maintain a larger database of contacts rather than carrying around your phone listings.

While some route drivers remain more comfortable with the pen-and-paper method, slowly more and more companies are opting for technical assistance.

Ode to Depreciation

Regardless of how you keep your data, a commonly overlooked line item is depreciation. Because it's not something you actually pay out, it's easy to miss the importance of tracking this expense.

The first important aspect of depreciation that you'll want to remember is that you can take it as a deduction on your tax return. This means that if you buy a machine for $2,400, you need to find out from the IRS what the life span is for a vending machine—in the view of the IRS (not in your opinion). If they say a vending machine (hypothetically) has an eight-year life span, then you can deduct $300 per year (2,400 divided by 8). Depreciation calculations are not always quite this simple, so you may need to confer with your accountant before doing your taxes.

The second part of knowing about deductions is that you can start a fund that will coincide with the life span of the machine—based on what you know about its history from other vending companies and the trade magazines. For example, some vending machines, such as a Dixie Narco, can last for 40 years. Therefore, you might not bother putting money into a fund for new machines until you've had the machine for quite a few years. Conversely (and you should try not to do this), if you buy a machine for $2,400 that traditionally lasts only six years, you will want to start putting away $400 a year toward buying a replacement. Obviously, you want to buy long-lasting machines and/or refurbished models that won't cost as much or require you to put aside much replacement money. For example, if a refurbished machine costs you $500 and should last around seven years from the time of purchase, as determined by reports in the trade magazines, you only need to put away about $72 per year to save up to replace it. Of course, with rising prices, you might set aside $80 or $85 per year.

One of the features Randall Sutherland's consulting service offers is a kit with everything the greenhorn needs to be prepared, including a depreciation breakdown for various machines. "There's a formula," says Sutherland. "You have to make sure you make a certain dollar amount per year from each machine to stay ahead. If you have a machine that cost you $3,900 and you're selling drinks for 50 cents and your profit is 25 cents per can, you're going to have to sell 15,000 cans before you even pay for the machine, not to mention what you have to put away for depreciation. There are several factors for staying ahead. Do you really want to vend soda for three years before you get one dime back on a single machine? Spelling it out like this really brings it home for some of the beginners who want to just throw down their money on high-end machines and think everything will just fall into place."

Beware!

Sending in taxes due to the IRS quarterly is how some of our operators stay ahead. It helps them budget more efficiently than if they sent in one lump sum at the end of the year. Meet with an accountant to figure out a quarterly deposit budget. If you can't afford a good personal CPA when you start your business, there are free accounting services in most counties for those who qualify financially (which you might in the beginning) and for senior citizens. Search "free tax help" in your city or county.

Taxing Questions

Talking about depreciation almost always leads to the subject of taxes, so now's as good a time as any to cover what a vending entrepreneur needs to know.

First, organized documentation is your friend. While the IRS watches every business, they scrutinize homebased ones even more. If the standard form letter with the "a" word in it (audit) comes to your door, the more documentation you have and the more organized you are, the better. Therefore, start and maintain a paper trail of expenses, starting with your receipts.

Even though you are not required to keep receipts below a certain amount, when you are sitting at your auditor's desk, you will wish you had. It's easy to do. Just make up some file folders for each line item on your income and expense statement. Then pop receipts inside. When you purchase with a credit card, simply staple receipts to the statement when it arrives.

This advice goes for sales as well as income tax. As a retailer, you are subject to both. But since you are not making face-to-face sales, your customers typically pay sales taxes as part of the product price. Thus, computing the sales tax you owe amounts to multiplying your gross sales by the sales tax percentage.

While sales tax laws vary by locality, you're likely to be required to factor in any items you purchased for resale but were consumed by you or someone else. Hence, if you donate products to an organization or eat a candy bar every day from your inventory, you'll be required to add in their retail value before computing your tax.

Because your sales taxes are less obvious than for businesses that can charge them separately on an invoice or a receipt, a pitfall for many startups is failing to put the tax money they owe aside. By tracking sales taxes as a separate line item on your income and expense statements, the total you owe will never be a surprise.

In general, you also want to watch that your tax-deductible expenses and cost of items consumed are about the same as any other vending business of your size and type. While local and federal tax agencies audit a certain percentage of taxpayers randomly, those with numbers outside the norm automatically trigger red flags in computers and get tagged for closer scrutiny.

Finally, if the whole issue of taxes and record keeping makes you squirm, consulting an accountant now can save you a bundle of headaches, not to mention dough, later on.

Be sure to review Chapter 7 for home-office deduction tips. The IRS website, hard as it may be to navigate, does have answers somewhere in there to your tax questions. You can also contact your state department of taxation or department of revenue.

Eggs in Many Baskets

Monitoring the progress of your business is also about managing its growth. While it's logical to conclude the more anchor accounts you have, the better off you are, the real key is diversity.

This not only means diversity in products that you sell, but also having various clients. While you want to continue to grow your relationship and add more machines to a business as that company grows, you want to have a number of clients so that when one suddenly downsizes, or in some cases, moves to another region of the country (or is forced to close up shop), you can better withstand the hit by having other businesses housing your vending machines comfortably inside.

You also need to concern yourself with companies where there is an increase in telecommuting among their employees. Telecommuting is an enemy of the vending business, since it means fewer people on site to buy your products. As this trend grows, you need to monitor your customers and get an idea of how many employees are no longer using the lunchroom, break room, or other locations where your machine may be set up.

To distribute your eggs properly, always be conscious of expanding your business. "A vending business is something you continually have to grow," says Vince Gumma of American Vending Sales. "I see people who get into it and plateau. They don't want to get bigger, and pretty soon they're getting smaller and they don't know why. Remember, you're going to lose locations eventually—nothing is forever."

Like too much of any good thing, too much growth too fast should also be avoided. "One of the most common mistakes I see is overextending oneself," notes Five Star Distributors' Ochi. "That is, growing too quickly without understanding your financial wherewithal and expecting your distributor to bail you out. Now that the industry is mature, we're not as inclined to take chances on operators who aren't good business managers."

17

Words of Wisdom

Although the industry has its idiosyncrasies, vending is really no different from any other business. To be successful in the field, it takes solid business management, old-fashioned elbow grease, plenty of persistence, and an ample dose of optimism.

▲

Many Perspectives

In addition to this tried-and-true wisdom, we asked the operators and experts interviewed for this book what the most important factors are for success in vending. Not surprisingly, their answers were very candid. Because entrepreneurs all have different learning styles and motivators, they each assign value to that which fills their cup. Only you can decide which path to take in the multifaceted field of vending, but we hope these mentors will help you reach for the stars and avoid common mistakes.

From a Position of Strength

When asked to name the most important factor for success, the first response from most who contributed to this work was, "Know what you're getting into from a hands-on perspective."

Northridge, California, full-line operator Becky P. explained the concept most eloquently. "Nobody—nobody—should try to go into this business without working one full year as a route person for a reputable operator. Lots of people go in, buy a business opportunity, get two weeks' training, and fall flat on their faces. The best way to get your education is by working in the trenches for a year and keeping your eyes and ears open. After three months, you may ask yourself if you're in your right mind. Then you can give your two weeks' notice and leave. But if you've got $50,000, $100,000, or $150,000 of your life savings invested, it's not so easy to say, Boy, did I make a mistake."

Behind Every Success Is a Support System

Surround yourself with those who believe in your mission and support what you are trying to do. It's OK to have critical thinkers in your life, but make sure they are working to a positive end for you and not just being naysayers.

Ask yourself how you feel after spending time with each connection in your life. If the answer is "like I'm capable of anything I set my mind to," then that individual should join the ranks of "personal advisor."

Make it a point to collect friends who empower you in some way and to not spend your energy on the rest. Starting a business is too consuming to waste any of your precious energy on those who don't nurture your dreams. Behind most innovative, successful trailblazers is usually at least one person, dog, or cat who was the "wind beneath their wings."

Hal Berdoll, Jennifer Berdoll Wammack's father, was the rock in her life when things got tough. Through countless trips to Precision Vending to develop the mechanisms that would allow the three-pound pies to be vended correctly, he was there with unwavering optimism.

"He encouraged me to resist changing the packaging (to smaller pies) the way Precision wanted us to," Berdoll Wammack fondly remembers. "He knew we could make this work and was the most persistent one through the process. Shoot, he didn't even want to stop there; he wanted our 5-pound bag of shelled pecans dropping from those coils. Maybe it'll be our next project!"

There Is Another Way

If, for whatever reason, you decide getting a job with a vending company just isn't for you, another industry veteran offers an alternative. "Before you get into the business, come ride along with our delivery drivers and see what it's like," invites product distributor John Ochi of Five Star Distributors in Vernon Hills, Illinois. "We'll show you the dredges of our stops and the best. Also, with the approval of one of our operators outside your competition area, we'll take you out and show you what it's like day to day. If you don't get firsthand experience, you're going to be an island unto yourself. You're going to make a lot of mistakes, and it's less likely that you'll succeed."

But why would an established operator let a potential operator peer into the inner workings of his business? "Because," says Ochi, "it doesn't do anyone in this industry any good when people fail."

Give Yourself a Break

No matter how much hands-on learning you do before you paint your business name on a shingle, you're going to make mistakes. Therefore, the next most important factor to your success is learning from your mistakes and moving on, and the sooner the better.

Erik A. Borger reflects on his journey: "I was the only one doing what I am doing in a city of 4 million, counting the suburbs. Starting Originally Organic Vending seemed like a no-brainer, but it's been much harder than I thought it was going to be. For me healthy vending is more of a passion

Smart Tip

Don't forget to take some downtime and address those sore muscles. Carting products around, driving all over town, and stocking machines can be hard on the back and joints. How about a little preventive maintenance in the form of a reasonably priced, bimonthly massage? Massage Envy (www.massageenvy.com) offers group and corporate rates and massages start at just $39 for 50 glorious minutes. Ask about package discounts.

than a great living. I've had many corporate jobs (which I hate), so these days I try and be myself. I wear street clothes, give out some free product to the people at the front desk, and try to have fun."

"One of the things I find is true with most businesses is they tend to get with something and stay with it," notes Burnsville, Minnesota's Wayne D., who worked his way up from a dozen snack and cigarette machines to becoming a full-line operator ready to hand over the reins to his son. "Be willing to be flexible and make the changes. Deep-six the things you make some mistakes on.

> **Fun Fact**
>
> Vending is historically a male-dominated industry, but full-line operator Becky P. attributes her success to having a woman's touch. "Men don't look at food the way women look at food," she says. "I can't have people coming up to my food machines without it looking like they're coming to my house for lunch."

"If you make a mistake, you make a mistake," he continues. "Be willing to admit to the mistake. Otherwise, you can save pennies on one side and lose dollars on the other side, and that's a pitfall for most small businesses."

Merchandise, Merchandise, Merchandise

The earlier you learn merchandising skills, the better, say our interviewees. "The object is to put a couple more of a good seller in a machine so [you] don't need to go back to this one machine every day just to fill a single column," says product broker Jim Patterson of Patterson Co. Inc. in Kenilworth, Illinois. "It's better to go back every three or four days and fill multiple machines.

"Managing that has a great deal to do with one's success," Patterson continues. "There's a fine balance between servicing too often and not servicing often enough. There's a cost to both." In the case of the former, it's wasted time, and in the latter, it's lost sales opportunities.

Be a Joiner

Budget three hours a week to join groups that will further your goals, whether they be trade, networking, or community focused. Follow the networking tips you learned in Chapter 14 and use them in every circle you become part of, and remember that follow-up is key.

While many startups only look at the cost of dues when considering membership in an industry organization, successful ones look at the benefits.

"It's absolutely important if you're starting out," assures B.J. S. "You find out what's going on in your industry and how your industry can help you." In B.J.'s case, this included learning about a tax break that cut his sales taxes from 8.5 to 1.5 percent.

"Some people say, 'I don't want to socialize with my competition,' " continues the full-line Tennessee operator. "I say, the only way to know your competition is to meet them."

Calling It Quits

Whether or not you're profitable, the long-term success of your business rests on your happiness. Because it's a lot of work and a lot of responsibility, you might discover that you'd be happier working for someone else. Remember that everything you've learned will make you an attractive candidate.

Should you decide to get out, industry magazine *Automatic Merchandiser* offers some savvy advice for selling your business. First, you're not just selling vending machines. You're selling locations as well as the information you've collected about past and current locations. You may have even worked out some unique systems for servicing locations and maintaining good customer relations.

Randall Sutherland sold Highlander Vending as a complete package to someone who chose to invest cashless technology in all his vendors. It says a lot that the new buyer had enough confidence in the package Sutherland presented to see the potential it held with a technology upgrade, and that it was worth the effort. Had he not maintained immaculate records and friendly, professional, and thorough customer service with all his accounts, he may not have been able to get as much value from the sale. Part of the appeal of that purchase was also Sutherland's competency and generosity with information and guidance, providing his mentorship to the buyer.

All this, and more, is valuable to a new owner.

But before you go shopping for a buyer, acquaint yourself with nondisclosure and noncompete agreements. *Entrepreneur* magazine has a number of helpful business and legal forms, including one for nondisclosure, that you can download for free at www.entrepreneur.com. Otherwise, during the course of selling your business, you may lose accounts to a competitor or—worse—to an unscrupulous buyer.

Determination Wins the Day

The final key ingredient for success is just plain grit. Jennifer Berdoll Wammack is still passionate about her pie and candy venture and encourages: "When you've got a unique idea that you believe in, don't let anyone tell you that you can't do it. You can make it happen and it's worth all the extra problem solving when you see your idea coming alive, starting to work and pay off."

Berdoll Wammack reminisces about the early days: "I remember in the early days when I'd get that email every morning from USA Technology with all of the progress data, replete with details on our new machine. I'd wake up and rush over to the computer to see which items did well the night before. It's interesting to see sales coming through at 1:30 in the morning and speculate that the people who were watching the football game last night just had to have some pecan pie when it was over. It's fun to track the patterns of sales."

"I usually tell new operators that they should be prepared to put in a lot of hours and to work very hard," Gumma asserts. "It seems to be a glamorous business because of the cash you collect from the machines, but people overlook the hard work. Vending is not something you can do five days a week from nine to five. I know successful operators who haven't had a vacation in 15 years; they may have five employees, but the owner just can't get away."

Five Star Distributors' Ochi concurs. "The typical successful vending operator is someone who's really willing to roll up the sleeves," he emphasizes. "It's a labor-intensive business. You have to lug machines up flights of stairs, fill them anytime of day or night, and burn the candle at both ends. You don't have to have technical or management skills; you can learn them. But it's a service industry and you have to do whatever it takes to satisfy the client."

To this, Baltimore pantyhose vending pioneer Janice M. adds, "Most successful businesspeople aren't that way because they had a lot of money to start out with, but because they kept at it and finished what they started. You have to decide whether you want a new pair of shoes or to be successful. You can't take that money and use it to live off of. You have to use it for your business," she says. "You have to commit to finishing the project."

This winning attitude seems especially key. If you go into business with the right stuff—a willingness to learn what vending is really about, to work hard, to merchandise effectively, to satisfy your customer—and the drive to get it done, chances are you will succeed.

Smart Tip

If you decide vending is not for you, consider retaining a professional who specializes in brokering business sales and acquisitions. Like a real estate agent, a broker will take a cut of the sales price, but in the final analysis, you're likely to gain more than you'll lose. To find a reputable broker, call the industry organization dedicated to your product specialty.

Appendix
Vending Business Resources

Becoming a successful vending entrepreneur requires doing your homework. To help you start out, we've compiled the following resources. Many of the sources listed were previously discussed in various chapters.

Although we've made every attempt to provide you with the most comprehensive and updated information, businesses and organizations do tend to move, evolve, expand, and fold. In addition to what's here, we urge you to contact the appropriate association for your intended vending specialty.

Every resource we've listed in the Appendix is linked to countless others. Practicing the following three great habits while using these leads will polish you to networking magnificence, and begin to weave the web of contacts you can count on for information and possibly referrals.

1. Always ask the person you originally contacted if they can refer you to anyone else with pertinent information.

2. Keep a notebook to record the details of any meaningful interactions you have with others.

3. Note the name and contact information, topics you speak of, and information someone shares with you. If that person refers you to another source, use that lead right away and record details for that new contact. Don't forget to connect the trail of who referred you to whom, because after you talk to the tenth fascinating referral, you'll forget the chain of favors. Immediately send both parties brief thank-you emails or even better, handwritten cards, and tell how they helped you. For example: "John proved to be a great resource. Thank you so much for your time and sharing his information with me."

Associations

American Amusement Machine Association, 450 E. Higgins Rd., #201, Elk Grove Village, IL 60007, (847) 290-9088, www.coin-op.org

American Beverage Association, 1101 16th St. NW, Washington, DC 20036, (202) 463-6732, fax: (202) 659-5349, www.ameribev.org

Amusement and Music Operators Association, 600 Spring Hill Ring Rd., #111, Elk West Dundee, IL 60118, (847) 428-7699 or (800) 937-2662, fax: (847) 428-7719, www.amoa.com

Canadian Automatic Merchandising Association, 2233 Argentia Rd., Suite 100, Mississauga, Ontario, Canada L5N 2X7, (888) 849-2262, fax: 905-826-4873, www.vending-cama.com

International Bottled Water Association (IBWA), 1700 Diagonal Road, Suite 650, Alexandria, VA 22314, (703) 683-5213, fax: (703) 683-4074, www.bottledwater.org

National Automatic Merchandising Association (NAMA), 20 N. Wacker Dr., #3500, Chicago, IL 60606, (312) 346-0370, fax: (312) 704-4140, www.vending.org, info@vending.org

Eastern Office: 1600 Wilson Blvd., Suite 650, Arlington, VA 22209, (571) 346-1900, fax: (703) 836-8262

Southern Office: 2300 Lakeview Pkwy., Suite 700, Alpharetta, GA 30009, (678) 916-3852, fax: (678) 916-3853

Western Office: 80 South Lake Ave., Pasadena, CA 91101, (626) 229-0900, fax: (626) 229-0777

National Bulk Vendors Association, 3240 East Union Hills Dr., Suite 129, Phoenix, AZ 85050, (888) NBVA-USA, fax: (480) 302 5108, www.nbva.org

National Coffee Service Association of USA Inc., 45 Broadway, Suite 1140, New York, NY 10006, (212) 766-4007, fax: (212) 766-5815, www.ncausa.org

Specialty Coffee Association of America, 330 Golden Shore, Suite 50, Long Beach, CA 90802, (562) 624-4100, www.scaa.org

Books

A Concise History of Vending in the United States, G. Richard Schreiber, Sunrise Books, NAMA

Business Networking and Sex by Ivan Misner, Ph.D., Hazel M. Walker, and Frank J. De Raffele, Entrepreneur Press

How to Start a Candy Machine Business [Kindle Edition], Douglas Cooper

Increase Your Website Traffic by Khoa Bui, Entrepreneur Press

Networking Like a Pro by Ivan R. Misner, Ph.D., David Alexander, and Brian Hilliard, Jere L. Calmes

The 29% Solution by Ivan R. Misner, Ph.D., and Michelle R. Donovan, Greenleaf Book Group Press

The Vending Start-Up Kit, The Vending Connection, 4303 Blue Ridge Blvd., #543, Kansas City, MO 64122, (800) 956-8363, (816) 554-1534, fax: (816) 554-1016, www.vendingconnection.com

Vending Business-In-A-Box: A Step-by-Step Guide to Starting a Profitable Vending Business without Getting Burned, by Bryon Krug

Vending Success Secrets—How Anyone Can Grow Rich In America's Best Cash Business! by Bill Way, Freedom Tech Press

▲

Blogs, Forums,
and Miscellaneous Resources

www.candymachines.com/blog/

http://bulkvending.blogspot.com/

http://vendingrules.blogspot.com/

www.vintagevending.com/

www.your-vending-resource.com

Vending Chat, www.vendingchat.com, featuring a vending chat room

Vending Connection, www.vendingconnection.com, is a vending resource directory, and the Vending Connection business directory and classifieds

Vendors Exchange International Inc., www.veii.com, technical news, new makeovers for old machines, repairs and blog

Branding, Social Media,
and Website Marketing Consultants

Chris Brogan, www.chrisbrogan.com

Gary Vaynerchuk, http://garyvaynerchuk.com, http://vaynermedia.com, 220 E. 23rd St., Suite 605, New York, NY 10010, info@vaynermedia.com

Guy Kawasaki, www.guykawasaki.com, kawasaki@garage.com

Khoa Bui, Khoa Bui International, 243/1 Heritage Cove, Maylands 6051, Western Australia, (08) 6102 1277, support@khoa-bui.com, www.khoa-bui.com

Shannon Paul, (734) 968-9065, shannonpaul5@gmail.com, http://veryofficialblog.com

Buyer's Guides

Blue Book Directory, *Automatic Merchandiser*, P.O. Box 803, Ft. Atkinson, WI 53538, (920) 563-1605, fax: (920) 563-1702, www.amonline.com

International Buyers Guide, *Vending Times*, 55 Maple Ave., Ste. 102, Rockville Centre, NY 11570, (516) 442-1850, fax: (516) 442-1849

Equipment, Suppliers and Classifieds, Pre-owned and New

American Vending Machines, Andy Hayes, 2035 Shenandoah, St. Louis, MO 63104, (888) 818-VEND or (314) 771-VEND (8363), andy@ americanvendingmachines.com, www.americanvendingmachines.com, www.vendingconnection.com/classifieds.html

American Vending Sales Inc., 750 Morse Ave., Elk Grove Village, IL 60007, (847) 439-9400, (800) 441-0009, fax: (847) 439-9405, TDD: (847) 439-9402, www.americanvending.com

Automated Merchandising Systems Inc. (AMS), 255 W. Burr Blvd., Kearneysville, WV 25430, (304) 725-6921, fax: (304) 725-6983, www.amsvendors.com

Automatic Products, A Crane Company, CMS Customer Service Center, 11685 Main St., Williston, SC 29853, (800) 523-8363, (800) 784-6438, fax: (803) 266-5150, www.automaticproducts.com

Dixie Narco, 3330 Dixie-Narco Blvd., Williston, SC 29853, (803) 266-5000, (800) 688-9090, fax: (800) 854-5852, www.dixienarco.com

Royal Vendors Inc., 426 Industrial Blvd., Kearneysville, WV 25430-2776, (304) 728-7056, (800) 321-8637, fax: (304) 725-4728, www.royalvendors.com

Saeco, 7905 Cochran Rd., Suite 100, Glenwillow, OH 44139, (800) 933-7876, fax: (440) 542-9173, www.saeco-usa.com

Seaga Manufacturing Inc., 700 Seaga Dr., Freeport, IL 61032, (815) 297-9500, fax: (815) 297-1700, www.seagamfg.com

Southern Equipment Sales, 1896 Forge St., Tucker, GA 30084, (800) 252-8363 or (770) 939-6740, www.southernequipmentsales.com

VE Global Solutions LLC, 8700 Brookpark Rd., Cleveland, OH 44129, (800) 321-2511, fax: (216) 706-7381, www.veglobal.net

Vencoa Vending Machines, www.vencoavendingmachines.com

Vending World, 10225 Philadelphia Ct., Rancho Cucamonga, CA 91730, (909) 944-9599, fax: (909) 944-7898, www.vendingworld.com

▲

Experts and Consultants for Vending

Jennifer Berdoll Wammack, Berdoll Pecan Farm Candy & Gift Company, 2626 State Hwy 71 West, Cedar Creek, TX 78612, (512) 321-6157, jennifer@berdoll. com, www.berdollpecanfarm.com

Erik A. Borger, originallyorganicvending@gmail.com, (816)-244-5460, www. originallyorganicvending.com

Vince Gumma, American Vending Sales Inc., 750 Morse Ave., Elk Grove Village, IL 60007, (847) 439-9400, fax: (847) 439-9405, TDD: (847) 439-9402, www. americanvending.com

David Murphy Consulting, (519) 428-8428, http://davidmurphyconsulting.com

John Ochi, Five Star Distributors Inc., 220 Fairway Dr., Vernon Hills, IL 60061, (847) 680-9900, fax: (847) 680-9910

Jim Patterson, Patterson Co. Inc., 425 Huehl Rd., Building 17, Northbrook, IL 60062, (847) 714-1200

Randall Sutherland, (727) 510-4195, St. Petersburg, FL, scotsman17@aol.com

Universal Vending Consultants, 19715 Oxalis Court, Spring, TX 77379, (877) 643-8363, fax: (281) 320-0667, www.universalvending.com

Helpful Government Agencies

Internal Revenue Service, 1111 Constitution Ave. NW, Washington, DC 20224, (800) 829-1040, www.irs.gov

SCORE Association, 1175 Herndon Parkway, Suite 900, Herndon, VA 20170, (800) 634-0245, www.score.org

U.S. Census Bureau, Washington, DC 20233, (301) 457-4608, www.census.gov

U.S. Department of Labor, Frances Perkins Building, 200 Constitution Ave. NW, Washington, DC 20210, (866) 4-USA-DOL, www.dol.gov

U.S. Small Business Administration, 409 3rd St. SW, Washington, DC 20416, (800) 827-5722, answerdesk@sba.gov, www.sba.gov

United States Patent and Trademark Office, (800) 786-9199, www.uspto.gov

Logo Design, Promotional Materials, and Printing

123 Print, www.123print.com, (800) 877-5147

BusinessLogo.net, (888) 352-5646, www.businesslogo.net

Modern Postcard, www.modernpostcard.com, (800) 959-8365

Vistaprint, www.vistaprint.com

Magnetic Signs

A Magnetic Sign, Lettering Specialist Inc., www.amagneticsign.com, (847) 674-3414

OC Signs, Quick Signs, (866) 267-4467, www.ocsigns.com, sales@ocsigns.com

Wholesale Magnetic Signs, (866) 769-SIGN, www.wholesalemagneticsigns.com

Merchant Accounts and E-commerce Solutions

Charge.com, www.charge.com

Credit Card Processing Services Inc., www.new-business-merchant-account.com, Kevin@ccps.biz

InfoMerchant, Infofaq, LLC, (971) 223-5632, www.infomerchant.net

Merchant Accounts Express, (888) 845-9457, www.merchantexpress.com

Square, https://squareup.com

Total Merchant Services Inc., www.totalmerchantservices.com, (888) 848-6825 ext. 9420

Webdean, www.webdean.com

Networking Groups, Consultants, and Blogs

BNI, Ivan Misner, Ph.D., (909) 608-7575, www.bni.com

Business Networking, www.businessnetworking.com

Hazel M. Walker, (317) 407-5331, hazel@hazelmwalker.com, www.hazelmwalker.com

The Referral Institute, (707) 780-8110, www.referralinstitute.com

Point-of-Sale Software and Hardware

First Data, (800) 538-0651, www.firstdata.com, paymentsoftware.support@firstdata.com

International Point of Sale, (866) 468-5767, www.internationalpointofsale.com, sales@internationalpointofsale.com

POSMicro, (800) 241-6264, www.posmicro.com, service@posmicro.com

POS World, (888) 801-7282, www.posworld.com, service@posworld.com

Printing Resources

48hourprint.com, (800) 844-0599, www.48hourprint.com

ColorPrintingCentral, (800) 309-3291, www.colorprintingcentral.com

Door Hangers.com, (704) 430-8242, www.doorhangers.com

Focal Point Communications, (800) 525-6999, www.growpro.com

Printindustry.com, (703) 631-4533, www.printindustry.com, info@printindustry.com

Printing for Less, (800) 930-6040, www.printingforless.com, info@printingforless.com

Print Quote USA, (561) 451-2654, www.printquoteusa.com

PSPrint, (800) 511-2009, www.psprint.com

Publications

Automatic Merchandiser, Vending Market Watch, 1233 Janesville Ave., Ft. Atkinson, WI 53538, (877) 382-9187, www.vendingmarketwatch.com/magazine/autm

Canadian Vending & Office Coffee Service, P.O. Box 530, 105 Donly Drive South, Simcoe, Ontario, Canada N3Y 4N5, (888) 599-2228, fax: (519) 429-3094, www.canadianvending.com

Candy Industry, 155 Pfingsten Rd., Suite 205, Deerfield, IL 60015, (847) 405-4000, www.candyindustry.com.

Play Meter, 6600 Fleur De Lis, New Orleans, LA 70124, (504) 488-7003, fax: (504) 488-7083, www.playmeter.com

Replay, 18757 Burbank Blvd. #105, Tarzana, CA 91356, (818) 776-2880, fax: (818) 776-2888, www.replaymag.com

Vending and OCS, 4016 Flower Rd., #440A, Atlanta, GA 30360, (770) 451-2345, fax: (770) 457-0748

Vending Times, 1375 Broadway, 6th Fl., New York, NY 10018, (212) 302-4700, fax: (212) 221-3311, www.vendingtimes.com

Wireless Dealer Magazine, (800) 862-2609, ext. 222, http://intelecard.com/

Security

BRW Control Systems Inc., 40222 La Qunita Lane, Bldg. B, Ste. 101, Palmdale, CA 93551-3629, (800) 235-6740, (661) 947-8800, fax: (661) 947-8859, www.brwcontrol.com

Locking Systems International Inc., 6025 Cinderlane Pkwy., Orlando, FL 32810-4754, (407) 298-9895, (800) 657-LOCK (5625), fax: (800) 895-0706, www.lockingsystems.com

Pacific Lock, 157 Fords Road, Honesdale, PA 18431, (888) 562-5565, fax: (570) 253-4292, www.paclock.com

Software and Technology

Cantaloupe Systems Inc. (vending machine communications equipment), 612 Howard St., Suite 600, San Francisco, CA 94105, (415) 525-8100 or (855) 956-7333, fax: (415) 680-2368, www.cantaloupesys.com/

InOne Technology, 190 Lakefront Dr., Hunt Valley, MD 21030, (410) 666-3800, fax: (410) 666-3872, www.inonetechnology.com

Premier Data Software, (800) 720-DATA (3282), fax: (888) 801-DATA, www.premierdatasoftware.com

Protel Inc., 4150 Kidron Rd., Lakeland, FL 33811, (800) 925-8882, fax: (863) 646-5855, www.protelinc.com

Software Essentials Inc., 24 Preble St., Floor 3, Portland, ME 04101, (207) 253-6067, www.softwareessentials.com

Validata Computer and Research Corporation, 428 S. Perry St., Montgomery, AL 36104, (334) 834-2324, fax: (334) 262-5648, www.validata.com

QuickBooks Pro 2011, Intuit Inc., (888) 729-1996, www.quickbooks.com

Peachtree, Sage, (877) 495-9904, www.peachtree.com

Suppliers—Products

(These are just a few of numerous possibilities)

CandyWarehouse.com, Online Candy Store, 215 S. Douglas St., El Segundo, CA 90245, (310) 343-4099, fax: (310) 615-9915, www.candywarehouse.com

The Hershey Company, Consumer Relations, One Crystal A Dr., Hershey, PA 17033-0815, (800) 627-8525, www.hersheys.com/vending

Kraft Vending and OCS, Marketing Services GV867, Kraft Ct., Glenview, IL 60025, (888) 879-0267, www.kraftvendingocs.com

Nabisco Inc., 7 Campus Dr., P.O. Box 3111, Parsippany, NJ 07054-0311, (800) 852-9393, (973) 682-6880, fax: (973) 682-7476, www.nabisco.com

Patterson Co. Inc., Northbrook, IL 60043-1097, (847) 714-1200, fax: (847) 714-1245

Vend Central, Vend Central Inc., 3914 Vero Rd., Baltimore, MD 21227, www.vendcentral.net

Vistar, Merchants Mart, (800) 880-9900, www.vistar.com

Welch Foods Inc., 575 Virginia Rd., 3 Concord Farms, Concord, MA 01742, (800) 340-6870, www.welchs.com

Tax Advice and Software

Internal Revenue Service, (800) 829-1040, www.irs.gov

Intuit TurboTax for Business, (800) 440-3279, www.intuit.com

Technical Assistance for Computers, Security Systems, Mobile Phones, GPS

Geek Squad, (800) 433-5778, www.geeksquad.com

Glossary

Many of the following terms are courtesy of www.vending.org and the National Automatic Merchandising Association.

4C's: an abbreviation standing for the basics of vending as it has evolved. The industry started with coffee, cup soda, candy, and cigarettes and grew to almost 8 C's (coffee, candy or confections, chips, cold drinks, canned drinks, cigarettes, cold cup, commissary).

Account retention: the maintenance of customer accounts, which usually requires a vending company to provide excellent service. For most customers, this includes having clean, working machines and an ongoing professional relationship with the company.

Account supervisor: a representative of the foodservice company involved in the day-to-day operations of several accounts.

Activity-based costing: an accounting method that enables a business to better understand how and where it makes a profit. In this method, all major activities within a cost center are identified and the costs of performing each activity are calculated—ncluding costs that cross functional boundaries.

Bank: two or more vending machines in a row; also refers to a route person's change fund.

Belt: the part of a vending machine that carries the product on a circular, revolving belt to the point of delivery.

Bill changer: see *changer*.

Bin: the individual dispensing space allotted for a product in a food vendor, most commonly used by the telecard industry to describe the place where telecards are stacked up to await dispensing; see also synonymous terms column and spiral.

Broker: another term for independent sales representative. Brokers represent manufacturers that are too small to—or choose not to—maintain their own internal sales force. Although they don't actually sell you products, they're an important source of information and leads for purchasing products at competitive prices.

Bulk operator: someone who specializes in vending machines offering gumballs, trinkets, and charms that sell for (typically) from 5 to 25 cents.

Bulk vending: sale of unwrapped or unsorted merchandise through coin-operated vending machines.

Buy-back: equipment purchased for a client by the foodservice operator; the cost is repaid through withholdings of commissions earned and/or through direct payments by the client.

Cash-and-carry: refers to a purchasing system that is between wholesale and retail. At wholesale, the quantity minimum is generally a case (box) of a given product at a significant discount from retail. Item selection is done from a catalog, and purchases are delivered by the wholesaler to the buyer. At a cash-and-carry, the minimum quantity is a single unit, but merchandise is sold in a no-frills manner out of cut-open cases; items are priced below retail. Generally, cash-and-carries offer a further discount if a case quantity is purchased. The term cash-and-carry describes the wholesale/retail hybrid system where customers (most often businesses) must pay cash or cash equivalent, such as credit card (rather than being invoiced later), and carry purchases out themselves (rather than have them delivered).

Category management: an objective system of merchandising products to maximize sales.

CFC: chlorofluorocarbon—compound used as a refrigerant, cleaning solvent, or propellant.

Change fund: coins carried by a route man that are used to replenish the money in change and coin mechanisms. Also the coins in those machines.

Changer: a machine that makes change for coins or bills without a vend of merchandise (also called a bill changer).

Channel of distribution: refers to the "retail sector" a product is being sold through (for example, vend, grocery, convenience, food service, or warehouse club).

Class of trade (also referred to as location): the classification of the site where the vending machine is placed by sector (for example, school, public, factory).

Client: the person or company who contracts with you to place vendors at their location. A client can also be a customer, but only when he or she is making a purchase from your machine.

Closed system: a drinks system that compels the user to buy ingredients from one source or supplier.

Coin mechanism: the mechanism within a vending machine that dispenses change or counts coins deposited.

Cold call: a sales technique that involves telephoning or personally visiting a prospect who has no prior knowledge of you or your business.

Column: the individual dispensing space allotted for a product in a food vendor; most commonly used when referring to a canned beverage machine where cans are stacked in individual columns to await dispensing; see also synonymous terms bin and spiral.

Commissions: payment of a percentage of vending sales by the vending machine service company to the client organization for the privilege of operating on its premises. Payments are usually made monthly. Rates differ according to size of location, types of products vended, and competitive factors.

Contract vending: the installation and operation of vending machines by a private contractor who retains title to his vending equipment while performing his services.

Cooperative (purchasing): an association of operators, usually small businesses, who join together for purchasing purposes. By soliciting distributors as a group, cooperatives assure a certain annual volume and therefore command a lower price.

Cup mechanism: a device that feeds cups in a drink vending machine.

Customer: a person who makes purchases from a vending machine. Often, a customer is an employee at your client's business.

Cycle: the length of time a machine takes to vend one unit.

Cycle menu: a food menu that repeats itself after a certain interval of time. Most common cycles are two-week, four-week, 20-day, and six-week menus.

Décor: the nonfunctional trim and decorative work installed around vending machines.

Delisting: dropping or discontinuing the stocking of a product at a machine, or aggregate warehouse level.

Delivery receipt: see *route card*.

Distributor: companies that sell equipment and consumables directly to operators. Distributors carry the products of a wide variety of manufacturers.

Drum: horizontal rotating shelves in a machine.

FIFO: first in, first out.

Fixed level: see *par*.

Food-service contract: a contract awarded on the basis of the specifications for proposals and the submitted proposal for food distribution.

Free-standing machine: a single machine installation, distinguished from a bank of machines.

Free vend: a machine purposely adjusted to vend product at no charge.

Full-line: complete food and refreshment service through vending machines.

Income statement (or income and expense statement): a report of all collections and disbursements for a business during a specific period, often monthly, used to determine net profit/loss.

Joint replenishment: the ability to buy two or more items from the same supplier on a single purchase order.

Legs: the leveling device on the bottoms of vending machines.

Location manager: a representative of the vending company who is permanently assigned to one particular account.

Location-owned operations: services similar to the contractor's but owned and operated by a college or factory on its own premises by its own staff; includes location-owned cafeteria, dining, and vending operations.

Locator: someone you pay to find you vending locations. You are still responsible for closing the deal to set up vending machines at that location. It is important to work with a reputable locator.

Machine settlement: see *par out*.

Management fee: the charge made by vending companies for providing an operating service.

Manual food service: conventional cafeteria, short-order, or table service where the customer is served by manual delivery rather than by vending machines.

Manufacturer: a company that produces vending equipment or consumables. Some manufacturers sell to operators directly, but most sell through distributors.

Marginal: applied to vending machine locations where traffic of potential customers is so small as to make vending machine placement feasible only if equipment is fully depreciated, or the placement fills a gap in route scheduling or is subsidized by the location so that operating costs are reduced to the point where the operator can make a profit.

Merchandising: the process of determining the exact brand, color, flavor, size, type, quantity, and placement of products consumers want to buy and then presenting the products to them in a manner that encourages them to do so. This can be accomplished anecdotally, by passively observing which products are being purchased, or systematically, by actively employing a measurable system often referred to as category management.

Meter: a machine-attached device that records the number of vending cycles.

Mixed route (or full-line route): a route that handles several types of products.

NAMA: National Automatic Merchandising Association; the umbrella trade association of the vending and contract food industry.

Net worth: a person or business's assets minus liabilities. Assets are generally tangible property such as buildings, vehicles, equipment, furniture, machinery, etc. Liabilities are generally intangible, such as loans, leases, or credit card debt.

OCS: an acronym for office coffee service, a specialized service provided by an operator who offers equipment, coffee products, and related (allied) products to offices and other locations.

Operating statement (or operating budget): an annual version of an income and expense statement used to determine actual net profit/loss or projected financial receipts and disbursements.

Operator: someone who owns a vending machine business. If you're reading this book, you're interested in becoming an operator. In the industry, the term vendor is also often used to mean operator, but generally, vendor is the term for a vending machine. In this book, operator is always used to refer to the owner of a vending business, and vendor is used to refer to a vending machine.

OSHA: the Occupational Safety and Health Administration. Its Hazard Communication Standard requires all companies to inform their employees of the potential dangers of any hazardous chemical substances used in their operations.

Par (or fixed level): the fixed inventory established for an individual machine.

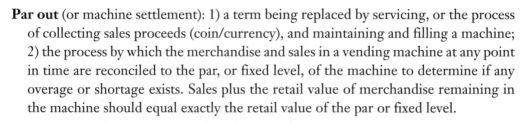

Par out (or machine settlement): 1) a term being replaced by servicing, or the process of collecting sales proceeds (coin/currency), and maintaining and filling a machine; 2) the process by which the merchandise and sales in a vending machine at any point in time are reconciled to the par, or fixed level, of the machine to determine if any overage or shortage exists. Sales plus the retail value of merchandise remaining in the machine should equal exactly the retail value of the par or fixed level.

Payout: length of time required for a location to return in profits the investment in the location.

Planogram: a simple diagram of an individual vendor with a specific product assigned to each spiral. Historically, as vendor capacity grew (most machines now include 40 or more spirals), more sophisticated selection and placement of products (aka merchandising) became necessary for profitability, and planogramming was born.

Pods: tea-bag-like ingredients used in high-quality closed systems.

Pro formula income: an anticipated operating statement of potential activity in a food-service location.

Proposal: a complete description of the type of food service to be provided.

Rehab (or renovate): to rebuild a changer or vending machine; also refers to the rebuilt machine.

Request for proposal (RFP): a request to various companies to submit proposals to provide food and vending services.

Resident vend: a vending operation at a client location that has one or more resident route persons or hostesses. It is thus distinguished from a location on a route, which is serviced by traveling route personnel.

Return on investment (ROI): the amount of money earned after taxes by a company at a particular location in relation to the total dollar investment required to operate in that location; usually expressed in a percentage form.

Return on sales: the amount of money earned after taxes by a company at a particular location in relation to the sales of that location; usually expressed in a percentage form.

Rotate product: to bring older products in a vendor forward and load them onto the route trucks, allowing for reordering of new product. Because many vending products have a short shelf life, companies want a regular rotation of products.

Route: a sequence of locations serviced by a traveling route person. The number of locations in a route is completely specific to each vending business. For example, you'd have two routes if you had 15 machines, which you serviced each week, going to seven one day and eight another.

Route accountability: a bookkeeping system whereby the retail value of merchandise issuances to a route person is equated to cash sales turned in by that route person to determine if overages or shortages exist on his route.

Route card: a card on which a route person keeps all manner of data about each vending machine he or she services (what sold, how much sold, what products were put into the machine, how much money was collected, etc.).

Route person: the individual who services one or more vending locations.

Route relief: when someone fills in to work the machines for a route person who cannot work on a particular day due to illness or vacation. Often called a utility person, this individual usually has knowledge of several routes and can work any of them as needed. If staffing is short, route supervisors may do the route relief work.

Route structure: the sequence in which a group of vending accounts is serviced by a route person.

Route vend: a group of individual vending locations serviced by a route person; today, the more commonly used terms are route or route structure.

Satellite: a site removed from the main location but serviced by the same resident vend.

Semi automatic: equipment that requires the user to do a little more than press a button, such as move a cup into place.

Servicing (or servicing a machine): the process of collecting coins/currency, cleaning, maintaining, repairing, and, most importantly, filling a vendor; in other words, servicing machines is what you do every day on a route.

Settlement figure: the amount required to settle an outstanding lease agreement when no new business is forthcoming.

Shelf life: the length of time a product will keep without deterioration that makes it unsalable.

Slotting: a fee charged by a vend operator to a product supplier for machine real estate to guarantee placement/distribution in an agreed-upon number of machines.

Slug: a coin-shaped object not recognized as a U.S. coin.

Spiral: the individual dispensing space allotted for a product in a food vendor; because today's snack machines move products forward via a mechanism shaped like a spiral, the term has been adopted to mean any individual offering, snack, sandwich, soda, etc.; see also synonymous terms bin and column.

Stock-keeping unit (SKU): a number assigned to a product by a manufacturer and used to identify that product; virtually every retail product in the United States has a SKU.

Stops: term used for different locations and accounts.

Subsidy contract: a contract that guarantees the operator a specific level of profit, normally a fixed fee or a percentage of sales. When the operation doesn't generate the guaranteed revenue, the operator bills the client for the balance. If the profit generated is greater than the contractual amount, the excess is generally returned to the client.

Supplementary vending: small banks or individual pieces of vending machines scattered throughout a location to provide backup service for a more complete centralized manual or automatic food-service operation.

Telemetry: a phrase used to describe the electronic communications between vending machines and operators using computer software.

Throw: the amount of product, usually liquid, dispensed per vending cycle.

Underwriters Laboratory (UL): a testing organization that certifies that electrical requirements of a piece of equipment meet federal standards.

U.S. Public Health Service (USPHS): the government agency responsible for the public health of the American people. In 1957, NAMA initiated a vending machine evaluation program to enable vending machine manufacturers to build equipment in conformity with USPHS sanitary requirements. Such a program also provides a means by which vending operators, customers, public health officials, military personnel, and other user groups can identify those machines that meet USPHS design and construction standards.

Vend: the delivery of a single unit of merchandise.

Vending (automatic vending): retail selling of merchandise and services by means of coin-operated dispensers.

Vending cafeteria: a location where all food and beverages are dispensed through vending machines.

Vendor: the abbreviated term for vending machine. In the industry, vendor also sometimes means operator, but in this book we keep the two terms strictly separate.

Index

▲